Clare Palmer is Lecturer in Ethics at the
University of Greenwich, and Visiting Research
Fellow in Philosophy at the University of
Western Australia.

D0024936

Environmental Ethics and Process Thinking

*

CLARE PALMER

CLARENDON PRESS · OXFORD
1998

GE/
4P
P36
1996

GE
42
P36
1998

Oxford University Press, Great Clarendon Street, Oxford OX2 6DP
Oxford New York
Athens Auckland Bangkok Bogota Bombay
Buenos Aires Calcutta Cape Town Dar es Salaam
Delhi Florence Hong Kong Istanbul Karachi
Kuala Lumpur Madras Madrid Melbourne
Mexico City Nairobi Paris Singapore
Taipei Tokyo Toronto Warsaw
and associated companies in
Berlin Ibadan

Oxford is a trade mark of Oxford University Press

Published in the United States
by Oxford University Press Inc., New York
The moral rights of the author have been asserted.

© Clare Palmer 1998

All rights reserved. No part of this publication may be reproduced,
stored in a retrieval system, or transmitted, in any form or by any means,
without the prior permission in writing of Oxford University Press.
Within the UK, exceptions are allowed in respect of any fair dealing for the
purpose of research or private study, or criticism or review, as permitted
under the Copyright, Designs and Patents Act, 1988, or in the case of
reprographic reproduction in accordance with the terms of the licences
issued by the Copyright Licensing Agency. Enquiries concerning
reproduction outside these terms and in other countries should be
sent to the Rights Department, Oxford University Press,
at the address above

British Library Cataloguing in Publication Data
Data available

Library of Congress Cataloging in Publication Data
Environmental Ethics and Process Thinking / Clare Palmer.
Includes bibliographical references.
1. Environmental ethics 2. Deep ecology
3. Thought and thinking I. Title
GE42.P36 1996 179'.1–dc21 97–32420
ISBN 0–19–826952–8

1 3 5 7 9 10 8 6 4 2

Typeset by Pure Tech India Limited, Pondicherry
Printed in Great Britain on acid-free paper by
Bookcraft (Bath) Ltd., Midsomer Norton

JESUIT - KRAUSS - McCORMICK - LIBRARY
1100 EAST 55th STREET
CHICAGO, ILLINOIS 60615

Acknowledgements

I AM grateful to my doctoral supervisor Revd Trevor Williams for his assistance, to Dr John Ashton for his continued support, to Queen's College, Oxford, for funding a research visit to the State University of Colorado at a crucial time in the composition of this work as a doctoral thesis, and to Professor Holmes Rolston for his hospitality there. In recent revision of this work, I am grateful to Professor Timothy Sprigge who provided a number of helpful and thought-provoking comments (on several occasions!) and to Revd Dr Paul Fiddes, the reader for OUP, who suggested a number of substantial improvements that could be made to the text. I am also grateful to Professor J. Baird Callicott for helpful comments made on a paper derived from parts of this book as well as his more general support.

The transformation of this work from a thesis into a book has been a difficult one, carried out in snatched moments over a long period of hard work as a new lecturer. For supporting me through this time, I am grateful to my parents, to my partner Quentin Merritt, and to my short-suffering friends Julie Clague, Sue Hamilton, Sarah Pearce, and Peter Jones.

Contents

Introduction

> One theological school in the West claims to have an intellectual alternative to the errors of classical Western metaphysics which brought on the alienation of humanity from nature and hence the eco crisis. Process theology therefore should be listened to with respect.
>
> (Mar Gregorias, 1980: 39)

WHILE Paulos Mar Gregorias follows this remark with substantial reservations about the metaphysics of process theology, he does not revoke his view that process thinking offers an intellectual approach peculiarly equipped to tackle what has become known as the eco crisis. In holding this view he is not alone. Prominent North American process theologians, such as Charles Hartshorne and John Cobb, as well as others working in the tradition of process thinking, have produced a number of publications advocating a process approach to environmental questions.[1] However, little has been published from outside the process tradition that critically examines this aspect of process thinking, in particular the interpretation of environmental ethics which might flow from it.[2] Indeed, some writers have expressed confusion (not without reason, as I shall argue) about exactly what the implications of a process approach to environmental ethics might be: 'It is quite unclear what kind of ethical relations could emerge with respect to the homunculi which inhabit 'occasions of experience' or how this esoteric reformulation is supposed to make a difference to our everyday behaviour' (Plumwood 1993: 130). This book aims to respond both to claims about the environmental significance of

---

[1] Hartshorne 1974a, 1979, 1981; Cobb 1973, 1979; Birch and Cobb 1981; Cobb and Daly 1990. This is by no means a complete listing.

[2] Sessions (Devall and Sessions 1985: 236–42) is critical of the environmental aspect of process thinking in his essay 'Western Process Metaphysics (Heraclitus, Whitehead, Spinoza)'. Some aspects of process thinking are also attacked (although a quasi-process position is adopted) in Keffer, King, and Kraft (1991: 23–47). Plumwood (1993: 130 offers a brief critique of process thinking based on what she argues is its human-hierarchical nature, a criticism to which I will return.

process thinking, and to questions about what the ethical implications of process thinking about the environment might be.

There are, undoubtedly, a number of ways of approaching such a project. I chose to begin by testing out some of the basic ethical themes of process thinking (Chapter 1) and thereafter adopted a largely comparative methodology, where interpretations of environmental ethics from within the process tradition were laid alongside other major approaches within environmental ethics. I called these approaches (in rather clumsy terminology) individualist consequentialist (Chapter 2), individualist deontological (Chapter 3), and collectivist consequentialist (Chapter 4). In Chapter 5, process thinking was compared with a philosophical movement which claims to 'go beyond ethics': that of deep ecology. This seemed an important comparison, both because deep ecology is an important popular movement in environmental philosophy, and because of the claims which are made by some deep ecologists concerning their links with process thinking.

The adoption of this comparative method throughout the book means that process thinking can be used to interrogate —and can be interrogated by—other approaches to environmental ethics, similarities and differences in approach can be characterized, and the vulnerability of process thinking to criticisms made of other environmental ethical approaches can be assessed. Such a method avoids the difficulties of judging process thinking against one single and absolute ethical standard, substituting instead a number of dialogues between process thinking and other environmental ethical positions. This method also throws up a number of questions, not only about the ways in which process thinking can address environmental issues, but also about the problems raised by any single, all-embracing approach to environmental ethics. Thus, in conclusion, the potential for more pluralistic approaches to environmental ethics is considered.

This comparative approach to process thinking and environmental ethics, together with the space limitations of a book, has resulted in a focus on a relatively small area both of process philosophy and of environmental ethics. I have concentrated on the later philosophical texts of A. N. Whitehead for my basic understanding of process thinking, although I have tried to take account of occasions when later process philosophers (in particular Hartshorne) have rejected or significantly developed Whitehead's thought. In the knowledge that Whitehead's philosophical ideas were still crystallizing in 1925 and the years subsequent to this, I have not quoted from his earlier philosophical writing about issues on which he later changed his mind.[3] I have also referred extensively to more recent writing by Hartshorne, Cobb, Jay McDaniel, and Daniel Dombrowski, which specifically discusses process thinking and the non-human natural world. I have also concentrated in this book on a small (if significant) group of positions in environmental ethics. This has resulted in the neglect of some important understandings of environmental ethics (such as those stemming from ecofeminism) and in the truncation of the presentation of some other approaches (in particular those of Lawrence Johnson and Robin Attfield). This restriction is a matter of regret, but also of necessity.

This book aims to examine process thinking in relation to environmental ethics. As such, it does not focus on wider issues—for example, process interpretations of the nature of being—although such questions are touched upon in Chapter 5.[4] Neither does it attempt to judge the truth or otherwise of claims by process thinkers about the presence of actual occasions of experience throughout a teleological universe. Such claims have been disputed elsewhere. Here the focus is primarily on the ethics of process thinking, and the environmental implications of such an ethical approach. I have written this book in the belief that, given the widespread assumption of the ecological significance of process thinking, such a critical study is now overdue.

[3] For a full analysis of Whitehead's changing views, see Ford (1984).
[4] Gare (1995) has developed process metaphysics in this direction.

I

Process Thinking, the Creation of Value, and Approaches to Ethics

I suggest that you take as a model for your essay on Whitehead's moral philosophy a well-known treatise on the Snakes
of Ireland.

(Schillp 1951: 593)

This response, received by Paul Schillp when he announced his
intention to write a paper on Whitehead's moral thinking, is an
understandable one. Whitehead's primary concern in his later
philosophical work was not moral philosophy, but the construction of a new metaphysics. It is to this task that his philosophical thinking was dedicated, and he never attempted to
construct an ethical system. Ethics were, in this sense, secondary
to his purpose.

The secondary nature of ethics in Whitehead's system means
that precise details of the source of value, and consequently of his
ethical position, can be obscure, and need on occasion to be teased
out. Broadly speaking, however, an evaluative structure does flow
from Whitehead's process metaphysics, a structure developed by
other process thinkers, in particular Charles Hartshorne. In this
chapter, I will consider the ways in which value is generated in
Whitehead's system, entailing a brief examination of the formation
of the 'actual occasion' or 'entity' and Whitehead's understanding
of the nature of God. I will also consider some developments of
Whitehead's position by Hartshorne. I will then move on to consider the human, macro-level of ethics which is underpinned by
this process understanding of value. Resemblances between this
ethical system and that of utilitarian ethical systems will be considered—in particular that of J. S. Mill. This opens the way, in
Chapter 2, to examine the more recent consequentialist systems
consciously constructed to take the non-human world into
account. These similarities raise the question of whether process
thinking is open to the same criticisms as utilitarianism, and
in particular whether it shares with utilitarian systems a difficulty

in coming to terms with many of the problems generated by environmental ethics. This examination will provide a foundation for the comparison of process thinking with other approaches to environmental ethics in Chapters 3 and 4.

The Actual Occasion

The 'actual occasion', or 'actual entity' (broadly, Whitehead uses these terms synonymously), is the fundamental component of Whitehead's system, and of all process systems that originate in a Whiteheadian context. As Whitehead (1978: 18[1]) states: ' "Actual entities" . . . are the final real things of which the world is made up. There is no going behind actual entities to find anything more real.' Everything which is actual in the universe is an actual occasion or is composed from actual occasions. Describing actual occasions is, however, difficult. Whitehead's first description of them in *Process and Reality* is as 'drops of experience, complex and interdependent' (ibid.).

In characterizing actual occasions as 'drops', Whitehead uses language directly dependent on that of William James.[2] It is, none the less, a peculiarly apt expression for his own position. The word 'drop' first suggests the spatial extension which actual occasions possess: 'Every actuality in the temporal world is to be credited with a spatial volume for its perspective standpoint' (ibid. 68). Secondly, it indicates a degree of discreteness, of self-completion. This is central to Whitehead's system—but should not be misinterpreted. An actual occasion is discrete as far as its contemporary occasions are concerned; 'contemporary events happen in causal independence of one another' (ibid. 61). Time is atomic, being composed from distinguishable and extended drops. This does not mean that any single actual occasion is unaffected by *past* actual occasions; they are vital to its formation. A third suggestion conveyed by the image of a 'drop' is that of constant process and growth, up to a point of fullness: 'Each actual thing is only to be understood in terms of its becoming and perishing. There is no halt

---

[1] All references are to the corrected edition.

[2] James (1911: ch. 10). Ford (1984: 52, 64) points out that Whitehead had developed his epochal theory of time before he came across James's description of experience 'growing by buds or drops of perception'.

in which the actuality is its static self, accidentally played upon by qualifications derived from the shift of circumstances. The converse is the truth' (Whitehead 1948). However, this statement also requires careful qualification. The fact that the actual occasion is a process does not, for Whitehead, mean that it is divisible, that at any point it has a past, present, or future. To understand this requires a closer examination of the nature of the actual occasion.

Actual occasions are, Whitehead argues, the drops of experience at the most fundamental level of the universe. This assertion forms part of Whitehead's case against dualism, and his rejection of the Cartesian view that the human mind is the only location of subjectivity in the created world. Human experience is not radically different from the rest of the natural world; it rather reflects the way that the world actually is.[3] Indeed, at root, Whitehead derives his concept of actual occasions from his understanding of human experience. Human experience is a very selective manifestation of the general experience of actual occasions. 'Consciousness', Whitehead (1978: 267) remarks 'is the crown of experience, only occasionally attained, not its necessary base.' Consciousness is a narrowing and a focusing, a highlighting of particular areas of experience, to the exclusion of more general experience. Actual occasions themselves, while they have subjectivity, have no consciousness.[4]

An actual occasion has no existence outside its own becoming. Being *is* becoming. Once an occasion is no longer in the process of coming to be, it has perished. There is 'no halt in which the actuality is its static self'; or, as A. H. Johnson (1983: 35) puts it: 'All you have are the processes of growth towards actual entityhood and the demise of actual entities. In a sense you don't have an actual entity as such, because you never catch one complete. It is either coming or going—never here.' Thus it is essential to consider the constituents and the development of actual occasions in order to understand them.

---

[3] In this subjectivization of the natural world, Whitehead is following a long-standing Continental philosophical tradition. Eagleton's (1990: 131) comments about Hegel's system 'modelling Nature itself after the freely self-generative subject, thus grounding that subject in a world whose structure it shares', could equally be made of Whitehead.

[4] For a detailed explanation, see Cobb (1966: 39).

The Development of Actual Occasions

Whitehead proposes that certain vital components make any actual occasion what it is: temporally preceding actual occasions which have now perished; eternal objects; the initial aim provided by the primordial nature of God; the consequent nature of God; and the subjectivity of the actual occasion itself. I will consider these constituents in turn.

Each actual occasion comes to be in the cradle of other, perished actual occasions. These perished occasions provide objective data which the currently actualizing occasion can incorporate into itself. The actualizing occasion is said to *feel* or *prehend* these perished actual occasions. However, it is not obliged to absorb all of them into itself. It may negatively prehend an objectified actual occasion, which means that it may exclude it. Every actualizing (or, in Whitehead's preferred term, concrescing) occasion prehends, either positively or negatively, every preceding actual occasion in the universe: 'An actual entity has a perfectly definite bond with every item in the Universe' (Whitehead 1978: 41). However, most of these are felt 'vaguely', providing a kind of background for the concrescing occasion.

Eternal objects provide a second kind of data for the actual occasion. Whitehead describes them as 'pure potentials for the determination of fact' (ibid. 22). They are abstract potentials for things which might be actualized: colours or shapes for instance. It is impossible to avoid a comparison between eternal objects and Platonic forms, but there are crucial differences between them. For Plato, it is the Form which is real, while for Whitehead and process thinkers in general, it is the *actual* which is real, and the abstract eternal object is dependent on the actual for instantiation. As Pols (1967: 7) points out, eternal objects ingress (into the actual world) and are meant to ingress; they do not, like Platonic Forms, have a life of their own. By its very nature, an actual occasion may only actualize some of the total array of eternal objects: for instance, it cannot actualize two different colours simultaneously. The context in which the actual occasion comes to birth also limits the eternal objects it may actualize. Only certain eternal objects are relevant to any one actual occasion: for example, the colour spectrum is not relevant to an actual occasion which forms part of something transparent. Relevant and compatible eternal objects, however, together with the array of perishing actual occasions which surround the concrescing actual occasion, constitute two of the factors involved in the creation of the actual occasion.

It is important to notice that Whitehead's concept of eternal objects is not accepted by all process thinkers. Hartshorne (1970: 59), for example, considers that eternal objects are regrettably Platonic, commenting: 'I do not believe that a determinate colour is something haunting reality from eternity, as it were, begging for instantiation, nor that God primordially envisages a set of such qualities.' Rather than these 'eternal universals, independent of time' Hartshorne (ibid. 64) suggests, following the philosopher Peirce, that all specific qualities are emergent and time-dependent. He comments, 'Something like this blue can occur over and over again, but not precisely this blue. Particular qualities in their absolute definiteness are irreducibly relational and historical.'

To consider the remaining constituents of the actual occasion, we will first have to examine Whitehead's understanding of God.

God in Whitehead's System

In *Process and Reality*, Whitehead presents his concept of God in its most developed form.[5] First, God is described as an actual entity, as is everything that is actual: 'God is an actual entity, and so is the most trivial puff of existence in far off space' (1978: 18).[6] For Whitehead, God is dipolar, with two aspects: a *primordial* nature and a *consequent* nature. The primordial nature is 'free, complete, primordial, eternal, actually deficient and unconscious' (ibid. 345). It is abstract and conceptual, 'the unlimited conceptual realization of the absolute wealth of potentiality' (ibid. 343). While the primordial nature of God does not create eternal objects ('his nature requires them in the same degree that they require him'), it orders them according to their relevance to each concrescing actual occasion. In this sense, the primordial nature *lures* each actual occasion

[5] See Ford (1984: 101–2) for detail on the way in which Whitehead's concept of God may have developed. It is worth noting, however, that Hartshorne does not accept Whitehead's description of God as an actual entity.

[6] See also (1978: 356). Suchoki (1988) argues, from a process perspective, that the subjectivity of actual occasions may be retained in the consequent nature of God. This position is a considerable development of Whitehead's thought, and I will not consider it further here.

to concresce in accordance with the ordering presented to it by God. This is what can be described as the initial aim, which determines 'the initial gradations of relevance of eternal objects for conceptual feeling; and constitutes the autonomous subject in its primary phase of feelings with its initial conceptual valuations [i.e. of eternal objects] and with its initial physical purposes' (ibid. 244). The consequent nature of God, in contrast, is 'determined, incomplete, consequent, "everlasting", fully actual and conscious'; 'the objectification of the world in God' (ibid. 345–6). In the consequent nature God feels the world and is affected by it. Every new occasion adds to the consequent nature; hence this aspect of God, in contrast with the primordial nature, is always incomplete, always growing and changing. Thus the experiences of the actual occasions in the world become part of God, and, while their immediate subjectivity has perished, they are preserved, or 'saved' objectively within the consequent nature of God.[7]

Whitehead describes the consequent nature of God as 'the weaving of his physical feelings onto his primordial concepts' (ibid. 345). This suggests that the consequent nature can be thought of as the integration of God's physical feelings of the actual world with the conceptual feelings of the primordial nature. Thus in his consequent nature God contains a conceptual awareness of possibility, as well as the physical feeling of actuality. It is the 'subjective form of this feeling of contrast' (between the 'in fact' and 'might be') which Whitehead describes as consciousness. The use of the term 'weaving' here indicates another important element of God's consequent nature. In the consequent nature, the multiplicity of objective actual entities are woven together in an ultimate harmony of patterned contrasts, which are felt by God. This will be of some significance in the consideration of value in Whitehead's system.

Whitehead also suggests, at the end of *Process and Reality*, that the consequent nature of God 'passes back into the temporal world, so that each actual entity includes it as an immediate fact of relevant experience' (ibid. 351). How this is possible is a subject of some discussion in process thinking. Ross (1983), for example, maintains that this cannot consistently happen within Whitehead's system. Hartshorne (1970: 277), however, develops this aspect of Whitehead's thought by suggesting that God and the world reflect

[7] Cobb (1966: 153); Pols (1967: 42); Ross (1983: 74).

(and enhance) one another's feelings. Whitehead himself does not examine in detail the effects on actual entities of prehending the consequent nature of God. Presumably the ability to feel the rich harmony of God's consequent nature enhances the potential satisfaction available to every actual entity. This in turn has value implications, which will be considered later.

The Initial Aim, and the Subjectivity of the Actual Occasion

Consideration of the aim of the actual occasion is a complex and difficult one in process studies, as many of Whitehead's interpreters agree.[8] Whitehead himself is not entirely clear what role he considers the aim of the occasion to play. As we have seen, he certainly speaks of an *initial aim* supplied by the primordial nature of God to the actual occasion. To make sense of this, of course, we will have to develop this consideration of the initial aim in the context of Whitehead's understanding of God.

The initial aim presents to the actual occasion a range of possibilities which it may choose to actualize. This initial aim is taken over by the subjective aim of the concrescing occasion itself, which, ultimately, makes what was potential become concrete and real. Thus, the initial aim of God—which grades the eternal objects— together with the actual world of perished actual occasions, 'jointly constitute the character of the creativity for the initial phase of the novel concrescence' (Whitehead 1978: 245).

The subjectivity of the actual occasion finally makes potentiality actual. Characteristic of the actual occasion is its freedom, or autonomy. Ultimately, the decision about self- actualization is freely made by the concrescing occasion, within its necessary contextual constraints—'no actual entity can rise beyond what the actual world as a datum from its standpoint—its actual world—allows it to be' (ibid. 83). It is important that the initial aim provided by the primordial nature of God, luring the occasion on to actualization, is seen as persuasive, rather than coercive. The occasion is never obliged to concresce in any particular way; it is a 'self-creating creature'.

Whitehead speaks of the *phases* of the actual occasion, internal stages in its self-actualization. This is problematic, since, as we

[8] This problem is tackled with great lucidity by Pols (1967: 42).

have seen, he insists that an actual occasion is indivisible. It appears that the phases of the occasion occur, in some sense, outside time; that the discrete occasion is what time is, what time is made from, as an indivisible whole.[9] Whitehead describes these phases as the conformal phase and the supplemental phase. The conformal phase of the actual occasion is composed from physical feelings of initial data: it can be called the physical pole of the actual occasion. These feelings are largely repetition of the data already existing in the world; the physical pole 'conforms' to the past. In contrast, the supplemental phase is composed from conceptual feelings of eternal objects; it can be called the mental pole of the actual occasion. It is here that originality or novelty can be generated, where new eternal objects are combined with physical feelings from already existing data to produce a new whole. Thus, the subjective aim of the actual occasion selects a combination of physical and conceptual feelings in order to generate its own, complete, subjectivity. Different actual occasions, however, coming to be in different contexts, have widely varying emphases on the physical and mental poles. The stronger the mental pole, the greater the degree of novelty possible; the stronger the physical pole, the more the occasion repeats, or conforms to, what already exists.

This examination of physical and mental poles, and degrees of novelty and repetition, provides a background to a consideration of the value generated by an actual occasion.

Process Thinking and Value

The Use of Intrinsic Value

Before examining Whitehead's understanding of value generation, it is important to clarify how I will be using the term 'intrinsic value'. This term has caused considerable confusion within (and outside!) environmental ethics. O'Neill (1993) has identified three main uses of the term: *Intrinsic Value 1* (*IV1*)—non-instrumental value, something being an end in itself (value can be subjective or

---

[9] Ross makes a number of apposite comments here about major differences between God and other actual entities in Whitehead's work. These include the inability of God to negatively prehend objective actual occasions, and the need for all actual occasions to be equally relevant to God. As pointed out in n. 5, Hartshorne entirely rejects the idea that God can be seen as an actual entity.

objective); *Intrinsic Value* 2 *(IV2)*—value an object has in virtue of its intrinsic properties, non-relational value (a use associated with G. E. Moore); and *Intrinsic Value 3 (IV3)*—objective value, value independent of any valuer. This classification, whilst not definitive, is a useful one. I will generally be using intrinsic value in the *IV1* sense identified by O'Neill—to indicate non-instrumental value. This conflicts with the usage of some environmental ethicists; where confusion may arise from this, I shall indicate in the text.

Intrinsic Value and the Actual Occasion

At the most fundamental level in Whitehead's system, what is actual generates intrinsic (non-instrumental) value, and since actuality is exclusively composed from actual entities, just by existing, actual entities generate intrinsic value. As Whitehead (1926: 100) comments: 'Value is inherent in actuality itself.' The locus of this value is the subjectivity or experience of the actual entities. To exist, in Whitehead's system, is to have some kind of self-enjoyment and thus, self-valuation:

> ...we see at once that the element of value, of being valuable, of having value in itself, of being an end to itself, of being something which is for its own sake, must not be omitted in any account of an event as the most concrete actual something. Value is a word I use for the intrinsic reality of an event. (Whitehead 1938*a*: 117)

Actual entities are the location of intrinsic value, and intrinsic value is located in, and only in, what is actual. Even the graded eternal objects envisaged by the primordial nature of God have only potential value. It is only when actualized that eternal objects have actual value. The identification of value with actuality means that value can only be present in the universe in the actual entities—and in the consequent nature of God.

God, of course, is vital to the generation of value in Whitehead's system. The consequent nature of God, as actual and conscious, generates intrinsic value within the universe on a different scale to that generated by all other concrescing actual entities. All actual entities contribute to God's consequent nature; the way in which an occasion actualizes itself, and thus the value it produces, affects God's own actualization and the intrinsic value God generates. God's aim in the universe is at the 'fulfilment of his own being'

(Whitehead 1978: 105). Since God's consequent nature is constantly growing, there can never be a time at which God reaches a completed state of fulfilment. The consequent nature 'can reach no final maximum, but is endlessly capable of increase' (Hartshorne 1970: 310). The aim is at maximum possible fulfilment in each fleeting moment of time. To speak of the maximum possible fulfilment of God at any time is the same as to speak of the maximum generation of intrinsic value at any time. The greater the intrinsic value generated by actual entities, the greater the intrinsic value possible for God, and thus the more fulfilled God's being may be.

Although intrinsic value is created by all that is actual, and thus contributes to God's fulfilment, all actual entities do not generate the same amount of value. To understand this, we need to know in more detail what Whitehead regards to be ultimately fulfilling to God's being. In *Process and Reality*, Whitehead (1978: 105) states that 'God's purpose in the creative advance is the evocation of intensities.' It is this which is ultimately fulfilling, and thus the amount of value an actual entity produces is dependent on the intensity of feeling it can produce for itself and for God. The more intensity it can produce, the more valuable it is.

How, then, do actual entities produce intensity for God's being? The first form of intensity Whitehead (1978: 102) discusses one might call 'trivial' or 'low-grade'. It is produced by narrowness. This occurs when actual entities, in the process of concrescing, 'block out all unwelcome detail', negatively prehending (excluding) all novel data. Thus each new actual entity closely repeats the old. There is, as Whitehead says, 'no originality in conceptual prehension'. This form of intensity, which Whitehead says is characteristic of what we know as material bodies, does not contribute significantly to God's intensity of feeling, though it does demonstrate some 'enhancement of the mental pole'.

The second form of intensity Whitehead discusses one might call 'creative' or 'high-grade' intensity. It is produced primarily by depth of contrast within concrescing actual occasions, usually derived from the prehension of novel data. The ability of an actual occasion to produce such intensity is largely dependent on the strength of its mental pole or supplementary phase. As we have seen, the physical pole, or conformal phase, of the actual occasion largely repeats the data which already exists in the world around it. In some actual occasions, the physical pole is extremely strong, outweighing the weak mental pole. Such occasions fail to integrate new eternal objects into their experience. Other occasions have a strong mental pole, with conceptual, as well as physical feelings, and integrate new eternal objects into their actualization to make a new synthesis.

However, caution is needed in explanation here. It is not because the synthesis achieved by occasions with a strong mental pole is new that it is valuable, it is because it provokes intensity. Originality or novelty is not in itself valuable, nor does it *necessarily* generate more value, as the process thinker Pols (1967: 67) points out: 'While it is true that novelty is a necessary condition for the heightening of intensity, it is not true that each novelty is a sufficient condition for the heightening of intensity.' Novelty is essential for change to happen; without novelty, there would be only repetition. However, novelty is necessary but not sufficient for creative advance. The aim of advance is greater satisfaction, which is expressed by Whitehead (1978: 83) as intensity of experience: 'the end is concerned with the gradations of intensity in the satisfactions of actual occasions'. The more intense the experience, the more it is valued by the actual occasion, and hence by God.

It is not, however, pure intensity that is of value. Intensity must be ordered, rather than chaotic. Chaotic or disordered intensity is intensity generated by conflicts or incompatibilities within the feeling of an actual occasion, caused when an occasion prehends conflicting perished actual occasions or eternal objects. Ordered or harmonized intensity is composed from *contrasts*, rather than *conflicts*. An actual occasion which produces a high level of ordered intensity is described by Whitehead as 'beautiful'. Other occasions, however, produce intense but inharmonious experience (aesthetic destruction) or harmonious but unintense experience (triviality). An intense experience which lacks harmony is described by Whitehead (1948: 295) as 'the feeling of evil in the most general sense, namely physical pain and mental evil, such as sorrow, horror, dislike'. Conversely, a harmonious experience which lacks intensity is described as 'the loss of the higher experience in favour of the lower experience' (Whitehead 1926: 95). In humans, triviality can be described as 'degradation—the comparison of what is with what might have been'.

Whitehead also suggests (although does not fully develop) a third way in which the intensity of God's feeling is enhanced:

God's feeling *about* the actual occasions concrescing within the universe. This relates closely to Whitehead's (1978: 110) understanding of God as an actual entity with an existence 'not generically different from that of other actual entities'. Like all actual entities, God has a 'perfectly definite bond with every item in the universe', and prehends objective actual occasions, synthesizing or 'weaving' them into a new unity.[10] Thus, as an actual entity, God not only feels the feelings of the actual occasions within the world, but can also feel contrasts between them. So within God as well as within all occasions, depth of contrast can enhance intensity of feeling, and contribute value to the universe.

It seems then that intensities for God, and hence value, can be produced in three ways in Whitehead's system. Most trivially, value is produced by 'narrowness'. The insignificance of this kind of value for process thinking is such that I will not be pursuing it further here. More profoundly, value is produced by ordered intensity in actual occasions felt by God, and by depth of contrast between actual occasions, also felt by God. One might summarize these by saying that value is generated both by God feeling the feelings of actual occasions, and by God having feelings *about* the feelings of actual occasions. The former of these has been the primary focus of study in process writing to date; the implications of the latter remain largely unexplored (although I shall look at them in more detail in this book). Whilst the difference between these sources of value creation may seem to be trivial, there are important implications here for value generation in Whitehead's philosophy, which will be developed later.

It will be clear from this description that value in Whitehead's system is aesthetic, rather than ethical. Ethical value, in process thinking, is a subset of aesthetic value. 'All order is therefore aesthetic order, and the moral order is merely certain aspects of the aesthetic order' (Whitehead 1926: 105). Aesthetic value is generated from harmony and intensity of experience; ethical value is defined, by Hartshorne (1984: 10), as 'not the value of

---

[10] Process ethics, like the majority of utilitarian systems, is totalizing as well as maximizing. Some utilitarian systems—in particular those developed with the ethical consideration of future generations in mind—aim at highest *average*, rather than highest *total* utility overall. This is still a maximizing approach. Process thinking, however, is clearly a totalizing approach, since the consequent nature of God integrates and sums all experience. I will only be discussing similarly totalizing approaches in this book.

experiences themselves, but rather the instrumental value of acting so as to increase the intrinsic value of future experiences of those of others than oneself'. Ethical acts (only possible for 'conscious' beings, rather than for the actual occasion, which lacks consciousness) are those which generate the greatest aesthetic value overall. This may mean the sacrifice of some present harmonious intensity, in order to generate greater harmonious intensity in the future; the renunciation of some aesthetic value now, in order to generate more total aesthetic value.

At the level of actual occasions, where to speak of 'ethics' is inappropriate, the initial aim provided by the primordial nature of God takes into account what one might call the 'ethical interest'. That is to say, the initial aim points towards the best possible actualization for that occasion—a 'patterned intensity of feeling arising from adjusted contrasts'—in the light of the effect of such an actualization on other, future occasions (Whitehead 1978: 244). As Cobb (1966: 128) expresses it: 'The initial aim is always that aim at the ideal harmony possible for that occasion. It is the aim at a balance between the intensity of that occasion's experience and its contribution beyond itself.' This does not mean that the occasion is determined by the initial aim. Some indeterminations are always present, to be decided by the freedom of the actual occasion. But even so, it is clear that actual occasions do not always actualize in accordance with the initial aim; that is to say, not every actual occasion produces maximum harmonious intensity, taking into account the effect on future occasions. This is because the subjective aim of the actual occasion, into which the initial aim is absorbed, can, through the phases of the occasion, modify the initial aim.

This, however, generates its own difficulty, aptly summarized by Randall Morris:

The freedom of the actual entity would appear to reside in the ability of the actual entity to modify its initial aim, to make some specific aim its own. However, since the initial aim includes a specific ideal, which is God's ideal for that occasion, the data and location of which the actual entity initially conforms to, must we not conclude that any modification is, in fact, degradation? (Morris 1986: 23)

Presenting the initial aim as a range of possibilities may be intended to resolve this difficulty, but as Morris correctly suggests, one of the possibilities must produce maximum harmonious

intensity, and so must be preferred over others as the specific ideal
for that occasion. Thus the concept of a range of possibilities within
the initial aim just pushes the problem one step back. The conclusion which can be drawn from this is that the greatest fulfilment
possible for the actual occasion is to conform to the aim presented
to it by God; that is, to act so that maximum total harmonious and
rich experience is generated for the consequent nature of God,
despite the possible sacrifice of harmonious and intense experience
which this might entail for the occasion itself. Thus, if the occasion
either concresces more trivially or more disharmoniously than it was
possible for it; or if it chooses its own maximal harmonious and
intense experience at the expense of future experience, it has failed
to generate maximum possible value in the world. That less value is
created does not, of course, mean that the occasion behaves uneth-
ically; ethics is only possible where experience becomes conscious,
in humans and conceivably a few other mammal species. This value
shortfall is, in a sense, the forerunner of ethics in the same way as the
subjectivity of the actual occasion is the forerunner of consciousness. Ethics is the supreme and most developed form known of the
decisions about concretion taken by the actual occasion.

Consideration of process ethics moves from the micro-level of
value generation by actual occasions to the macro-level of the
human being. In process thinking, human beings, like all other
living and non-living objects, are societies of actual occasions.
Together with some other mammals, they are marked by the
peculiarly powerful mental poles of their constitutive actual occasions. This means that they have a high potential for the generation
of harmonious and intense experience. This high-value potential of
human beings, together with their ability to make ethical decisions,
is of central importance in this study. But whether on a micro-or a
macro-level, the ultimate aim is still to generate maximum harmonious and intense experience for the consequent nature of God. I
will now move on to consider the ethics which might be engen-
dered by such an approach.

Process Thinking and Utilitarianism

As we have seen, Whitehead's system is clearly teleological. The
primordial nature of God acts in the world, luring the concrescing

actual occasions on to ever greater levels of harmony and intensity. These actual occasions, when they are complete, are absorbed into the consequent nature of God. Thus God, by acting in this per-suasive manner in the world, lures it towards 'depth of satisfaction as an intermediate step towards the fulfilment of his own being'. The consequent nature of God is thus 'ever enlarging itself' to integrate all the actual occasions that have ever existed (Whitehead 1978: 349). Process thinking, then, subscribes to a contributory theory of value: all value generated by the harmony and intensity of the actual occasions, and by depth of contrast between them, contributes to God's consequent nature—a nature which, as we have seen, is endlessly capable of increase.

From this, certain characteristics of process ethics emerge. Since process thinking as a metaphysical system is teleological, so also is process ethics. Ethical behaviour consciously conforms with God's aim at harmonious intensity. Thus, process ethics is consequenti-alist: to behave ethically is to act in a way which produces the best consequences—the production of harmony and intensity of experi-ence for the consequent nature of God. Process approaches to ethics thus contrast with deontological ethics, where ethical beha-viour is determined by rules of right and wrong which are inde-pendent of their consequences. This consequentialist rather than deontological approach is of key significance. In addition to its consequentialist nature, process thinking is a maximizing ethical system. Within God is summed all valuable experience. The more value that is generated by actual occasions, the more fulfilment is possible for God's being. The ultimate aim of ethical behaviour is to produce the greatest possible value for the consequent nature of God.

In possessing the characteristics of consequentialism and value-maximization, process ethics is, in structure at least, similar to many utilitarian approaches, in particular classical utilitarianism.[11] What is important for utilitarianism is changes in states of affairs, that is to say, the process, rather than things in themselves. This is, Bernard Williams comments, due to the consequentialist nature of utilitarianism: 'I take it to be the central idea of consequentialism that the only kind of thing that has intrinsic value is states of affairs,

---

[11] The similarity is also noticed by Morris (1986: 124–6), who comments 'Mor-ality consists in the maximization of experience. Each philosopher provides his own version of the principle of utility.'

and that anything else that has value has it because it conduces to some intrinsically valuable state of affairs' (Smart and Williams 1973: 83). Many utilitarian systems also aim at maximizing value or utility—however it might be defined—by achieving the best balance of good consequences over bad.

Thus some utilitarian and process approaches to ethics share several crucial methodological characteristics: those of consequentialism and value-maximization. Obviously, there are also important metaphysical differences, primarily that Whitehead's process system is theistic. In fact, the presence of the consequent nature of God summing experiences gives process thinking an anchor for its ethical perspective which is lacked by utilitarians, where locating a 'general good' is somewhat problematic (since there is nothing which corresponds to the sum of experience). A second metaphysical difference is the central role of the actual occasion in process thinking: human beings, and other sentient organisms, rather than being the primary individuals, are complex societies of actual occasions. Value, then, in process thinking, is focused on the actual occasions of which everything is composed and on the consequent nature of God. However, despite their deeply divergent metaphysical frameworks, process thinking and some forms of utilitarianism at least, share an ethical affinity.

Process Thinking and Mill's Utilitarianism

Mill's utilitarianism is, as is well-known, based on pleasure and pain. Value (which, as a consequentialist, Mill locates in 'states-of-affairs' rather than 'things-in-themselves') is experiential, relating to the states of feeling in organisms which have this capacity. Here, Mill's approach differs from some forms of consequentialism, which are not experience-centred (for instance, that of Robin Attfield, as will become evident in the next chapter). Mill's locus of value in experience is, of course, congenial to a process understanding of value, as relating to the subjective feelings of actual entities. At first sight, however, Mill's focus on pleasure and pain seems very different from the value criteria of harmony and intensity of experience adopted by most process thinkers.

However, Mill's understanding of pleasure and pain is considerably more complex than this initial comparison would suggest. In particular, Mill differentiates between different qualities of pleasure, as well as quantities of it; and these qualities closely resemble concepts of valuable experience identified by process thinkers. As Mill comments in *Utilitarianism*:

It is indisputable that the being whose capacities of enjoyment are low, has the greatest chance of having them fully satisfied; and a highly endowed being will always feel that any happiness which he can look for, as the world is constituted, is imperfect. But he can learn to bear the imperfections, if they are at all bearable; and they will not make him envy the being who is indeed unconscious of the imperfections, but only because he feels not at all the good which those imperfections qualify. It is better to be a human being dissatisfied than a pig satisfied; better to be a Socrates dissatisfied than a fool satisfied . . . (Mill 1979: 260)

The broadening of the concept of pleasure here in Mill brings it very near to the idea in process thinking of harmony and intensity of experience. The contentment of a pig, or of a fool, is like a harmonious experience which lacks intensity; it is of less value than an experience with a greater degree of intensity, even if it lacks the same amount of harmony. Mill also considers that value is lost if a less rich or less intense way of life is adopted, through electing to take the 'nearer good'. This is identical to the process concept of triviality, where the most intense experience possible is not actualized, and hence generates less value than it might otherwise have done. Whitehead, for instance, comments that: 'Good people of narrow sympathies are apt to be unfeeling and unprogressive, enjoying their egotistical goodness. Their case, on a higher level, is analogous to that of a man completely degraded to a hog' (Whitehead 1926: 96). Mill and Whitehead thus consider intense, complex experiences to be of more value than simple, trivial experiences. Mill argues for this as a matter of human preference: we would all prefer an intense, even if dissatisfying experience to a trivial, satisfying one; we would all rather be a sad Socrates than a happy fool. While issuing in the same conclusion, Whitehead's reasoning here is rather different; while it may be true that the generation of more intense experience may be preferred by human beings, its ultimate importance is the contribution which it makes to the consequent nature of God.

The similarity between Mill and Whitehead has passed largely unnoticed in process writing. Indeed, John Cobb, one of Whitehead's most widely known interpreters, attacks utilitarianism vehemently. Equating utilitarianism, it seems, with a simple,

Benthamite position, Cobb rejects its ethical approach: 'An old example [of the case against it] is that many of us would prefer to share with Socrates an experience of pain than to share with a pig the experience of contentment...Values must be correlated with reflective preferences, or assertions about them are meaningless and arbitrary' (Cobb 1966: 101). In fact, Cobb is here making the same objection as Mill to Benthamite utilitarianism: Bentham's calculus of pleasure and pain is an over-simple one, failing to take into account, for instance, the more profound experiences that would be preferred after thought rather than immediate and thoughtless pleasures. Mill most definitely thinks, like Cobb, that to have a more complex experience is a better state, even if this brings more dissatisfaction. Bube, in his consideration of value in Cobb, comments that Cobb is 'ironically borrowing from John Stuart Mill's version of hedonism' by using Mill's very example of a pig and Socrates (Bube 1988: 47). But if Cobb is borrowing this example, he is doing so unconsciously (he does not appear to realize that this example comes from Mill). The real irony is that, despite his attack on utilitarianism, by a different system, Cobb has come up with something very close to it.

A similar argument concerning the resemblance between process thinking—in particular of Hartshorne's approach—to Mill's understanding of pleasure and pain has been made by J. Moskop (1980) and stimulated a response by T. Nairn (1988: 170–9). Their exchange is of considerable interest to this study. Moskop (1980: 18) likens process thinking to Mill's utilitarianism in a broader context than purely that of his complex understanding of the qualities of pleasure. He suggests five key theses on which Mill and Hartshorne agree. These are (1) that the aim of ethical behaviour is to further the good; (2) that the good is experiential; (3) that there are morally significant differences of quality between experiences; (4) that the experience of all sentient beings is morally considerable; and (5) that experience is valuable as a balance between two poles—which Mill calls tranquillity and excitement, and which Hartshorne calls harmony and intensity.

The accuracy of Moskop's points 1–3 has already been argued in this chapter; and point 4 will be considered in the following chapter. However, there are serious problems with Moskop's point 5: here his argument seems to have been carried too far. Moskop argues that tranquillity and excitement for Mill are equivalent to intensity and harmony for Hartshorne. This is, however, problematic. Tranquillity and excitement are, first, of limited significance to Mill, being merely one of the ways in which he elaborates the concepts of pain and pleasure. In contrast, harmony and intensity are of crucial importance to process thinking. More importantly, Moskop accurately describes tranquillity and excitement as 'poles' for Mill: people oscillate between them, and one is a preparation for the other. A pleasurable life would be composed from both tranquil and exciting experiences. But it is clear that they are mutually *preclusive* experiences. It is impossible to be both tranquil and excited simultaneously. The two are at different ends of one scale. However, this is not true of harmony and intensity in process thought. In the papers which Moskop cites, as he points out, Hartshorne (1974*b*: 215) discusses the nature of *contrast* and intensity, and even goes so far as to say: 'It is an aesthetic principle that intensity of experience depends on contrast.' But Moskop seems to have confused *contrast* with *conflict*. It would only be the case that intensity is on the other end of the scale from harmony if intensity *meant* conflict. But intensity should be, as Whitehead (1978: 115) makes clear, an ordered state, not one of conflict. It is *possible* to have an intense and harmonious experience at the same time, although this is uncommon because a greater capacity for intensity makes conflict more likely. But it does not *necessitate* it. It is perfectly *possible* for Socrates to be satisfied and hence to have an intense and harmonious experience which would be of more value than an intense but non-harmonious experience. The aim, in process thinking, is to maximize both harmony and intensity as much as possible. Thus, Moskop (1980: 23) is mistaken to argue that both Mill and Hartshorne 'recognise the importance of a balance between simple, harmonious experiences (tranquillity) and more complex or intense experiences (excitement)'. In fact, only Mill recognizes this balance. For Hartshorne, the balance is that of an experience which neither has intensity but lacks harmony (the sad Socrates) nor one which has harmony but lacks intensity (the happy fool). The more intensely harmonious, or harmoniously intense, an experience is, the better. Certainly, there is no virtue for Hartshorne in oscillating between the two positions.

Moskop also comments that excitment and tranquillity are not used by Mill as synonyms for higher and lower pleasures. Yet a process thinker *does* consider that a more intense experience is a higher one. A very intense experience with very little harmony is valued far more than a very harmonious experience with very little intensity.[2] So an unhappy Socrates (intense but not harmonious experience) is of much more value than a happy pig (harmonious, but not intense experience). Thus they do not act as value balances for one another in the way that tranquillity and excitement do.

While this comparison between Mill and Hartshorne pushes the resemblance between them too far, it does not destroy Moskop's underlying contention. In many respects, both of structure and of content, process ethical thinking does resemble the utilitarianism of John Stuart Mill.

The Problem of Justice

Thomas Nairn, in his article responding to Moskop's argument, makes several criticisms of the view that process thinking is closely related to Mill, or indeed to hedonistic utilitarianism in general. His initial remarks concern the metaphysical divide between process thinking and utilitarianism—in particular, the theistic nature of the process system. However, as we have seen, the acknowledgement of a different metaphysical foundation does not mean that there can be no ethical similarity between the two positions.

Nairn's more substantial criticism concerns the question of justice in process and utilitarian ethics. His fundamental argument is that, if process ethics behave like utilitarianism, and God is at the root of ethics, then God must be behaving, or wanting others to behave, in a utilitarian way. This, for Nairn, is a violation of his own as well as Hartshorne's concept of God. He comments: 'An unjust God, however... would be unloving, and therefore would not be God at all' (Nairn 1988: 175).

Fundamental to this criticism is Nairn's belief that utilitarianism is an unjust ethical system. If God were to behave in the way in which Moskop describes—a way akin to utilitarianism—then God

---

[12] In opposition to this, Cobb (1966: 102) does say that 'great strength accompanied by serious discord may be inferior to a simple and placid harmony'. However, this is not reinforced elsewhere in his own work, or in that of other process thinkers who argue that a discordant intense experience is of more value than a trivial harmonious one. (Indeed, this appears to be the whole point of the Socrates/fool analogy.)

would be unjust.[3] Since God cannot be unjust, either Moskop's interpretation of Hartshorne, or Hartshorne himself, must be wrong. Nairn chooses to defend Hartshorne against Moskop, and to argue therefore that process ethics does not support a utilitarian position. Lying behind this accusation that utilitarianism is unjust is Nairn's understanding of utilitarianism as a maximizing value system. We have already seen that process thinking can be accurately so characterized. Some philosophers have expressed doubts as to whether Mill himself intended to be thus understood. Sprigge (1990: 18), for instance, suggests that, by distinguishing different qualities of pleasure and pain, Mill may have understood them to be incommensurable. Such value incommensurability could make summing pleasures impossible.[4] If this is a correct interpretation of Mill, then he differs in this respect from process thinking, and indeed from most utilitarian approaches, which do aim at the best overall consequences or production of maximum utility (however utility may be understood). It is this aggregative, maximizing nature of utilitarianism that leaves it open to the criticism that it is unjust. Since process ethics adopts the same maximizing methodology, one would expect process thinking to be vulnerable to the same justice critique. After all, as Hartshorne (1974*b*: 214) comments: 'to be ethical is to seek aesthetic optimization of experience for the community'.

It is essential to have some kind of definition of what is meant by justice in this context. In general, justice concerns that which is fair or impartial, usually when making decisions about the treatment of individuals, or arbitrating in a situation of conflict. However, when the 'problem of justice' in both utilitarian and process thought is being considered, a slightly more precise understanding is usually in mind: that of the limits of what one may do to someone else, the issue of personal inviolability. Bernard Williams describes justice in this sense as 'respect for the integrity of the individual' (Smart and Williams 1973: 108). Both process thinkers and utilitarians have been accused of failing to respect this integrity and putting no ultimate limits on what may be done to create more utility or harmony and intensity of experience. J. L. Mackie, for instance,

---

[13] Mill himself, of course, deals with just this problem and argues that a moral God 'must fulfil the requirements of utility to a supreme degree' (Mill 1979: 273).

[14] The question of difficulty of summation in process ethics will be developed later.

argues that; 'On a utilitarian view, transferring a satisfaction from one person to another, while preserving its magnitude, makes no morally significant difference' (Mackie quoted in Frey 1985). In other words, so long as the same amount of satisfaction is generated, the *distribution* is immaterial. Thus an action may cause some individuals acute suffering, but if their suffering is outweighed by the much increased happiness of others, then the action is morally justifiable—indeed, desirable. Similarly, it could be argued that in a process ethical system an action that trivializes or deharmonizes the experience of some individuals, but that, overall, increases harmonious and intense experience for the consequent nature of God is morally desirable. Yet such behaviour appears to be unjust. In other words, utilitarianism and process thought can allow, or even provide, a moral imperative for acts that seem to be unjust or reprehensible to someone who accepts an idea of personal inviolability. Regan (1984*a*: 209), a critic of utilitarianism, argues that utilitarianism treats individuals as 'mere receptacles of what has positive value (pleasure) or negative value (pain). They have no value of their own; what has value is what they contain.' As an analogy for utilitarianism, Regan describes individual organisms as cups containing either sweet or bitter liquids (pleasures and pains). The aim of moral decisions must be to achieve the best aggregative balance of sweet and bitter between the cups, involving redistribution or the breaking of cups if necessary. The cups in themselves are not of value; the value is in the balance of sweet and bitter that they contain. What matters is the best possible distribution of the liquids between the cups—even if some end up without any liquid at all.

It is difficult to avoid the suggestion that this picture also gives a powerful expression of the ethical approach adopted by process thinkers. Max Stackhouse (1981: 108), for instance, describes process thinking as a philosophy where concrete entities are dissolved in a web of relationships.[5] As he goes on to comment, this throws up great problems for process thought: 'There is a "thinginess" about life that does not easily dissolve into its relationships; there is a reality about a self—a Socrates or Jesus, a John Smith or Jane Doe—that is not easily accounted for by appealing to a "synthesis of a multiplicity of relations".' It is this lack of 'thinginess' that is

---

[5] The parallels between process philosophy and so-called deep ecology are very striking at this point. This will be further examined in Ch. 5.

the fundamental cause of unease concerning process attitudes to justice. Henry Clark (1981: 136) argues that process thought, on this count, becomes unable to 'productively address the issues of personal inviolability, equity and rights'.

However, a number of responses can be made to this attack. It might be suggested, for instance, that Hartshorne's understanding of the human being as 'dipolar' protects his thinking at least from such difficulties. Hartshorne maintains that all human individuals—and God—have an 'essence' which constitutes one part of their nature. This essence can be defined as 'the individual in abstraction from all in him which is accidental or without which he would still be himself' (Hartshorne and Reese 1953: 4). This 'essence' is what constitutes our personal identity, but as Hartshorne (1974b: 201) maintains, 'Personal identity is a partial, not complete identity; it is an abstract aspect of life, not life in its concreteness. Concretely each of us is a numerically new reality every fraction of a second.' This constantly changing concreteness constitutes, in Hartshorne's account, the other pole of being. These poles resemble, at least, Regan's image of the cups (the essence of personal identity, the self) and the water (the constant flow of changing experience). If Hartshorne were to maintain that the abstract pole, the essence, was of *ethical* significance, then this might allow him to resist the charge that his philosophy, at least, is unable productively to address 'personal inviolability, equity and rights'. However, further study of Hartshorne's work does not tend to support this position.

First, when making ethical decisions, Hartshorne (1974b: 203) insists that to concentrate on one's own thread of personal identity is 'an illusion of egoism'. This is not true only of one's own thread of personal identity but also of that of any particular others. 'Both you and the other, as individual animals, are passing phenomena whose careers may cease at any time' (ibid. 206). Ethical behaviour, therefore, according to Hartshorne, should not be about protecting individual threads of identity, but rather about the general good. The general good will, of course, attach to abstract threads of personal identity (in the same way as in Regan's example the water is contained in cups). But the particular threads of identity, like the cups, are not what is important: 'Our ultimate obligations are to the future in an impersonal or suprapersonal sense, to humanity, nature and God' (Hartshorne 1981: 105).

Hartshorne clearly emphasizes, in utilitarian fashion, the ethical importance of the general good, 'the ongoing communal process of life as such'. Anything other than this 'subordinates the concrete to the abstract' (Hartshorne 1974*b*: 207) and is 'not quite ethics in the clearheaded sense' (ibid. 213). Hartshorne's dipolar concept of the self, then, does not seem to offer a defence against the criticisms of such writers as Stackhouse and Clark.

Paul Custodio Bube (1988: 119), however, in his consideration of the ethics of John Cobb, explicitly argues that process thinkers such as Cobb do have a concept of rights and a belief in personal inviolability. In support of this contention, he turns to Cobb's conception of the soul, which Cobb argues is composed by the close unity of the actual occasions composing the human individual (an idea which performs a similar function to Hartshorne's abstract pole of personal identity). This uniquely integrated soul, Bube claims, provides a process basis for human rights. A human is irreplaceable; no other human individual can have identical rich experience, and therefore each human is more than just part of a wider web of experiences. Bube (ibid. 139) thus describes human individuals as inviolable, although he later qualifies this by commenting that Cobb himself would not consider inviolability to be absolute (in fact, to my knowledge, Cobb does not use the word at all).[6]

By his use of the language of human irreplaceability and inviolability here in relation to Cobb's work, Bube raises an issue of some importance. Is there any way in which such terms can be justified in process thinking? First, and most obviously, it is clear that process thinkers accept that human beings generate large amounts of value. Due to the strength of the mental poles of the actual occasions which constitute them and build up their capacity for mentality, human beings are capable of generating very intense experiences. Thus, for process thinkers, human lives are frequently inviolable in practice because of the rich experience which they can produce. However, in circumstances where overall richness of experience would be enhanced rather than damaged by taking life, all that we have seen so far from process thinkers (like utilitarians) would indicate that overall richness of experience has ethical priority over protection of life. As my consideration of

[16] Birch and Cobb (1981: 166) also explicitly deny that human life is sacred or of infinite value.

Hartshorne's dipolar concept of the person suggested, it is the general good not individual personal life-threads that are important. This indicates that inviolability of life in a process ethical system, as in a utilitarian one, cannot be guaranteed.

However, there is a further element to be considered here. An important part of Bube's argument is that no human can have experiences identical to those of another; the experience of each is unique. This argument is clearly important, since if every human generates unique experiences, contrasts are created between different human beings. These, it could be argued, cause greater value for God. Indeed, at first sight it would seem possible to argue that the value generated by such contrasts is sufficient to render a life inviolable. The taking of life would significantly reduce the depth of contrast in the world, and hence reduce the intensity of experience that God could receive from such contrasts.

This, however, is not enough to render human life inviolable as Bube suggests; nor does it necessarily support the position that human lives are irreplaceable. Again, this is because process ethics is consequentialist in form. What matters is the generation of rich experience for God. It is not the *source* of the value which is significant, but the *quality* and *quantity*. This has important implications for inviolability in a process system.

An example may make this clearer. An individual human being—Clare—is born. In process terms she is a society of constantly changing actual occasions, producing harmonious and intense experiences enjoyed by God. Her experiences are unique, thus contrasting with the experiences of those around her, and contributing to intensity of feeling in the consequent nature of God. Clare is now painlessly killed. The harmonious intensity of Clare's experiences, and the contrast these made with other human experiences, is lost. But in Clare's place a child, Julie, is born, who would not otherwise have existed. She generates harmoniously intense experiences, and these experiences contrast with those humans around her, generating intensity of feeling for God, and hence producing value. Assuming that there was no great grieving for Clare, and that Julie lived a satisfying life, it would not seem unreasonable to assume that the value generated in the world would be much the same whether Julie existed or Clare existed.

A number of issues are raised here which will be explored in subsequent chapters. The basic point being made is that even though human experiences may be very intense and harmonious and may produce great depth of contrast, they are not inviolable in a process system such as Whitehead's. Even Bube repeats that the realization of maximal beauty is the aim of God, and thus should be the aim of all life. This statement is without caveat, and clearly stands in tension with inviolability.

Cobb's writing supports this understanding of process thinking. Whilst he does use the language of rights, he rejects any 'absolutist arguments' for them (Birch and Cobb 1981: 175).[7] He concludes: 'There are no absolutes here. There is the general principle—to act so as to maximize value in general...' and again: 'The ethical requirement is that we provide circumstances which promote richness of feeling' (ibid. 174, 205). Cobb repeatedly asserts the primacy of maximizing rich (that is, harmonious and intense) experience for God as the fundamental ethical principle. Of course, this usually corresponds with what is best for an individual human being. But where there is conflict, it is the promotion of total ordered intensity of feeling at which, according to process thinking, ethical decisions should aim. In the face of this, Bube's argument that the unity of the human soul is such that it is inviolable is little supported in the rest of process writing.

We can now return to Nairn's contention that Hartshorne's process ethics cannot be utilitarian, since this would make God unjust. His statement in itself begs a question, since Nairn is working with the assumption—from outside process thinking—that God must be just in the sense of protecting personal inviolability and rights. Coming with this assumption, if he wishes to defend Hartshorne as a theologian, he has to assert that process ethics does not resemble utilitarianism and look for evidence for this. In doing so, he side-steps the real ethical questions, and charges Moskop with ignoring or even opposing views with which Moskop does not in fact quarrel. For instance, Moskop has no argument with Nairn over the location of value in God, nor with the idea that God suffers with the occasions that make up the world and appreciates all individuals. It is, in fact, Nairn who avoids

---

[7] Rights language is frequently used in process ethical writing, particularly among those who write on animal rights. However, to anticipate later conclusions, rights can always be overridden if harmony and intensity of experience are thereby increased. This echoes Mill's (1979: 309) understanding of rights, where rights are based on utility.

confronting the important ethical issues which are raised by his own work.

Nairn himself argues that 'the aim of ethics is not the balancing of interests, but rather the creating of a more harmonious world as a gift for God' (Nairn 1988: 173). Although this is a partial definition (since Nairn has neglected to mention intensity, which is more significant) it is essentially a process one, and one with which Moskop would not quibble. No one has suggested that the purpose of process ethics is to balance interests; this is not essentially a process position at all. Nairn's alternative, 'to create a more harmonious world', includes the maximizing element 'more', and is far closer to a process ethic. Moskop's concern, however, is in how this rather vague aim translates in practice, that is to say, when conflicts arise, as they inevitably do in a world where there is freedom. Nairn accepts that such conflicts requiring ethical solutions must happen (ibid. 175). At this point he introduces Hartshorne's concept of *tragedy* (also used by Bube). It is not God's will that any individual should suffer, and when they do, it is a tragedy for the individual, and also for God, who shares in the suffering. Again, this is a perspective that Moskop would not contest. That God shares in suffering, and that suffering is tragic, is a contention put forward by all process theologians (and a large number of other besides). However, this does not help in answering the questions: 'How should one behave morally in a situation of conflict?' 'How should one make ethical decisions?' The only answer to these questions which can be drawn from Nairn's paper is that since God 'is not indifferent to any suffering but in fact shares in all' one should act so as to minimize suffering, i.e. in a directly (negative) utilitarian way!

At root, the problem seems to be Nairn's much stronger understanding of the centrality of the individual human being (or other organism) than that which process thinking can countenance. It is not that God wishes the weal of one and the woe of another, but rather that God wishes to generate maximum value or richness of experience from the inevitable conflicts of existence, and that ethical behaviour is action according to this end. If this means woe to some actual occasions or societies of actual occasions, overall it is still for the best—an outcome which again sounds utilitarian. Nairn's argument, while developing the theistic element, has failed to change the basic conclusion: that process ethics behaves in an aggregative, maximizing way, and in this respect resembles many utilitarian approaches; that both are vulnerable to a justice critique; that the process understanding of an individual is even less well defined than that of utilitarianism.

It is important, however, to reinforce at this point that while this analysis may undercut the substantiality of organismic individuality, it is not intended to deny the importance of individuals such as human beings in the process system. Human beings, and some other animals, are often described as 'monarchies' in a process system: that is to say, they have a dominant or presiding actual occasion which generates a degree of unity and control among the actual occasions which actualize within its sphere of influence. This contrasts with other societies of actual occasions, 'democracies', which lack such co-ordination and which have no controlling centre. The closeness and co-operation of monarchical societies allows for the generation of much more valuable experience than could be a characteristic of the more disparate democracy, or possible for the individual actual occasion if it were outside the society. In this sense, the whole is more than the sum of its parts, since as a whole it is capable of generating far more rich experience than its parts. However, this does not mean that a whole, such as a human being, is more valuable than its experiences. None the less, monarchical societies—human beings, and some higher animals—generate the most harmonious and intense, rich, and valuable experience known in the universe (other than that of the consequent nature of God). These monarchical societies of actual occasions are thus the most important components of the process system. It is for this reason that I have called process thinking an *individualist* consequentialist system: its focus is on the experience of individual organisms. This is not intended to be an absolute label; indeed, process thinking, in the context of environmental ethics, is less individualist in focus than the (broadly) utilitarian approaches to be considered in the next chapter. However, it stands in contrast with the collective consequentialist ethical systems to be considered in Chapter 4.

In summary then, process ethics is consequentialist, maximizing, and totalizing and to this extent resembles many utilitarian approaches. As with Mill, value is exclusively experiential, although in process thinking the experience of God is the key factor. Like Mill again, quality of experience as well as quantity is of significance. This quality is expressed by process thinkers in terms of ordered intensity generated by depth of contrast. Individual higher animals, in both hedonistic utilitarianism and process thinking, are the primary generators of such value. The similarity of process thinking to utilitarianism opens process ethics to some traditional criticisms of utilitarianism: in particular to the charge of injustice. In the less traditional field of environmental ethics, however, new problems with the process position arise, and I shall begin to examine these in the following chapter.

2

Process Thinking, Individualist Consequentialism, and Animals

Individualist Consequentialist Positions

From Bentham to the present day, utilitarian philosophers have, to a greater or lesser degree, extended ethical concern to non-human animals.[1] It was Bentham, after all, who wrote the famous words, 'It may one day come to be recognized that the number of the legs, the villosity of the skin, or the termination of the *os sacrum* are reasons equally insufficient for abandoning a sensitive being to the same fate . . . The question is not, Can they *reason*? nor Can they *talk*? but, *Can they suffer*?' (Bentham 1943: 411). Admittedly, in the past, many hedonistic utilitarian philosophers have ignored the pleasures and pains of animals. That this cannot be logically supported is increasingly acknowledged even by these same philosophers. J. C. C. Smart, for example, who previously doubted the moral value of animals, has subsequently revised his views: 'It is a merit of utilitarianism, with its stress on happiness and unhappiness, that lower animals must be considered along with human beings so that they are not debarred from full and direct consideration because they are not "rational"' (Smart 1987: 283).

Alongside hedonistic utilitarians such as Bentham and Smart, other individualist consequentialist writers have also insisted that the consequences of human actions for animals should be taken into account when making ethical decisions. In this chapter three such approaches will be examined: those of Peter Singer, Donald VanDe Veer, and Robin Attfield.

Hedonistic and Preference Utilitarianism: Peter Singer

Peter Singer's *Animal Liberation: Towards an End to Man's Inhumanity to Animals* (1976) presented a hedonistic utilitarian

[1] I will subsequently refer to 'non-human animals' by the shorthand 'animals'—whilst recognizing the inbuilt separation of 'human' from 'animal' suggested by such linguistic usage.

position which took animals into account. Singer subsequently developed this account in a number of articles, most prominently in *Practical Ethics* (1979*b*) and 'Killing Humans and Killing Animals', *Inquiry*, 22 (1979*a*). His developed position is a coalition of hedonistic and preference utilitarianism.

Fundamental to Singer's hedonistic utilitarianism, as indeed it must be, is the capacity of an organism to have subjective experience. It is this capacity which allows it to feel pleasure or pain, and hence to have valuable experiences. Value, or at least intrinsic value, is identified with pleasurable subjective experiences; having such experiences means that an organism should be taken into account when moral decisions are being made. (In Singer's terms, the organism is 'morally considerable'.) The capacity to have painful or pleasurable experiences also means that an organism has interests; such a capacity is in fact a 'prerequisite for having interests at all' (Singer 1976: 27). An organism which can feel pain has an interest in avoiding it; an organism which can feel pleasure has an interest in sustaining or increasing it. This presentation of utilitarianism in terms of interests, rather than directly as pleasures and pains, allows Singer to consider interests that would not normally fall directly into the narrow categories of simple pleasure and pain. However, as he points out, this does not substantially change his position. Mill's broad sense of pleasure would encompass most of what Singer wishes to consider by interests (Singer 1979*b*: 13).

Only those organisms that can have subjective experiences, and hence interests, are, for Singer, morally considerable. Where 'a being is not capable of suffering, or of enjoyment, there is nothing to be taken into account' (Singer 1976: 27). This generates a boundary beyond which moral behaviour is inapplicable. Into this category fall molluscs, insects, plants, and non-living objects, natural or artificial. They have no experiences, and hence no interests. In *Animal Liberation* this is the only boundary which Singer accepts. Sentient organisms are morally considerable, insentient organisms and objects are not. All morally considerable animals, including humans, have, according to Singer (ibid. 25), an equal interest in avoiding pain and in generating pleasure: 'The interests of every being affected by an action are to be taken into account, and given the same weight as the like interests of any other being.' However, even on his earlier and simpler account, this does not mean that if, for example, an amount of suffering must be inflicted on either an animal or a human being, there is no moral difference between the two. While this may be the case in so far as the suffering alone is concerned, other interests may be affected. Human beings have extra interests not possessed by animals that would make the infliction of the pain on a human being worse. A human may, for instance, anticipate pain, or subsequently remember it vividly, which means that the same amount of pain may generate greater bad experience for a human being than for an animal. Similarly, other human beings, or human society as a whole, may be affected by human suffering in a way that would not be the case for an animal. These side-effects may make it preferable, overall, to inflict suffering on an animal than on an adult human being. Given these conditions, however, a human being with a severe mental handicap, or a baby, may not have the same 'protection by side-effects' (such as anticipation or memory) as an adult human being. It might be preferable to inflict suffering on a baby than an adult, and indeed, there are circumstances where it would be better to inflict suffering on a baby than on an adult non-human mammal, such as a chimpanzee. It is the interests of the organism that are morally relevant, rather than its species. This allows Singer to avoid being charged with the word he popularized himself: speciesism.

However, Singer later acknowledges that this position, being a kind of expanded classical hedonistic utilitarian one, was seriously flawed. Hedonistic utilitarianism focuses on the value of experiences, rather than on the organism which has them. The aim of ethical behaviour is to maximize pleasurable experience. This not only has the consequence, as we saw earlier, of ignoring the distribution of such experiences; it also carries the suggestion that if an organism can be painlessly killed (so as not to produce painful experience) and replaced by an organism that would not otherwise have existed, with the same or greater level of pleasurable experience, this would be morally acceptable. Thus hedonistic utilitarianism seems to support a 'replaceability' hypothesis, where one organism can be substituted for another. Human beings are not excluded from this position, although possible negative side-effects are greatest in the human case (such as anticipation, grief, and disturbance in the community that can generate offsetting negative experiences). But the existence of such side-effects is by no means guaranteed.

As Singer realizes, his interest utilitarianism, based very heavily on pleasurable and painful experience, is also open to this interpretation. His awareness of the problem of 'replaceability' leads him to adopt a form of preference utilitarianism, which he adds on to his hedonistic utilitarianism. Thus, in more recent writing, Singer divides the 'morally considerable' into two groups: the conscious and the self-conscious. The conscious are organisms which have pleasurable and painful experiences, but have no self-awareness, no conception of themselves as persisting into the future, and hence no preference to go on living. They are purely the sums of their experiences: 'This kind of being is, in a sense, impersonal . . . in killing it, one does it no personal wrong, although one does reduce the quantity of happiness in the universe. But this wrong, if it is wrong, can be counterbalanced by bringing into existence a similar being which will live an equally happy life' (Singer 1979b: 102). Thus they are replaceable; as Frey (1983: 161) puts it, they can be replenished as a glass of water, once drunk, can be refilled.

This is not the case with self-conscious organisms. They have conceptions of themselves as individuals who endure through time. They have desires and preferences about the future, primarily the preference to go on living. These preferences are morally significant in preference utilitarianism, which takes into account 'the preferences of all affected by an action and weighs them according to the strength of preference under certain conditions of knowledge and reflection. Preference utilitarians count the killing of a being with a preference for continued life as worse than the killing of a being with no such preference' (Singer 1979a: 152). Thus preference utilitarianism acts, for Singer, as a ring-fence to guard self-conscious organisms—normal adult human beings, and adult higher mammals such as primates and whales—against painless destruction and replacement. Their awareness of their own individuality and their preference to go on living gives them a moral significance not available to those who are sentient but not self-conscious.

Singer thus developed a hybrid utilitarianism which provides different levels of moral considerability for different kinds of sentient organisms. This can be described as a three-tier ethical system. The third, or bottom tier, consists of insentient organisms and objects that have no experience and no moral considerability. The second tier is composed of organisms that are sentient and conscious but which lack self-consciousness and preferences about the future. These organisms are of moral significance, but they can be painlessly killed and replaced without there being a loss of value in the world. The first or top tier, however, is composed from sentient self-conscious organisms with preferences about the future. The organisms in this top tier, Singer claims, cannot ethically be painlessly destroyed and replaced. This three-tier system assists Singer in making ethical decisions where interests conflict. The problem of resolving conflicts also occupies VanDe Veer.

Two-Factor Egalitarianism: Donald VanDe Veer

Both stimulated and concerned by Singer's account in *Animal Liberation*, VanDe Veer attempted to develop a more discriminating and detailed account of the relative weighting of human and non-human animals when making moral decisions—which he calls a 'theory of interspecific justice' (1979: 57). Alarmed both by accounts that failed to take animals into consideration at all, and equally by those which claimed to be strongly egalitarian, VanDe Veer proposed a middle way, which he called Two-Factor Egalitarianism.

Like Singer's view, VanDe Veer's 1979 position is not far removed from classical hedonistic utilitarianism. The ability to feel pleasure or pain and hence to have interests gives an animal moral considerability. The difficulty, however, is to make decisions when the interests of different sentient individuals, in particular humans and animals, conflict. In contrast with Singer, however, VanDe Veer does not turn to the problem of painless killing and replaceability, and adopt a principle of adjudication based on whether or not sentient animals have preferences. Indeed, VanDe Veer misses the force of this difficulty, commenting that 'generally, when it is in some creature's interest not to suffer, it is also in its interest not to die (and hence not to be killed)'. This assumption, as was clear from Singer's account, is by no means a secure one. VanDe Veer instead develops a discriminatory principle based on psychological or mental capacities. Thus, although, like Singer, he has a relatively clear demarcation of moral considerability (the ability to feel pleasure or pain) he does not have two clear tiers above this, but rather a grading of superior and inferior psychological capacities. Alongside this discriminatory principle, he also distinguishes between different categories of interests: basic, serious, and peripheral. A creature has a basic interest in something that is essential for its survival, a serious interest in something that 'although it can survive without... [it] is difficult or costly (to its wellbeing) to do so' and a peripheral interest in something that is of only mild significance to its welfare (ibid. 63).

Thus, VanDe Veer grades both organisms and interests. The more serious the interest and the more psychologically complex the organism, the stronger the positive weighting. This leads to several clear-cut conclusions. If, for instance, conflicting interests are of equal weight, the psychologically more complex organism takes priority. A basic interest will always trump a peripheral interest, however psychologically complex the organism with the peripheral interest may be. However, the situation is less straightforward where the serious interest of a psychologically superior organism conflicts with the basic interest of a less complex one. Under such circumstances, VanDe Veer thinks that the psychologically more complex organism should have priority, and the basic interest should be sacrificed to the serious one.

The aim of VanDe Veer's discriminatory principles—as Peter Singer's—is to achieve maximum total utility. The subordination of peripheral to basic interests and of psychologically inferior to psychologically superior organisms is aimed at achieving this end. The more psychologically sophisticated an animal, according to VanDe Veer, the better the experience produced; the more basic the interest, the more satisfaction in having it met. Failure to acknowledge VanDe Veer's principles, then, at least in a broad sense, will result in a loss of total utility. If one were to be, in VanDe Veer's terms, a 'radical speciesist', holding it to be morally acceptable to inflict suffering on non-human animals for a trifling reason, a loss in total utility would result. The small gain in human utility would be vastly outweighed by the loss to suffering non-human animals. Similarly, the 'species egalitarian' position which would treat members of all species equally, 'blatantly ignores relevant differences' and by doing so fails to maximize the utility which would be gained by a positive weighting to the psychologically more complex (ibid. 66).

Thus, VanDe Veer elaborates a position in many essentials similar to that of Singer. Unlike Singer, however, he integrates the tiers of moral considerability into one scale of psychological complexity and categorized interests into different degrees of significance. He thus provides a more detailed account of the prioritization involved in making moral decisions. In this respect, Attfield is even more meticulous.

Robin Attfield: Practice-Consequentialism

Attfield acknowledges a considerable philosophical debt both to Singer and to VanDe Veer. This debt is, however, more obvious in his earlier book *The Ethics of Environmental Concern* (1983) than in his later articles and in *A Theory of Value and Obligation* (1987) although in his earlier work, it is sometimes not clear whether Attfield should be regarded as a consequentialist at all.[2] In his later work, however, he makes a characteristically consequentialist statement about intrinsic value: 'I in fact hold that it is not objects as such which are of intrinsic value, but rather their states, activities and/or experiences. Beings can therefore be *bearers* of intrinsic value' (Attfield 1990: 63, italics mine). What state of affairs does Attfield consider to be intrinsically valuable? Here he diverges significantly from both Singer and VanDe Veer, and indeed from hedonistic utilitarianism in general. For both Singer and VanDe Veer, intrinsic value is experiential. The ability to experience is the prerequisite for having interests or preferences, and hence for moral considerability. However, Attfield severs this exclusive link between experience and value, an uncoupling of central import- ance in environmental ethics. He extends moral considerability beyond the boundary of sentience or experience, thus rendering some items in Singer's third tier morally considerable. Hedonistic utilitarianism is rejected as being 'severely impoverished and defective' (Attfield 1987: 32). He argues that intrinsic value is located in the state of flourishing, of exercising the basic capacities of a species, and in order to do this, of having basic needs met. An organism which has the capacity to develop and flourish has an interest in doing so.

It is clear from this description that such categories do not apply only to human beings or even to sentient organisms, but to all organisms that can be said to have a well-being—that is, all living

---

[2] A point also made by Taylor (1986: 270).

organisms.³ All organisms, regardless of their sentience, can be bearers of intrinsic value. Plants, insects, and bacteria, for instance, have a well-being and can flourish. Inanimate objects, however, which have none of these capacities, cannot generate intrinsic value and are still morally inconsiderable. This position makes the development of interspecific priority principles vital. The greater the number of organisms admitted to moral considerability, the greater the potential for conflict and the need, in a consequentialist system, to establish which behaviour will produce the best overall consequences.

Attfield, especially in *The Ethics of Environmental Concern*, is clearly impressed by VanDe Veer's Two-Factor Egalitarianism. VanDe Veer's failure to take insentient organisms into account, and his willingness to sacrifice basic interests to serious ones where psychologically more complex organisms are concerned is, however, questioned. Attfield (1987: 177) initially concludes that 'it has to be understood that creatures with capacities for more valuable forms of life receive priority over others only where the ability to exercise those capacities is genuinely at stake'. This would, he argues, nullify the argument that eating meat from factory farms is a case where a serious interest of a psychologically superior organism conflicts with a basic interest of a psychologically inferior organism, and hence takes priority. Not eating meat (unless it is a necessity for survival) does not threaten the capacities of superior organisms and hence cannot be justified on this principle.

In *A Theory of Value and Obligation*, Attfield develops a much more sophisticated set of priority principles which are intended to govern interhuman relationships, as well as human/non-human ones. It is the latter, however, with which I am particularly concerned. This schema still resembles VanDe Veer's, although Attfield introduces a considerable number of new elements. Like VanDe Veer, Attfield retains a sliding scale of psychological complexity and hence the amount of intrinsic value which can be generated. Humans are at the top of such a scale, with varying degrees of psychological complexity in sentient animals beneath. Plants and insentient organisms fall below this. The intrinsic value generated by an individual plant is close to negligible. Large groups

---

³ VanDe Veer (1979: 58) hints at such a position, but fails to develop it, by commenting that even protozoa have a well-being and something which is in their interest.

of plants, such as forests, may have greater value (although a forest is not distinctly valuable as a whole, but only as a collection of individual trees).

The second part of Attfield's weighting process is a scale of significance for needs and wants, resembling VanDe Veer's emphasis on interests. Attfield divides needs into 'survival' needs and 'basic' needs, where the former normally have priority. (Under exceptional conditions—if survival would be literally staying alive but without opportunity to flourish or develop essential capacities—this might not apply.) Beyond needs are wants and preferences, over which basic needs have priority. In addition, Attfield adds the category of the length of time the satisfaction of a need or want could last: the longer the time, the greater the total utility to be derived from it. Thus, Attfield's weighting system, like VanDe Veer's, gives priority to the basic and survival needs of the most sophisticated organisms over those of less sophisticated organisms, but basic needs of less sophisticated organisms have priority over wants or preferences of the more sophisticated. This system, Attfield (1987: 95) claims, can 'bring about an optimal balance of intrinsically valuable states of affairs over intrinsically undesirable ones'.

One further point should be made about Attfield's position as developed in *A Theory of Value and Obligation*. He describes his system as 'practice-consequentialism'—a form of rule-utilitarianism. There are, Attfield (ibid. 107) contends, 'various practices which make for or would make for, a much better world than would be possible either in their absence or through alternative practices'. Practices such as promise-keeping should be followed in each case, even where the results in that particular instance may be less optimal than they would have been had the promise been broken. Overall, the belief that promises will be kept will, for example, generate a climate of trust in society, and hence lead to better overall consequences. In this respect, Attfield's work differs from the act-utilitarianism of Singer and VanDe Veer.

Problems with Individualist Consequentialism in Environmental Ethics

The difficulties faced by individualist consequentialist ethics when applied to the non-human world are myriad. Many specific areas

that such an ethic finds difficult to accommodate, such as predation, wilderness, species, and ecosystems, will be explored in
later chapters, and will be passed by at this point. The focus here
will be on several more general issues that are, one might say,
foundational problems, from which many of the more specific
difficulties stem. Three main areas will be examined here, falling
under the broad headings of 'Experience and Value', 'Replaceability', and 'Subjectivity of Relative Judgements'.

Experience and Value

> They pick a quality that is conceded to be normally possessed
> by humans; they make it the basis for a capacity of rights, then
> they find it 'writ large' beyond the human pale
>
> (Rodman 1977: 93).

Although rights are not at issue here (Rodman's attack is directed
at Stone, a rights advocate, as well as at Singer) the process
described above is an important one. A central objection to
an individualist consequentialist basis for environmental ethics
focuses on its assignation of intrinsic value to qualities supremely
possessed by humans. This objection is, however, unevenly aimed
at Singer, VanDe Veer, and Attfield, each of whom have different
emphases in this context.

For Singer, the capacity to feel pleasure and pain, and so to have
interests, together with (on a higher level) the ability to have preferences, bestow moral considerability and degrees of moral significance. VanDe Veer, like Singer, takes sentience as the basic
requirement for moral considerability, and uses psychological complexity to differentiate degrees above this. Both take as a premiss
that intrinsic value must be experienced value: pleasurable subjective experiences, preferences, and psychological complexity are all
value-generating factors. Since experience, for both Singer and
VanDe Veer at least, is confined to animals, and reasonably
sophisticated ones at that, such criteria render all non-sentient
living beings—and collectives, such as ecosystems—morally inconsiderable. They can only be of instrumental value, to fulfil the
needs of, satisfy the preferences of, or give complex and pleasurable experiences to sentient animals.

Animals which are morally considerable (on the basis of their
ability to experience) are further ranked according to other human

qualities (psychological complexity, preference- having). Animals are thus implicitly—and frequently explicitly—categorized with so-called 'marginal humans'—those humans who lack some of the abilities of normal human adults. VanDe Veer, for instance, uses a 'bright chimpanzee' and a 'Down's syndrome child' in order to make a value comparison. Rodman (1977: 94) finds this categorization unacceptable, putting his argument with characteristic force: 'Is this then, the new enlightenment—to see non human animals as imbeciles, wilderness as a human vegetable?...It is perhaps analogous to regarding women as defective men who lack penises, or humans as defective sea mammals who lack sonar capacity...' At the heart of this criticism is the contention that individualist consequentialism of this kind fails to accept animals on their own terms, judging them by inappropriately human-centred standards. Of particular concern is the exclusive link of intrinsic value with experience, and the consequent inability of Singer and VanDe Veer to accept the generation of intrinsic value from anything other than organisms with nervous systems and subjective experiences.

Both Singer and VanDe Veer are aware that this criticism may be levelled at their work. VanDe Veer (1979: 73) comments:

Two-Factor Egalitarianism is not anthropocentric in the way that a view is if it regards species membership in homo sapiens as relevant per se...if others were to claim that Two-Factor Egalitarianism is also invidious and arbitrary in its 'psychocentric' emphasis, reasons need to be stated other than that it takes species membership per se as relevant; for it does not.

VanDe Veer is surely suggesting here that, while his position is not speciesist, it may well be called anthropocentric because it is geared to valuing the psyche. While human qualities, rather than species membership, are the indicators of value, value is still measured on a human-biased scale.

Singer, similarly, is aware of the accusation of anthropocentrism. He contends, however, that the connection of sentience and moral considerability is not arbitrary, but rather the only sensible position to adopt. It is not because human qualities are better than non-human ones, but because it makes no sense to argue that a non-sentient being can be treated badly. Since a non-sentient being cannot feel, nothing can matter to it, and consequently it is impossible to behave either morally or immorally towards it. This debate is a central one in environmental ethics, and one which spans the divide between deontologists and consequentialists. Regan, for example, in many ways vehemently opposed to Singer, puts forward a similar view concerning moral considerability in *The Case for Animal Rights*. Others, both deontologists and consequentialists, reject the link between experience and value, and some between any quality particularly possessed by humans and value.

Robin Attfield, for instance, as we have seen, does not insist that all value must be experienced. Thus he is not vulnerable to accusations of anthropocentrism in this way. None the less, like VanDe Veer, Attfield does argue that complex psychological capabilities generate more intrinsic value. Thus, although his criterion for moral considerability is not the ability to experience, the more psychologically human-like a non-human is, the more intrinsic value it can generate. Some environmental ethicists might still argue that Attfield's presentation is thoroughly anthropocentric. His emphasis on flourishing and fulfilment of capacities, while not uniquely human characteristics, are ones he argues that humans do supremely possess. In addition, Attfield focuses exclusively on individuals. Ecological systems, or species, can have no value other than that generated by the flourishing and the fulfilment of an individual's capacities. There is no place for collective value (which will be examined in Chapter 4). It is only individuals, who are by their very individuality like humans, who can have moral considerability.

Replaceability

There must always be the possibility of replaceability, or the substitution of one individual for another, in ethical systems aimed at the maximization of total value. Singer's acceptance of the principle of replaceability for lower organisms which are merely 'sums of their experiences' makes explicit this implicit characteristic of totalizing utilitarianism. However, Singer attempts to limit replaceability to the second tier of moral considerability, and to exclude the first tier. This has been questioned by both Lockwood (1979: 157) and Frey (1983). As Lockwood (1979: 160) comments:

He seems not to notice that a preference utilitarianism [*sic*] will support this thesis only if it is formulated in such a way as to render preferences themselves non-replaceable, in the sense that the frustration of one preference (or set of preferences) cannot be morally counterbalanced by the creation of another preference or set of preferences which would not otherwise have existed.

Lockwood does not find a satisfactory solution to this problem, which is acute. If Singer is advocating, as he seems to be, preference maximization, he cannot contend that the preference to go on living is ultimately inviolable. The individual's preference to live could be frustrated if the strength of other preferences for the individual's death were greater. Frey puts this more bluntly by suggesting that it could equally well be argued from Singer's position that providing a new life was created with an equal preference for life as the individual to be killed, killing could be justified.[4] This argument, without further development, is enough for some critics to describe Singer's utilitarian position as morally unacceptable. However, the implications of such a position even for the second ethical tier, the conscious but not self-conscious, are worth examining.

As part of his campaign not to be 'speciesist' Singer points out that his category of those without the preference to go on living is not restricted to the non-human. Babies, people with some kinds of mental handicaps, and those in comas, for example, are also in this position. The inexorable conclusion of this is that they, too, are replaceable; indeed, Singer gives an example of this with 'defective infants' being allowed to die painlessly, if the parents are prepared to try again for a non-defective one. However, as Lockwood right-fully points out, this actually applies also to 'normal' babies (presumably justifying the widespread practice of infanticide of female babies when they are born, to try again for the preferred boy). Replaceability also applies to those animals which are considered not to have a preference to go on living. Lockwood (1979: 168) makes this point powerfully by imagining the existence of a fictional service which he entitles 'Disposapup Ltd.'. In brief, Lockwood supposes that families enjoy the happy, playful nature of puppies, but that they are not so enthusiastic about fully grown dogs. He also supposes that they take an annual holiday each year, perhaps abroad, where it is inconvenient to take the puppy—or dog as it now is. A company, Disposapup Ltd., is set up to remove and painlessly kill each dog when the family goes away, and they return

---

[4] Regan (1984*a*: 208–11) also examines this argument.

from their holiday to another happy, playful puppy. He argues that Singer's ethical position makes this morally acceptable.

There is no apparent way in which Singer can resist this argument. Neither, it seems, can VanDe Veer, who is, in this respect, in a very similar position to Singer. Like Singer, VanDe Veer advocates maximization of total utility, where utility is measured by the satisfaction of interests—the more psychologically complex the better. Since interests are totalizable, there is no reason why one interest should not be replaced by another, if it would not otherwise have existed, provided that side-effects such as 'dread of impending disaster' do not create counteracting disutilities (VanDe Veer 1979: 70).

Attfield, however, is in a slightly different position, both in his rejection of the exclusive link between intrinsic value and experience, and in his practice-, rather than act-utilitarianism. Like Singer and VanDe Veer, however, he is a totalizing consequentialist, aiming at the generation of maximum total intrinsic value. It is not experiences which are totalled, but rather fulfilment of graded species-specific characteristics for the maximum length of time. However, this difference does not exclude him from the possibility of replaceability. As a consequentialist, it is not organisms themselves that are valuable. The value lies in the states of affairs that are generated by organisms. As with Singer and VanDe Veer, it must then be true for Attfield that, providing total value remains the same, which individual generates the value is irrelevant. Thus, it is inevitable that, within Attfield's system, one organism is replaceable by another. The killing of an organism would, of course, prevent it from flourishing and fulfilling its capacities; but the creation of a new organism which would not otherwise have existed, with the same opportunity to flourish and fulfil its capabilities, replaces the lost value.

It would seem possible, however, that Attfield's practice-consequentialism might constrain replaceability in a way impossible for act-utilitarianism. We have already seen that Attfield advocates, for example, keeping promises even where in the specific instance more immediate value might be generated by breaking them. Greater overall value, he contends, would result from the higher level of trust in the community when promises are kept, than would result from the mistrust when there is an expectation that promises will be broken. In similar vein, Attfield could argue that greater total value for society would be generated by not killing individuals and replacing them, even though total value might remain the same or even increase on some occasions (for instance by killing a handicapped baby in order to try for a non-handicapped one). The security which humans might derive from the knowledge that neither they nor their offspring would be painlessly killed and replaced would override the benefit gained from the specific occasions where total value might be increased by doing so.

This practice-consequentialist argument, however, is centrally flawed, at least in the context of the treatment of non-humans. Attfield (1987: 110) makes it quite clear that 'Practice-consequentialism does not call on agents to consider whether each and every action, whether important or trivial, should become part of a social practice, but rather to adhere to optimific practices which are already in force, and also to comply with ones of whose adoption by the relevant agents there is a significant prospect.' While (generally speaking) not replacing human beings is an 'optimific practice' already in force for human beings—this is not true of human attitudes to non-humans. While Lockwood's Disposapup example may shock, this is largely because of the status of dogs as pets, rather than any widespread belief that the idea of replacing animals is repugnant. In fact, a policy of replaceability of both wild and domestic animals is widely accepted. Animals are frequently described as 'resources' or 'stocks' which, unlike coal and oil, can be replaced or replenished. They are renewable. The widely held nature of this belief makes it unlikely that the non-replaceability of animals would ever become a social practice and hence fails to be supported by practice-consequentialism. It is doubtful in any case whether the replaceability or otherwise of animals would generate optimific feelings of security in the human community. Replacing animals would not, after all, pose a threat to human individuals. As Regan (1984a: 205) comments of Bentham in a similar context, 'Since humans can have no serious worry that the employees in the nation's slaughterhouses . . . will any day now turn to slaughtering human beings, our knowing that these animals are killed will not cause "the slightest inquietude" in our breast.' Thus, Attfield's position, like that of VanDe Veer and Singer, is also open to the criticism that he would allow replaceability, although his practice-consequentialism may protect humans from such a fate. That a sentient organism can in this way be replaced by another is an implication of individualist consequentialist ethics which many environmental ethicists find unacceptable.

The Variety of Relative Judgements

> There is a very good reason why we should be suffered to eat such of them as we like to eat; we are the better for it, and they are none the worse.[5]

While Bentham is much lauded for his remarks on the moral considerability of animals (quoted earlier) he himself was not a vegetarian. This fact causes Singer (1976: 213) to comment that Bentham 'flinched' at changing his diet; that he had 'lowered his normal standards of argument' and 'turned his face away from the ugly reality'. Singer considers Bentham to be inconsistent at this point, to have failed to prosecute his argument to its logical practical conclusions. But Bentham's argument is, in fact, quite logical. He argues that the slaughter of animals for food gives humans greater pleasure than it gives animals pain (because, he continues, their slaughter is speedy, less painful than death in the wild, and they do not have the facility to dread it). Thus, killing animals for food maximizes utility and is entirely consistent with Bentham's principles.

Singer's objection to Bentham, then, is based not on the principle of maximizing utility, but rather on a different evaluation of the relative experiences of humans and animals. Bentham rates highly the pleasure humans gain from eating meat; Singer (1976: 164) considers it to be merely a 'gustatory preference', a 'taste for a particular kind of food'. For Bentham, the gain to humans outweighs the loss to animals; for Singer, the loss to animals outweighs the gain to humans. In VanDe Veer's terms, Bentham considers meat eating to be a serious human interest, which outweighs the basic interests of non-human animals; while Singer regards it as a peripheral interest, over which the basic interests of animals have moral priority.

This raises the crucial question of how relative value judgements can be made. Is it possible to compare human gustatory pleasures with the suffering of animals? How can one compare a non-human animal with a Down's syndrome child? VanDe Veer (1979: 74)

---

[5] Bentham, quoted without footnote reference by Singer (1976: 213).

acknowledges this difficulty, but fails to address it: 'Most evident, the principle [Two-Factor Egalitarianism] is vague. There is no precise way of determining which interests are basic, which serious and which are more peripheral, and how to rank interests precisely. Similarly, no adequate account has been offered of how to determine levels of psychological complexity.' This vagueness makes it difficult to assess the detail of his position. Are meat eating, cosmetic testing, and hunting for sport serious or peripheral interests? The answers to these questions are not self-evident. However, this lack of certainty means that, depending upon how one judges pleasure and pain, anything might be permitted. Rodman (1977: 90) notices this problem:

The location of value in the subjective experiences of sentient entities allows for no small amount of subjectivity in our moral appraisals, since our judgment about the inner experience of others is either inferential, utilizing a criteria of evidence (the presence of a nervous system, the exhibition of what we acknowledge as pain behaviour, etc.) or sympathetic, depending on our imaginative/emotional capacity to identify with others' sufferings, to put ourselves in their place . . .

This can have even more problematic implications where personal criteria, unrelated to the evidence, are used in making relative moral judgements. Singer (1979b: 81), in fact, demonstrates this in his comments on the morality of fishing: 'The fish's struggle against danger and pain does not suggest that the fish is capable of preferring its own future existence to nonexistence.' By saying this, Singer places fish firmly into the second tier of moral considerability, the replaceable according to his system. But as Regan (1984a: 207) remarks in response: 'But if the *fish's* behaviour is insufficient to establish that the fish has this particular preference, how can the behaviour of other animals show that they do?' Although he does not make this point explicitly, Regan seems to be saying that, faced by similar behaviour from other animals, Singer would deduce that they did have a preference to go on living. He refuses to deduce this from the fish, because he has a preconceived idea of the capabilities of a fish; fishes cannot be preference-havers; they are merely the sums of their experiences. Thus, the same behaviour which would have counted as evidence that another organism has preferences is discounted because Singer is importing a personal judgement from outside the system (perhaps because, in Rodman's terminology, he cannot sympathetically identify with fish).

The basis of value in experience, then, and its accompanying refinements, in both Singer and VanDe Veer, leads to relative value judgements being based on frequently unsubstantiated personal opinions. Attfield, however, is less vulnerable to this criticism, since he has severed the link between value and experience. Value is generated by the state of flourishing, or of fulfilling capacities. Certainly for Attfield, the more psychologically complex an organism is, the more value it can generate. But this is a far less subjective criterion than one based on experience. One can only imagine or infer the experiences of a caged tiger, probably with varying degrees of inaccuracy; one can, however, make objective statements about the frustration of its species-specific characteristics and its inability to flourish when confined in a cage. One need make no comment on either the experience or preferences of a fish to recognize that, when being landed, a fish is being deprived of one of its basic needs: that of breathing.

At this point, I will move on to consider how process thinking compares with the positions of Singer, Attfield, and VanDe Veer, and consider how it might respond to these three basic points of difficulty.

Individualist Consequentialism, Process Thinking, and Non-Humans

In the preceding chapter, it was argued that process thinking shares some characteristics with individualist consequentialist systems resembling classical hedonistic utilitarianism. Thus, when considering ethical concern for non-humans in process thinking, one would expect to find some resemblance to Singer's or VanDe Veer's utilitarianism. This initial impression is confirmed by examining process thinking more closely.

As with Singer and VanDe Veer, experience and intrinsic value are inextricably linked in process thinking. However there are of course several key differences. Valuable experience in a process system is located in the subjectivity of the actual occasions and in the consequent nature of God. Since actual occasions are the components of everything that is, experience is universal.

Organisms, as societies of actual occasions, are matrices of this valuable experience. This has important implications for process thinking about the non-human. At a very basic level, there is no demarcation where experience ceases to exist, and therefore where value ceases to exist. To exist is to create at least a minimal amount of value. Process thinking, thus, has some points of correspondence with Singer and VanDe Veer and some with Attfield. Like Singer and VanDe Veer, but unlike Attfield, process thinking contends that value is experiential; unlike Singer and VanDe Veer, but like Attfield, process thinkers extend experience, and therefore value, into plants and other non-sentient organisms.[6]

This apparent coincidence of views with Attfield is, however, not more than superficial. It is not the generation of experience which Attfield considers to be valuable, but the fulfilling of capacities. There is obviously a connection between the two kinds of value, since the flourishing and fulfilment of any organism, in process terms, is likely to produce rich experience; but for process thinkers it is the experience (both of the actual occasions and of God) rather than the state of flourishing, which is valuable. It seems clear from this that process thinking is in closer agreement with Singer than with Attfield.

Does this experiential understanding of value make process thinking open to the same critique as Singer and VanDe Veer? For instance, has value been assigned to a quality which humans supremely possess? Whitehead (1938*b*: 91) openly takes human experience as his starting point, using it as a model of the way in which the universe works. In fact it provides not only a model of the way the universe works, but also a standard by which to judge it (Whitehead 1978: 112). Human experience is 'an extreme instance' of the experience which occurs throughout the universe—extreme because it generates the most harmonious and intense, and hence the most valuable, experience known to exist anywhere (except, of course, for the experience of God) (Whitehead 1948: 215). However, process thinkers can escape the accusation of speciesism, because their value criteria do not relate to species membership. Harmonious intensity of experience, and contrasts between kinds of experience, are not confined to human beings alone. Although for process thinkers most humans, most of the time, generate more

<hr>

[6] And also into inanimate objects, although as will be made clear in the following chapter, this does not make them morally considerable.

value than any non-human, some humans—babies, those in comas, and those with mental handicaps—generate less valuable experience, perhaps even than some other adult mammals, and hence the other mammals could be preferred when taking ethical decisions. Again here, however, there is an explicit comparison of animals with humans who in various ways lack abilities normally associated with adult humans. The question whether this is an appropriate way to treat individuals of other species is raised.

Process thinking is not as vulnerable to the criticism that only states of affairs generated by individual organisms can be valuable. Since the fundamental unit in process thinking is the actual occasion, even individual organisms are societies rather than true individuals. That other kinds of value-generating societies can exist, such as, perhaps, species and ecosystems, is not ruled out by a process approach since, as we have seen, it is not only sentient animals that can experience. (This will be considered in Chapter 4.) In addition, the possibility of valuing contrasts between *kinds* of experience, not possible for Singer and VanDe Veer, adds complexity to the process position. These factors explain the reservation expressed earlier about entitling process thinking an individualist consequentialist system. None the less, there is no doubt that, for all process thinkers, sentient animals produce the most intense experiences and the highest degrees of value.

This identification of value with experience within an individualist consequentialist structure indicates a fundamental closeness between Singer, VanDe Veer, and process thinking. This similarity is strangely passed over in recent process writing, even where it is directly concerned with value in the non-human world. Singer's *Animal Liberation* is mentioned, as far as I can discover, by only three process writers, Jay McDaniel, Charles Birch, and John Cobb; none of Singer's other writings, or any work of VanDe Veer is mentioned at all. The omission of *Practical Ethics* and 'Killing Humans and Killing Animals' is a significant one, since this means that all three process theologians miss Singer's advocacy of preference utilitarianism, concentrating solely on the hedonistic utilitarianism of *Animal Liberation*. In the case of Birch and Cobb, this concentration is in the form of attack. Yet this attack conceals a remarkable resemblance between the two positions: and, oddly, an even more striking likeness between Singer's later three-tier ethical position, and that of Birch and Cobb in *The Liberation of Life*.

While McDaniel merely summarizes Singer's position in *Animal Liberation*, Birch and Cobb level several criticisms at it. First, they attack his understanding of suffering:

> The recognition of degrees of analogy of animal behaviour to human behaviour is commendable, but it is unfortunate that it seems to be associated in Singer with the view that everything depends on whether there is any capacity to suffer at all. To us, it seems more plausible that there are degrees of the capacity to suffer and that it is much worse to inflict suffering on creatures with highly developed capacity to suffer than on those where this capacity is rudimentary.   (Birch and Cobb 1981: 158)

Even if the development of Singer's position in later articles is ignored, Birch and Cobb are inaccurate here. Even in *Animal Liberation*, Singer (1976: 38) does not claim that 'everything depends' on the capacity to suffer, rather that 'the capacity for suffering and enjoyment is a prerequisite for having interests at all'. Beyond this, other factors are important: he cites, for instance, the ability to plan for the future, close personal ties, higher degrees of self-awareness, and a greater capacity for meaningful relations, among others, concluding that 'a rejection of speciesism does not imply that all lives are of equal worth'. The possession of these other capabilities, for Singer, means that a human being, for example, has more interests than an animal, and can thus have extra positive and negative experiences. There is no suggestion in Singer's work of an ethical system where all sentient animals are worth the same and all non-sentient beings are worthless. In fact, it is highly probable that Birch and Cobb hold an identical position to Singer here. Their interpretation hinges on their understanding of 'increased capacity to suffer'. Presumably they refer here not so much to the physical pain from damaged nerves, but instead to the very human qualities to which Singer refers: the ability to remember and anticipate pain, and the degree of self-awareness involved in the experience of pain.

While Birch and Cobb thus indicate differences between themselves and Singer which do not really exist, they generate a position strikingly close to that of Singer's hybrid act- and preference-utilitarianism, even using the same example to make the same point. Like Singer, their ethical schema arises from considering what is wrong about killing. In a process system, such as Birch and Cobb's, killing any living organism results in the loss of future rich experience from that organism. Killing humans, however, according to Birch and Cobb (1981: 159), is a special example of this, because 'each [human] individual is unique'. Thus, when a human is killed, the depth of contrast that he or she provided in the world has been lost. As well as the loss of rich and even unique experience, Birch and Cobb suggest that anticipation of death and grief in others also generate negative experience, and hence add to the wrong of killing.

An initial resemblance to Singer is not difficult to trace. Anticipation of death, and grief to others, are standard utilitarian side-effects which, because of the suffering they generate, act as constraints to killing. Singer (1979a: 145) himself makes the same points; but, as he argues, these 'do not deal with the real wrong of killing'. The primary loss at death, for Singer as any hedonistic utilitarian, is pleasurable experience. If a pleasurable life is cut off, there is less pleasure in the world. This sounds very like Birch and Cobb's worry about loss of experience; if a life rich in experience is cut off, the consequent nature of God is deprived of future rich experiences. However, both of these positions then become open to the replaceability hypothesis. If it is total pleasure or total experience that is important, then as long as an adequate substitute is created, killing is not wrong—new life for old. It is at this point that Singer introduces his preference utilitarianism: the category of those who, as I said earlier, have a concept of themselves as individuals who endure through time and who have desires and preferences about the future. That is to say, they are not replaceable; they are unique. The production of another happy life in their stead is not good enough.

This is precisely how Birch and Cobb view the situation. With their earlier suggestion that human life is unique, it is clear that they are building towards a position of irreplaceability for human individuals. To illustrate this, Birch and Cobb compare the killing of a chicken to the killing of a human being. Side-effects are immediately dispatched. A chicken, they argue, cannot anticipate its own death; neither does the chicken community grieve for its loss. With regard to the 'real wrong of killing' the loss of experience involved, Birch and Cobb (1981: 159) comment:

First, it is true that the killing of a chicken prevents the occurrence of the additional experiences that the chicken would have had. But it is not clear whether the distinction between those prevented experiences and the experiences of another chicken is of much consequence. If the death of one chicken makes room for the raising of another, the values lost are largely replaced by the values gained.

Thus, chickens are merely the sums of their experiences, and are therefore replaceable. Birch and Cobb imply here that the experience of a chicken is not unique—it seems to feel something which one might call generic 'chickenness' rather than the feelings of a unique individual. Thus a chicken is replaceable both because the harmony and intensity of its experiences can be matched by a new chicken, and because the contrast which the chicken produces in the world is by virtue of its 'chickenness', rather than by virtue of its individuality. Chickens are merely sums of chickeny experience and hence can be replaced. They experience as species-representatives, not as individuals. Human beings, however, cannot be replaced: 'The future experiences that are cut off are unique and irreplaceable. That is because they derive from a unique individual with a unique history, whose particular capacity to generate new experience is forever destroyed. In the chicken's case the element of uniqueness is trivial' (ibid. 159).

The closeness of Birch and Cobb's position to that of Singer in *Practical Ethics* should by now have become clear. This closeness is compounded by the curious coincidence that Singer (1979*b*: 104) also uses a chicken to illustrate the same point. A chicken falls into Singer's second tier, and is thus replaceable: 'The replaceability argument will justify killing the birds, because depriving them of the pleasures of their existence can be offset against the pleasures of chickens who do not yet exist and will exist only if existing chickens are killed.' Humans and some other adult mammals, however, with their conception of self-identity and preference to go on living, cannot be replaced.

Birch and Cobb, then, like Singer, appear to have a first and second tier of moral considerability: the first being composed from humans and perhaps extended to include adults of other higher mammal species such as chimpanzees, the second being such creatures as chickens which are replaceable. The difference between Singer's criterion of preference-fulfilment and Birch and Cobb's of uniqueness-preservation are not substantial. Both have a top, irreplaceable tier, and a second, replaceable tier. The only significant difference is the process extension of the second tier to include organisms which to Singer are insentient, but which, to process thinking, experience and therefore produce value.

Can process thinking, then, withstand Lockwood's criticism both that replaceability even in the second tier leads to some conclusions which would normally be considered morally repugnant, and that the first tier of moral considerability is not exempt from replaceability? In his essay 'Christian Obligation', Charles Birch discusses Lockwood's Disposapup example, received through the filter of Attfield (1987: 170). Here, Birch (1990: 65) condemns the Disposapup organization as 'immoral': 'It is immoral to deliberately deprive the puppies of lives of possible pleasure and fulfilment of their canine possibilities...' In the light of views expressed in *The Liberation of Life* this is a confusing conclusion. We have seen that Birch and Cobb accept a replaceability argument for a chicken; why not a puppy, which is, after all, an immature member of a species only on the borderline of first-tier consideration? Birch does not here, after all, explicitly suggest that the reason the puppy cannot be replaced is that it is unique. Birch's earlier argument would suggest that, provided another new, fulfilling canine life is created, the Disposapup system is perfectly moral. His repugnance at Disposapup Ltd. suggests that his ethical intuitions are at odds with his ethical system. He must either, as Tom Regan suggests (appropriately enough) 'bite the bullet' and accept ethical conclusions which he may find distasteful, or fundamentally revise his ethical system. Where process thinking is concerned, this might require a fundamental metaphysical, as well as ethical, revision.

What, then, of the first tier? Can Birch and Cobb maintain a unique and irreplaceable first tier of moral considerability? It should already have become clear that this would be very difficult. It is certainly the case that Birch and Cobb consider adult human beings at least to be unique as individuals, rather than as generic representations of the type of experience produced by their species. Every unique human being thus provides God with depth of contrast. However—a point which I made earlier—this is not enough to guarantee inviolability. The experience of a human being can be valuable because it is (1) harmoniously intense and (2) contrasts with the experience of other humans (and presumably non-humans). However, the painless killing of one human and the replacement by another, equally harmoniously intense and equally unique, appears to compensate for the loss, assuming there are no side-effects. Uniqueness is valuable, not because of its specific content but because it is not something else. Its value is relational—the feeling that God gains from the contrast between it and the other types of experience around it. So long as the same total amount of value is produced in the world, nothing has been lost. This is much the same argument as Lockwood uses to attack Singer's preference utilitarianism. If equal, or greater, preferences-to-live can be generated, then the loss of the preferences is not significant. Similarly if equal, or greater, contrasts can be generated, then the loss of *this* contrast is not significant in process thinking. Birch and Cobb's unique individuals could be out-weighed by other unique individuals. Thus, like Singer, the first and second categories of moral considerability do not fall into watertight compartments of replaceability and non-replaceability. While the occasions when adult humans and adults of the highest mammal species may be treated as replaceable are rare they cannot be ruled out.

Birch and Cobb, then, put forward a process position which closely resembles that of Peter Singer's later work. However, while structurally Birch and Cobb describe a classic process system, their conclusions are not the only possible ones to which a process methodology might lead, any more than Singer's is the only possibility for hedonistic utilitarianism. As with utilitarianism, process thinking has a wide scope for decision-making where relative judgements are concerned. We have already seen that Birch seems to consider a chicken to be replaceable, but a puppy not to be. Different process thinkers may make other judgements. Like hedonistic utilitarianism, the process system provides a structure by which ethical decisions can be guided. It indicates which kinds of experience are most valuable. But the way in which the scale of value is weighted is largely left open. Is a rich human cultural experience worth more than the life of an adult mammal, if the two should come into conflict? Is a puppy worth more than an adult chicken? Or, to return to the earlier question, is the human richness of experience generated by eating meat greater than the loss of rich experience caused to animals? Is a small amount of high-quality human experience more valuable than a large amount of low-quality insect experience? A similar point can be made about the significance of contrast. It is clear that process thinkers consider that 'patterned contrast' in the world produces greater intensity of feeling for God. It is not clear, however, how in situations of conflict, the value of contrasts might be weighed. Is the kind of experience generated by a human life, for example, worth more than the kind of experience from an entire non-human species? Who is to decide?

An interesting example of the way in which, even within process ethical structures, value judgements can differ, is given by comparing passages on whaling by two different process thinkers:

A recent instance occurred when the United States government agreed to much larger quotas of whale kills for other countries in order to allow an Eskimo tribe to maintain its distinctive traditions. We suspect that too much was sacrificed here for too small a gain. If the Eskimos could have been allowed their hunt without raising the quotas of other nations, we would have supported the decision. There are no absolutes here. (Birch and Cobb 1981: 174)

We can deduce from this that Birch and Cobb consider whales to be sentient creatures (i.e. that they have rich experiences). However, clearly they are not inviolable in the way that humans were argued to be earlier in their book. (This is, in itself, a strange conclusion, since they certainly include chimps in their 'first tier'.) In addition, Birch and Cobb may have had in mind the scarcity of whales and the contrasts which the existence of whale species could provide for the divine life. Due to the whales' rich experience, and the rarity of the species, whaling should not be increased, or at least, not among nations for whom it does not have great cultural significance (although Birch and Cobb do not advocate here that it should be banned, even in these nations). Whaling is, however, important to ancient Eskimo culture. If their whale hunting was restricted, it would damage their culture, a loss not only to them but to humanity as a whole, as well as, presumably, depriving God of the depth of contrast which could be derived from different cultures. Thus, we are faced with a trade-off of richness of experience. Does the richness of experience lost to individual whales when slaughtered, and the risk of species extinction, outweigh the richness of experience lost to Eskimos and the rest of humanity when their lifestyle is lost? Is human culture worth more or less than the lives of whales and whale species in general? For Birch and Cobb, human cultural experience seems to be worth more.

In vivid contrast to this, Franklin Gamwell (1981: 49), another process thinker, treats whaling very differently: 'If a species of whales becomes extinct while whalers become prosperous, the potential loss to human happiness is great, and only if greater human possibilities are created is the deed justified...' Gamwell clearly considers whaling in a very different light. The whales' experience does not enter the calculation; there is no trade-off between human cultural experience and whales' living experience. Instead, two different kinds of human experience are pitted against one another. If whalers exterminate whales the loss to human happiness will be great (presumably he refers to human aesthetic experience, the pleasure given to future generations by seeing whales). However, Gamwell is prepared to countenance this loss if greater human possibilities are created—perhaps whalers can afford better lives and education for their children, or international co-operation increases through continued whaling. While Gamwell admits that animals do have experience, and hence value, he concludes: 'Since human experience is the most important, it can add most to the importance of the inherited world.'

Phrased in VanDe Veer's terms, Birch and Cobb are advocating a position similar to that of Two-Factor Egalitarianism: the serious interests of more psychologically complex animals (humans) take priority over the basic interest of less complex animals (whales). Gamwell, however, is advocating a position, which VanDe Veer calls Extreme Speciesism, where if human and non-human interests conflict, the former always trump the latter. It would be perfectly possible, however, for a process thinker to adopt a third position, closer to that of Species Egalitarianism, and argue that the difference of richness of experience between humans and some animals, in this case, whales, was so slight that humans should be given very little ethical priority at all (although no process thinker has, to my knowledge, approached anything like this view).

That the structure of process thinking can support so many differing interpretations of relative values is an indication of just how vague the criteria both of richness of experience and of patterned contrasts can be. As with hedonistic utilitarianism, process thinking has the problem of making judgements about the relative subjectivity and uniqueness of other organisms. The result of this ambiguity is that judgements made by process thinkers independently can be read into the system and then presented as its inevitable conclusion. Owing to the very nature of this activity—judging the subjective experience of other organisms—there can be no definitive statement of specific relative values.

To summarize, then, the arguments of the last two chapters: value in process thinking is located in the harmony and intensity of experience of the concrescing actual occasion. Thus value is aesthetic and, in a very primitive sense, universal; and the value generated by each actual occasion and societies of actual occasions (an issue developed further in Chapters 3 and 4) is taken into the consequent nature of God. Within the consequent nature of God, all actual occasions are woven together, and ordered contrasts between them enhance the intensity of God's feelings, thus generating increased value in the universe.

At the human level, ethical behaviour is behaviour which maximizes the amount of value in the world. This fundamental principle suggests a comparison with utilitarian ethics. Seen in this light, process ethics resembles classical hedonistic act-utilitarianism, with close similarities to Mill's qualitative understanding of pleasure and pain, and to Singer's approach to animals. However, this means that it is open to several key criticisms, both in a general sense, and specifically related to environmental ethics.

The emphasis on maximizing total experience leads to the twin problems of distribution and replaceability. Since total experience is what matters, who has how much is ethically irrelevant, providing that the greatest amount is generated. Uneven distribution of valuable experience, or the replacement of one organism by another may thus be ethically permissible. The association of value with experience, which characterizes all hedonistic utilitarianism and process thinking (although excluding Attfield) also means that relative values are based on inferred conclusions about the subjectivity and uniqueness of other organisms. Thus a variety of different ethical conclusions based on the same ethical structure is possible, as was indicated by contrasting attitudes towards whaling.

Both these criticisms, together with attacks on the identification of value with experience, are made by the environmental ethicists who will be considered in the following two chapters. Both the individualist deontologists considered in Chapter 3, and the collective consequentialists considered in Chapter 4 develop approaches to environmental ethics which contrast sharply with the individualist consequentialists considered in this chapter.

3

Process Thinking and Individualist Deontological Environmental Ethics

This chapter will examine what I have called individualist deontological approaches to environmental ethics: 'deontological' because these ethicists reject consequentialism, and 'individualist' because their ethical focus is on individuals rather than collectives or systems. This is not to say that all those to be considered in this chapter are opposed to collectivist or systemic approaches to ethics, although all are opposed to consequentialism; Goodpaster (1983) and Regan (1982) hold the possibility of systemic value open (while putting emphasis on individual values), and L. Johnson (1991) explicitly affirms it. However, inasmuch as Johnson considers ecological systems and species to be *individuals* of some kind, his work is appropriately included here.

I will first examine those individualist deontologists who, ostensibly at least, affirm that all individual organisms are of equal value; beginning with the work of Schweitzer, as perhaps the father of such individualist, deontological positions. I will move on to look at more recent exponents of deontological individualist views, including those who propose some sort of value hierarchy, before considering criticisms of these approaches and comparing them with process thinking.

Individualist Deontological Positions

The Will-to-Live: Albert Schweitzer

> The essential nature of the will-to-live is determination to live itself to the full. It carries within it the impulse to realize itself in the highest possible perfection.
>
> (Schweitzer 1987: 282)

Albert Schweitzer's comments on the will-to-live, while hardly systematic, provide interesting access to this kind of environmental ethic. The above quotation introduces several of Schweitzer's key concepts, some of which seem to be developed (although without any acknowledgement to Schweitzer) by Paul Taylor. The concept of the will-to-live (derived largely from Schopenhauer by whom Schweitzer was deeply influenced) forms the basis of Schweitzer's ethical philosophy. It is for Schweitzer almost a religious concept, a force fragmented in nature into individual lives, which each struggles to express and to realize in her or his own way. Within the non-human world, the will-to-live expresses itself in the cruel battle for existence between competing life-forms which survive by destroying one another. Only humans 'can escape and catch a glimpse of the light' by ethical behaviour which Schweitzer (1970: 121) describes as 'reverence for life'. It involves the fundamental recognition that 'I am life that wills to live, in the midst of life that wills to live' (Schweitzer 1987: 309). Recognition of will-to-live parallel to our own in other lives should engender reverence, and the desire that they too should reach realization, as we wish it for ourselves: 'At the same time, the man who has become a thinking being feels a compulsion to give to every will-to-live the same reverence for life that he gives to his own. He experiences other life as his own' (Schweitzer 1986: 131). Since ultimately the will-to-live is a single force, Schweitzer can suggest a strong degree of identity with other living beings: their will-to-live is not only similar to our own, it is identical. By allowing other beings to realize the will-to-live in their own individual ways—most prominently by assisting them to continue to live—humans can achieve the reunification of the divided will-to-live: 'If I save an insect from a puddle, life has devoted itself to life, and the division of life against itself is ended. Whenever my life devotes itself in any way to life, my finite will-to-live experiences union with the infinite will in which all life is one' (ibid.). Schweitzer's concept of the will-to-live is clearly focused on individual organisms. He never discusses the possibility of ecological systems or species having a collective good, value, or will. While Nature 'does sometimes act purposefully in a magnificent way' she never seems 'intent on uniting these instances of purposiveness which are directed to single objects into a collective purpose' (ibid. 273). It is only humans who can unify the fragmented and conflicting wills within nature by acting ethically.

Alongside the individualist emphasis of Schweitzer's ethic is a deontological one. Schweitzer refuses to accept that any kind of calculus or trade-off can resolve situations of ethical conflict.

'Having the will-to-action, it can leave to one side all problems regarding the success of its work' (Schweitzer 1987: 312). Whereas a utilitarian may consider that an ethical deed is one which produces the greatest happiness, for Schweitzer any loss of life, irrespective of the fact that it may produce the 'best consequences', is unethical. 'All life is sacred.' 'All killing is a "sacrifice"' (Schweitzer 1986: 189). The taking of any life, however necessary, whether to survive oneself or to protect one organism against another, generates a burden of guilt and responsibility—even the killing of bacteria, which was routine for Schweitzer as a doctor.[1] This rejection of consequentialism is bolstered by Schweitzer's pessimism that any individual can ever do more than a little to reduce the suffering in the world, and that if one were to concentrate solely on the insignificant consequences of one's actions, however ethical, one would feel permanently disheartened.

That Schweitzer's ethic is individualist and deontological seems to be without doubt. The third important characteristic to consider here is equality. Schweitzer certainly intends us to think that all living things are of equal value: 'The ethics of reverence for life is found particularly strange because it establishes no dividing line between higher and lower, between more valuable and less valuable life' (ibid. 189). Since Schweitzer's ethical system is based on the will-to-live, or, in Callicott's terms, it is a conative ethical theory,[2] no distinction can be made between different wills-to-live. Everything which is alive wills to go on living; it is the one essential aim of all organisms, and equally important for them all. Different wills-to-live and their value cannot be distinguished. Any such attempt 'will end in judging them by the greater or lesser distance at which they seem to stand from us human beings—as we ourselves judge. But that is purely subjective interest. Who among us knows what significance any other kind of life has in itself and as a part of the universe?' (Schweitzer 1987: 189). Schweitzer's question here dissolves any possibility of discrimination between the value of living things. The will-to-live is vital to all organisms; we cannot know what significance they have in

---

[1] Singer (1979c: 200) attacks Schweitzer over this—a critique which seems a little harsh, as Schweitzer was well aware of the contradiction in which he stood. If Singer is trying to suggest that Schweitzer is working with a hidden (hierarchical) agenda, there may be some substance to his point.

[2] See Callicott (1984: 299–308).

themselves or to the universe. Thus we must treat all life equally. To kill a flea is as bad as to kill a cat; to tear a leaf from a tree as bad as to mutilate a whale.

Leaving aside for the present the practical problems of upholding such views, at least one major inconsistency can be found in this aspect of Schweitzer's work. Contrary to his affirmation of equality, there is the constant suggestion in his writing that he does have at least a two-level hierarchy in operation—humanity, and everything else. In humanity (in Hegelian fashion) will-to-live has become conscious of itself; ethical behaviour is possible; reunification between divided will-to-live can be achieved. That humans are the only species capable of ethical action does not, of course, mean that they are necessarily of higher value. However higher value for humans is implied in some of Schweitzer's comments; for instance, he remarks that the aim of reverence for life is ... 'to create values, and to realize progress of different kinds which shall preserve the material, spiritual and ethical development of mankind ... the thinking world and life-affirmation sets up the spiritual and ethical perfecting of mankind as the highest ideal, and an ideal from which alone all other ideals of progress get their true value' (Schweitzer 1986: 132). Here Schweitzer leans towards the Kantian view that cruelty brutalizes the perpetrator, that it is bad for the human character not to enact reverence for life.[3] The aim of ethical behaviour thus becomes the spiritual and ethical perfecting of humanity. Only humans can 'fulfil' the will-to-live and become ethically perfect, thus achieving for the world what no other kind of animal can do (Schweitzer 1970: 38). This suggests that the preservation of a human will-to-live has priority over that of other species.

Schweitzer makes only one formal exception to his principle of reverence for life: self-protection or defence (also adopted by Paul Taylor): 'The fundamental commandment of ethics, then, is that we cause no suffering to any creature, not even the lowest, unless it is to effect some necessary protection for ourselves, and that we be ready to undertake whenever we can, positive action for the benefit of other creatures' (Schweitzer 1987: 260). But 'self-protection' has a wide interpretation. Schweitzer insists that one may only injure life 'when it is necessary'. But what constitutes necessity? He suggests

---

[3] A view recently restated by Carruthers (1992).

that mowing a meadow to feed cows is acceptable. More significantly—and surprisingly—he allows animal experiments which
'bring help to mankind with the results gained'. Indeed, introducing
another principle taken up by Paul Taylor, he comments:

By the very fact that animals have been subjected to experiments, and have
by their pain won such valuable results for suffering humanity, a new and
special relation of solidarity has been established between them and us.
From that springs from each one of us a compulsion to do every animal all
the good we possibly can. By helping an insect when it is in difficulties, I
am only attempting to cancel out part of man's ever new debt to the animal
world.   (ibid. 318)

Schweitzer's use of the term 'solidarity' here has an important, as
well as unfortunate, connotation. Certainly any solidarity between
animals and humans as a result of experimentation may seem to be
a rather one-sided relationship. However, the solidarity is supposed
to be one of human *restitution*. To compensate for damage done to
some living creatures, others must gain. The debt must be
cancelled.

    This theme—and criticisms of it—will be considered in the work
of Paul Taylor. It suffices here to note that acknowledging the
possibility of compensation to one organism for causing suffering
and death to another compromises the deontological nature of
Schweitzer's system, as the suggestion that humans are more valuable than other living beings compromises its egalitarianism. These
are examples of what I call the *slippage* between positions: where
one position is openly advocated, yet the writer slips into other,
often conflicting, positions elsewhere, usually without noticing the
discrepancy. This is particularly prevalent where upholding
the original position leads to very difficult practical consequences
as is the case with affirming the equality of all living beings.

    Schweitzer's work is, as his critics repeatedly affirm, unsystem-
atic. He offers no guidelines as to the resolution of ethical conflict
and suggests, in the end, that other forms of life can be used as long
as they benefit humans in some significant way. This can mean
almost anything: as Lindhart (in Langfeldt 1979: 22) comments,
'Reverence for life has aroused much enthusiasm because it can
mean anything and everything.' However, it is too easy to dismiss
Schweitzer. His environmental ethic combines concepts which
recur time and again in the more recent, more systematic writing;

concepts such as conation, equality, self-realization, self-defence, and restitution to name but a few.

Grounds for Considerability: Goodpaster and Regan

Within many ethical systems, including some approaches to environmental ethics, sentience (roughly defined as the ability to experience pain or pleasure) is thought to bestow moral considerability. If a being can have pleasurable or painful experiences, if it can suffer, then what happens to it, it is argued, is morally relevant. While this is obviously the basis of classical utilitarianism, as we have seen, some animal rights advocates such as Regan have developed deontological positions heavily dependent on a sentience criterion. However, of primary interest in this chapter are environmental ethical approaches which do not base moral 'standing' or 'considerability' on sentience.

The expression '*moral considerability*' was first used in this context by Goodpaster (1979). By this expression, Goodpaster means only that something falls within the sphere of moral concern, that it is morally relevant, that it can be taken into account when moral decisions are made. He reserves the expression '*moral significance*' to indicate how far it should be taken into account, its relative weighting in situations of moral conflict. Moral considerability merely indicates the baseline for inclusion: as Rolston (1988a: 102) comments: 'the point here is to get the theory clear: who counts, not how much'.

Goodpaster suggests that being alive is the criterion of moral considerability. 'As far as I can see, X's being a living thing is both necessary and sufficient for moral considerability so understood' (Goodpaster 1979: 34). Sentience, for Goodpaster, does not go far enough; it is 'an adaptive characteristic of living organisms which provides them with a better capacity to anticipate and so avoid threats to life—ancillary to something more important, an indicator, not a goal'. That a creature can suffer is not, then, a necessary criterion for moral considerability: suffering points towards something else, the protection of life, which does not require sentience.

Like Singer and VanDe Veer, Goodpaster emphasizes the importance of 'interests'. Unlike them, however, he draws a distinction between 'being interested in' something and something 'being in one's interest'.[4] While only a sentient creature can be interested in something (one could hardly say that a Venus's fly-trap is interested in a fly in the way that a cat is interested in a mouse), it is perfectly possible to say that something is in the interests of a non-sentient creature (that it is as much in the interests of the Venus's fly-trap to catch a fly as it is for a (hungry!) cat to catch a mouse). Anything which is alive can be harmed or benefited and thus, according to Goodpaster, has an interest in being benefited and not being harmed. On this account, it is possible for humans to have duties and responsibilities towards non-sentient living beings. This point is of crucial significance to individualist deontological environmental ethics. That duties are posited towards non-sentient individuals means that living beings beyond the ethical concerns of utilitarians such as Singer are morally considerable.

Goodpaster's criterion of moral considerability draws a firm line between the living and non-living. Some environmental ethicists, however, have proposed a move in the other direction: assigning non-living natural objects moral considerability. Regan (1982) tentatively argues that neither conscious nor sentient creatures exhaust the class of the morally considerable. This is based on a criterion of *inherent goodness* or *inherent value* in natural objects, a goodness unrelated either to their ability to value themselves or to anyone else's ability to value them. They need not be alive; Regan uses a river as his example. The use of inherent value here seems very close to the Moorean definition of intrinsic value I gave in Chapter 1 (*IV2*), since Regan (ibid. 199) goes on to say, 'The presence of inherent value in a natural object is a consequence of it possessing those other qualities which it happens to possess.' But what such qualities are, Regan (ibid. 199) fails to suggest:

If we could establish that there is something, (X) such that, whenever any object (Y) has X it is inherently good, we could then go on to try to establish how we can know any object has X. Unfortunately, I now have

---

[4] Many articles have been written on this distinction, some disagreeing with this interpretation. Sapontzis (1982: 345–58) concludes that plants cannot have interests. P. Miller (1983: 319–34) distinguishes between psychological interests which he calls 'motivated attention' (interest in) and beneficial interest, which he calls 'welfare' (having an interest). Miller's distinction here is in essence identical to mine. A similar debate is at present current concerning press freedom: something may not be 'in the public interest' (welfare) despite the fact that the public are interested in it (motivated attention).

very little to say about such questions, and what little I do have to say concerns how not to answer them.

This rather unhelpful response is followed by a rejection of Schweitzer and Goodpaster as drawing an 'arbitrary' line between moral considerability and the lack of it. Despite this vagueness, the existence of such inherent values in nature should, according to Regan, generate an attitude of 'admiring respect' in humans and lead them to adopt the 'preservation principle' of 'nondestruction, noninterference, and, generally, nonmeddling'.

Regan's suggestions here are problematic (as he himself is aware). In *The Case for Animal Rights* (1984*a*) Regan retreats from this position. Rejecting the Schweitzer/Goodpaster criterion of being alive, he comments (ibid. 242) that it is 'not clear why, or how, we could have direct duties to, say, individual blades of grass, potatoes or cancer cells'.[5] Instead, he proposes a new criterion: being a subject-of-a-life. In doing this, Regan shifts to a position where it is necessary not only that an organism has interests, but also that it is able to *take* an interest in its own life before it is morally considerable. By taking this step, Regan removes non-mammals, all plants, and all non-living natural objects from the sphere of moral considerability. Indeed, he equates *rights* with moral considerability: an organism either has both equally, or neither. This animal-rights (or rather, mammal-rights) position is plainly individualist, deontological, and egalitarian, but its value base—being subject-of-a life is narrow in comparison with the positions of Goodpaster and Schweitzer.

Absent from Regan (1982) and Goodpaster (1979) are any possible principles for resolving ethical conflict, although Goodpaster hints that such conflicts might be resolved by examining moral significance rather than moral considerability. Schweitzer offers a few suggestions, but also fails to develop any rigorous principles. Paul Taylor, however, in *Respect for Nature* (1986), has developed a rigorous (if not unproblematic) individualist deontological egalitarian ethical system drawing together suggestive threads from all these sources.[6]

---

[5] Rolston (1988*a*: 103) has an interesting response to the question concerning cancer cells.

[6] It would be appropriate at this point to consider the ethics of the deep ecology movement. However, since deep ecologists seem to have moved away from

Respect for Nature: Paul Taylor

Taylor (1981: 205) intends his ethical system to have three major strands: a belief system, a moral attitude, and rules of duty/standards of character. It is the rules of duty which are particularly significant here, but it is impossible to consider them outside the context of the other components.

Like Schweitzer's 'reverence for life', Taylor's concept of 'respect for nature' is a human attitude, a comprehensive world-view, 'the fundamental kind of moral commitment one can make'. It involves the recognition that humans are part of an interconnected and interdependent ecosystem to which they are not inherently superior; and that all organisms, as well as humans, are 'teleological centres of life, in the sense that each is a unique individual pursuing its own good in its own way' (Taylor 1986: 100). This claim is the bedrock on which Taylor's system is built, and around which he locates his criterion of inherent worth. Everything which is alive has its own *telos*; it 'pursues its own good in its own unique way . . . It is a unified system of organized activity, the constant tendency of which is to preserve its existence by protecting and promoting its well-being' (ibid. 45). This criterion is very close to that of Goodpaster (as Taylor acknowledges), and reminiscent of Schweitzer. Taylor's concept of inherent worth is thus rather different from intrinsic value, as I have been using the term; organisms with inherent worth not only have non-instrumental value, but also a good of their own.[7] Thus, a very distinct boundary is drawn between the living and non-living; the latter must be sharply separated from the former. Taylor dismisses, for instance, the idea of having 'duties to a river' (suggested by Regan 1982)—one can only have duties towards living organisms with a good of their own.

Acceptance of the idea that all living organisms have inherent worth, Taylor argues, is the only coherent position for someone who has adopted the attitude of respect for nature. Humans who respect nature, and who consider their own lives to have inherent worth as people with their own good, cannot but endorse the view that this is true of all living organisms. While their good is not the

advocating 'biocentric equality in principle', and since the metaphysics of deep ecology will be considered in Ch. 5, I have chosen to omit them here.

[7] Taylor only applies the term '*intrinsic value*' to organisms which are *conscious valuers*, a far stronger usage than my own.

same as a human good—different species have different goods to fulfil—their good is as vital for them as a human good is for a human. By locating his concept of 'inherent worth' and the duties which follow from recognition of this, in a complete belief system, Taylor is attempting to avoid the accusation that he is deriving an 'ought' from an 'is'. There is no *logical* entailment between accepting that an organism has its own good and that it has inherent worth which imposes duties of respect on us (Taylor 1986: 71). Recognition of the inherent worth of all living organisms and acknowledgement of corresponding duties is part of an ecologically informed coherent ethical system of respect, rather than a simple derivation from biological fact.

If Taylor's belief system in *Respect for Nature* is examined more closely, we can see that his ethics are individualist, deontological, and egalitarian—a development from his views in 1981, where he accepts both that species and communities have a telos and also that his system is open to deontological or consequentialist approaches. By 1986, Taylor (ibid. 69) maintains that one can only speak of species and ecological communities as having a 'stat-istical good', where the 'good of its individual members [is fur-thered] in such a way that the median level of their good-realization is raised'. The good of the community or the species is the good of the individuals who compose it. Similarly, Taylor has sharpened the deontological nature of his system. He stresses the attitude with which and *motivation* by which actions are carried out, rather than their *consequences*. Even if, for instance, conservation of wildlife for hunting has good consequences for living organisms, Taylor con-siders it to be unethical behaviour, since it is not motivated by the attitude of respect for nature, but ultimately for its exploitation (ibid. 185). His egalitarianism—in intention at least—is clear from his criterion of inherent worth. Everything that is living has inherent worth; and everything that has inherent worth has it equally. It is the organism as a whole, as a structure working together to preserve itself, that is valuable, rather than any particular capacities that it might have, or states that it might be in. This leads Taylor to the strictly egalitarian principle of *species impartiality.*

From within this belief system Taylor puts forward four basic principles of duty to the wild non-human world: non-maleficence, non-interference, fidelity, and restitutive justice. In summary, non-maleficence is the duty not to harm any individual organism;

non-interference is the duty to refrain from constraining organisms and to allow them to seek self-realization unhindered and to avoid disturbing natural ecosystems (all negative duties); fidelity is the duty not to break a trust placed by a wild animal in a human; restitutive justice is the duty to make good wrongs done to individual organisms through human action—that is to say, when one of the other three rules has been broken. Application and elaboration of these four principles should govern human moral behaviour towards other living organisms. Taylor acknowledges that there are occasions when these duties clash with one another, and develops a general priority structure with non-maleficence at the top, fidelity and restitutive justice with priority over non-interference (providing that no creature is permanently harmed) and restitutive justice over fidelity, if great good is produced without serious harm (ibid. 218).

These duties are accompanied by a series of five priority principles which aim to direct conflict resolution between human and non-human organisms. Obviously, for an individualist deontological egalitarian ethical system, conflict resolution must be a key issue. Since this is a problem presented by Schweitzer, Goodpaster, and Regan, as well as Taylor, these principles will be considered in some detail.

The first principle listed by Taylor is that of *self-defence*. It is, Taylor (ibid. 265) states, 'permissible for moral agents to protect themselves against dangerous or harmful organisms by destroying them'. This condition only applies where the agent could not avoid the danger, where the danger threatens 'life or basic health' and minimum effective force must be used. The second and third principles Taylor calls *proportionality* and *minimum wrong*. To explain these he introduces a distinction between basic and non-basic interests. He begins by explaining his understanding of organismic interests as events or conditions in their lives which are conducive to the realization of their good; while detrimental events or conditions are 'against their interests' (ibid. 170). But different interests are of different significance to organisms; they may contribute more to the realization of their good, or they may be vital to their survival. An interest of the second sort is basic; an interest of the first sort is non-basic.

In addition, Taylor comments that different organisms have different basic interests. For humans, basic interests not only include prevention of physical and mental damage, but also 'what people need if they are going to be able to pursue those goals and purposes that make life meaningful and worthwhile' such as autonomy, security, and liberty (ibid. 272). (How these are to be interpreted, of course, could make for a substantial difference in the way humans may, morally, treat non-humans.) Human non-basic interests, however, differ between people. In situations where interests conflict, basic interests, initially at least, have priority over non-basic ones.

Both proportionality and minimum wrong concern situations of conflict between *non-basic human interests* and *basic non-human interests*. Taylor divides such conflicts into two categories. Into the first category, governed by the principle of proportionality, fall actions which are, according to Taylor, 'intrinsically incompatible' with the attitude of respect for nature. Hunting for recreation or for fur provide examples of this—a non-basic human interest which does not respect nature here conflicts with a basic non-human interest. Since greater weight should always be given to basic over non-basic interests, and the non-basic interest is incompatible with respect for nature, the basic interests of non-humans must win. Into the second category, governed by the principle of minimum wrong, fall actions which are not directly incompatible with respect for nature but which threaten basic non-human interests, such as construction projects in a wilderness. Here, Taylor's attitude is ambiguous. Some such projects may be rejected by those who have respect for nature; but others may be valued too highly to forgo, even though the human interest is non-basic. Such projects include those of cultural significance, such as a concert hall, or legal and political centres which allow 'civilized life' to continue (ibid. 281–3). If such projects are carried out, they must involve minimum wrong: the 'lowest number of violations of the rule of maleficence in the ethical system of respect for nature'. Such actions are still violations of duty, still wrongs; no utilitarian calculus is acceptable; 'It is not the aggregate amount of disvalue or harm which is relevant here, but the number of cases in which one fails to carry out one's duty to another being' (ibid. 284).

Taylor's fourth principle is *distributive justice*, where *basic human* and *basic non-human* interests are in conflict (the basic non-human interests being harmless ones). All interests in such circumstances have the same moral weight, since all interests are basic and all organisms have the same inherent worth. This might suggest that eating is wrong, since for humans at least it almost inevitably involves the taking of life. However, of course, not to eat would also result in the taking of life, and eating is thus justified—humans would only have duties to sacrifice their lives if they were of less inherent worth than other living organisms.

The egalitarian position taken by Taylor would seem to suggest that eating plants and animals is equally wrong. However, he comments, causing suffering to animals when killing them is worse than killing plants because 'any form of suffering is an intrinsically bad occurrence in the life of a sentient creature' (ibid. 295). Thus Taylor suggests a preference for killing plants over killing animals. However, his main argument here for vegetarianism is that more food can be produced on less land by growing plants, and hence fewer organisms need die. It is, on the principle of minimal wrong, far less destructive of life.

Taylor's final principle is that of *restitutive justice*. This involves recompense being made when damage has been done to organisms. Taylor first comments that 'the greater the harm done, the greater the compensation required'; and suggests that a comparative amount of good should be generated to compensate (ibid. 305). Secondly, he suggests that restitution should be concentrated on ecosystems, where the 'good of the greatest number of organisms can be furthered'. Setting aside wilderness in one area, for instance, could be an act of compensation for damage in another, similar area.

These priority principles allow Taylor to argue that an individualist deontological egalitarian environmental ethic can be put into practice, albeit not without a serious change in human attitudes. Some individualist deontologists (although surprisingly few, and mostly in some kind of response to Taylor) have rejected the egalitarian nature of his system and proposed their own hierarchical deontological approach. Lombardi and Johnson will be considered in this context, before I move on to consider a critique of both approaches.

A Scale of Value: Lombardi and Johnson

Lombardi (1983: 257–70), in response to Taylor, argues for a hierarchical individualist deontological ethic based on the different capacities of individuals. He argues that the telos possessed by a living thing is a capacity it possesses, and inherent worth is assigned to it on the basis of that capacity. He then advances the argument that many organisms have *additional* capacities which can bestow added degrees of inherent worth, depending on the kind of being concerned. Lombardi (ibid. 263) states this as a basic principle 'P' where 'a type of being that (1) has the capacities of other beings and (2) has additional capacities which differ in kind from the capacities of other beings, ought to have more inherent worth'. Thus, a plant, which has 'vegetative capacities', has some inherent worth, but not much; animals also have vegetative capacities; but, on top of this, they have the capacity to feel pleasure and pain, and demonstrate some self-directedness. These additional capacities give them additional inherent worth. Humans have both vegetative and sentient capacities, and also others, such as reflectiveness, which gives them greater inherent worth again. This difference in inherent worth only extends to differences between species—members of the same species have the same capacities and hence the same inherent worth.[8] The higher level of inherent worth among humans gives them, uniquely, rights. (This is a term which Taylor also uses for intra-human relationships, but unlike Lombardi, he does not regard it as indicating greater inherent worth.)

Lombardi, therefore, sets up a value hierarchy which resolves many of the practical difficulties generated by a strictly egalitarian position: 'killing crops for food, killing trees for paper and killing animals to cure significant human infirmities can be justified if there are differences in inherent worth between animals, plants and human beings' (ibid. 267). This graded individual deontological environmental ethic is built on *difference of capacities between different species*.

This contrasts with L. Johnson's position in *A Morally Deep World*, where a value hierarchy is built on the basis of differing *interests*.[9] Interests spring from well-being—the most fundamental kind of good an organism can have. Like Goodpaster, Johnson considers that pain and pleasure are important for the protection

---

[8] This raises the obvious question of humans who lack capacities such as reflectiveness, a question which Lombardi does not address.

[9] Johnson ascribes similar interests to species and ecosystems as he does to individual organisms. In this sense, he is not an individualist—although in another sense his focus of concern is always on the individual, because he ascribes interests to species and ecosystems on the grounds that they are like individuals. The significance of species and ecosystems will be considered in Ch. 4.

of something else: well-being. He rejects preferences and desires as the root of ethical concern: one may desire things that are contrary to one's well-being, or fail to desire things which are beneficial to it. Prudent desires are judged, like pleasure and pain, with reference to something else: well-being. Disengaging well-being from pains, pleasures, and preferences enables Johnson to claim that one need not be sentient nor have preferences in order to have a well-being. Johnson understands well-being primarily as health, possessed by all living things. While some organisms, primarily humans, may have psychological as well as physical health, lack of sophisticated psychology does not mean that one cannot have a well-being.

Johnson, like Goodpaster, links well-being with interests. The most basic interest is the 'well-being interest in life', possessed by all organisms. All organisms have the basic interest to go on living— a 'will-to-live' in Schweitzer's terms. But here Johnson diverges from Schweitzer and Taylor and moves towards a hierarchical value theory. Differing values are based on differing interests; different organisms are worth differing amounts: 'It may be that a plant's need for the necessities of life are morally significant on some level, while not so morally important as a human's need for the necessities of life. I see no reason to assume that interests are atoms that all have the same moral weight' (L. Johnson 1991: 80).

While all organisms have a life-well-being, beyond this point different kinds of organisms have different well-beings and different interests. Mammals, for instance, have a well-being that involves avoiding pain and increasing pleasure, and hence have an interest in not being hurt which plants do not. Humans have psychological well-being which few non-humans have; it is in their interests not to have this damaged. Thus the same interests (e.g. an avoidance-of-pain interest) have the same weight, but extra interests give extra weight according to the importance of the interest to the individual involved. Thus Johnson proposes, as his fundamental discriminatory principle: 'Give due respect to the interests of all beings that have interests in proportion to their interests.'

Critical Responses to Individualist Deontological Positions

Numerous problems are generated by the ethical approaches considered in this chapter, clustering around the key words

deontological (or non-consequentialist), individualist, and egalitarian. Correspondingly, my consideration of these criticisms falls
into three sections.

The Problem of Non-Consequentialism

The problems of a non-consequentialist approach to ethics in
general are well known and will not be dwelt on here. However,
specific problems are generated within environmental ethics, particularly within the systems considered earlier, by such an
approach.

The first and perhaps most obvious difficulty is that just by living
one is constantly forced to destroy life. There is no escape from the
guilt involved in this; in eating, walking, washing, lives are being
lost. While this may be morally *permissible* behaviour, it can hardly
be described as morally good. One could not, for instance, in
Taylor's system, eat a morally good diet. At best, it would be less
bad than any other option. Unlike consequentialist ethics, even by
doing the best thing that one can do, one is violating a duty.
Schweitzer (1987: 318) gloomily summarizes this position, 'The
good conscience is an invention of the devil.' Such a comprehens-
ively depressing position where all actions to survive are bad
(although some are worse than others, especially for Lombardi
and Johnson) hardly adheres to the principle of 'ought implies
can'. If one does not act at all, one dies oneself; and this is also bad.

A second problem centres around the concept of restitution,
which was hinted at by Schweitzer and developed by Taylor.
Despite the fact that Taylor is one of the very few environmental
ethicists to put forward this concept and to argue for it with rigour
and conviction, his is one of the systems which cannot support the
principle. No non-consequentialist is able to accept restitution,
which, in many ways, resembles Singer's concept of replaceability
or substitution. As Schweitzer presents it, our debt to the non-
human world can, in part at least, be paid off by protecting the will-
to-live of all the individual organisms that cross our path. However,
these are different individuals from the ones which have been
harmed—or killed—by ourselves or others. Thus it is not restitution to the damaged or destroyed individuals, but to other organisms. This resembles Taylor's more developed concept of
restitution: where harm has been done, compensation should be

made: the more harm, the more compensation. Setting aside one wild area to compensate for damage done elsewhere is an example of this. Again, compensation is not to the actual organisms that have been damaged, displaced, or killed, but to other (albeit similar) organisms elsewhere.

However, *such compensation is not possible for an individualist, deontological environmental ethic.* A duty has been violated, whether or not compensation is paid, and especially if it is paid to something else. No compensatory calculus exists. It is the organisms themselves which have inherent worth and will-to-live; creating or assisting a different organism does not affect this.[10] One cannot compensate a dead organism. As Wenz (1988: 290) points out in his interesting examination of this concept in Taylor, Taylor's individualist deontological system cannot reasonably support restitution. Yet, as Wenz also indicates, restitution is an important idea for environmental ethics. As a practical suggestion, it provides grounds for resolution in situations of conflict (such as the building of Taylor's concert hall). Taylor's acknowledgement of this, despite the ensuing 'slippage', is a sign of the importance with which he credits it. His system cannot support all that he wishes to say about environmental ethics; a fact which will be revealed even more prominently when considering his egalitarianism.

The Problem of Moral Considerability and Significance

The egalitarian (or ostensibly egalitarian) nature of Schweitzer's and Taylor's systems have evoked much criticism and restatement: hence the hierarchical approaches of Johnson and Lombardi. To adopt Goodpaster's distinction, however, it is impossible to examine the moral *significance* of individual natural objects and organisms without first turning to the question of moral *considerability*. This is, of course, a central concern of environmental ethics— indeed, of ethics in general. It is impossible to give more than a cursory consideration of the complex issues involved here and to summarize the main arguments in the debate about individual considerability in environmental ethics.

---

[10] Schweitzer's system is perhaps more amenable to restitution than Taylor's, since the will-to-live could be regarded as a universal force with particular manifestations. This would lead, however, to a consequentialist ethic, which Schweitzer explicitly rejects elsewhere.

Regan's (1982) suggestion that natural objects have 'inherent goodness' and should be treated with an attitude of 'admiring respect' is the broadest of the positions I discussed earlier. Such a position is widely rejected, for two fundamental reasons. The first is that non-living natural objects have no good of their own. Nothing matters to them; nothing is bad for them or harms them. They have no well-being and no interests. How can non-living natural objects be morally considerable (other than instrumentally), when the set of actions that corresponds to 'treating them wrongly' is empty?[11] The second criticism is found most clearly in Partridge (1986: 96–110). He argues that Regan's concept of good is unbounded: 'If the concept lacks bounds, then everything is "inherently good", and "goodness" fails to qualify anything at all. That which denotes everything, connotes nothing' (ibid. 101). While Regan does say that not everything in nature is inherently valuable, he fails to give any idea of what the non-valuable things might be. Frankena, whose criticism is similar to that of Partridge, concedes that clearly Regan does not intend everything to be morally considerable: 'not junk, useless cars and artifacts generally' (Frankena 1979: 19). Thus Regan could refute Partridge's criticism by arguing that it is non-living *natural* objects (using natural to mean 'of non-human origin') that have inherent goodness. Such a position, however, would be difficult to maintain. A theistic or pantheistic approach might be adopted to affirm, *contra* Partridge, the inherent goodness of all non-living (as well as living) things. To recognize non-living natural objects as having inherent goodness because God made them, or is in them, is to give them moral considerability of a sort (although based on God as valuer).

Some sort of defence then, can be mounted to defend the moral considerability of non-living natural objects, but this is difficult to maintain. Human cultural and aesthetic values, as Johnson concludes, seem to be the most convincing reasons, within an individualist framework, for the preservation of non-living natural objects.

---

[11] Objections to this argument do exist. For instance Sylvan (n.d.) argues that inherent goodness does not imply moral considerability, a position that Sprigge (personal communication with the author) supports with reference to works of art. Pantheists and panentheists have metaphysical systems which could support such a position (a route similar to that taken by process systems, as we shall see). Collectivist ethical approaches could also value non-living natural objects as part of ecological systems. However, the majority of philosophers (including Regan himself) would think this criticism telling.

The inclusion of all *living* things within the sphere of the morally considerable is a different question. It is a fact, as Taylor states, that all living things (including plants and bacteria) have their own good, a *telos*, and attempt to preserve their own life. Things can be bad for them; they have a well-being. The question remains, however, whether having a well-being in this sense qualifies them for moral considerability. Here, views among individualist ethicists are divided. Frankena (ibid. 11), for instance, is negative about the possibility of non-sentient individuals without subjective experience having intrinsic value:

I can see no reason why we should respect something which is alive but which has no conscious sentiency... Why, if leaves and trees have no capacity to suffer should I tear no leaf from a tree? Why should I respect its location any more than that of a stone in my driveway, if no benefit or harm comes to any sentient person or animal by my moving it?

Regan (1984*a*) and Frey (1983) make similar arguments. However, Schweitzer, Taylor, Goodpaster, Lombardi, and L. Johnson, as we have seen, consider that being alive, having a will-to-live, a well-being, or a good, is enough to qualify for moral considerability.

It would be impossible even to attempt to resolve this issue here, if, indeed, such an issue is resolvable. It may be more helpful to focus, not on the question of moral *considerability*, but rather moral *significance*. Where to have moral considerability entails a high degree of moral significance, it is unsurprising that there is great reluctance to admit plants to moral considerability. This is particularly true of positions which conflate moral considerability with moral rights, and even more so with equal moral rights such as Regan (1984*a*) and Feinberg (1974). Indeed, any individualist egalitarian deontological ethical system faces the problem that admission to moral considerability means equal considerability for all—plant, animal, human. To avoid this, many ethicists consider it better not to admit plants and many animals at all. For those with hierarchical systems, the problem is far less acute: plants can be acknowledged to have some moral significance, but this need be little more than negligible. However, hierarchical systems face different problems avoided by egalitarian ones. The dilemma is pithily summarized by Dooley (1986: 52): 'Biocentric views' he comments, must either 'rank life integrities assigning relative standing against a standard' or 'refuse to discriminate amongst life, and hence to rank it'. But the former option is 'homocentric' while the later is 'morally absurd'. L. Johnson and Lombardi adopt the first option and rank life by interests and capacities. Not to do so, in their view, leads to the kind of moral absurdity where washing one's hands and hence destroying micro-organisms 'might be just as bad as Hitler's extermination programmes' (L. Johnson 1991: 136).

The seeds of destruction for egalitarian positions such as Taylor's and Schweitzer's (or, indeed, of Regan's in *The Case for Animal Rights*) are found within their own writing, in the form of slippage into other positions. We have already seen that Schweitzer is subject to such slippage. That Regan also slips positions is frequently noted.[12] Even Paul Taylor's seemingly rigorous approach is not exempt—for instance, in his principle of self-defence where moral agents may destroy harmful organisms (since their own inherent worth and that of the aggressor is equal). The situation, however, frequently arises where the aggressor is not a single organism, but organisms in the plural—disease bacteria for instance. Surely, if thousands of disease bacteria are dependent on me to survive, I have a duty to sacrifice myself to them?[13] Although one cannot tot up worths, as one might in a consequentialist system, the loss of my life or health is surely a lesser loss than that of many bacteria, who each have equal inherent worth to me? This certainly follows from Taylor's principle of minimum wrong, where ethical behaviour minimizes violations of duty.[14] That Taylor does, however, accept the medical profession suggests that, in actuality, he does consider one human to be worth many bacteria.

A second example of slippage is found in Taylor's attitude to vegetarianism. As we have seen, Taylor (1986: 295) comments that 'Where there is a choice between killing plants and killing sentient animals, it will be less wrong to kill plants if animals are made to suffer when they are killed for food.' Killing an animal painlessly, then, is equally as bad as killing a plant; killing an animal and inflicting pain on it is worse. By introducing the 'painless killing'

---

[12] Regan (1984a: 351) comments that in a lifeboat situation, he would save a human over a dog. This prompted a typical response from Sylvan (n.d.): 'Despite his disclaimers, Regan's egalitarian principles ring hollow when it comes to the crunch, for then humans always outrank animals.'

[13] Wenz (1988: 284) suggests a similar example.

[14] It thus resembles Regan's 'Miniride' principle (1984a: 305).

clause, Taylor is attempting to hang on to his egalitarianism. But a new value has been added on top of that of inherent worth: that of painful experiences. When a decision must be made between killing two beings of equal inherent worth, sentience has now become a deciding factor. Here, surely, Taylor is moving close to espousing a 'capacity' view, similar to that of Lombardi, although without apparently changing his position on inherent worth.

The most outstanding example of slippage in Taylor's work is incorporated into his principle of minimum wrong, and picked up effectively by Wenz (1988: 286). This principle allows humans to undertake projects important to civilized society, even at the expense of killing or displacing thousands of organisms. Such actions, he argues, may still cohere with the attitude of respect for nature. Leaving to one side the possible cultural snobbery implicit in Taylor's work (why a concert hall, rather than a motor-racing track?) this principle of minimum wrong is plainly inconsistent with Taylor's fundamental position of equal inherent worth. Human non-basic interests are explicitly given preference over non-human basic interests.

These examples make it quite clear that egalitarian positions of the sort championed by Taylor and Schweitzer cannot be sustained—not even by their advocates, who slip, sometimes unconsciously, into inegalitarian positions where humans are concerned, and frequently also with sentient animals. It seems impossible to escape some kind of hierarchical value system in an individual deontological environmental ethic. Yet, as Dooley suggested, hierarchical systems have problems of their own. Existing forms of ranking have meant that other organisms are being judged by their similarity to humans—their possession of sentience, intelligence, or interests for example. Humans always remain the paradigmatic possessors of such qualities, and always possess them in the most perfect form. (Such a criticism can, in fact, be extended to individualism in environmental ethics in itself, as was suggested in Chapter 2.) Rodman (1977: 94), as we have already seen, is the most powerful critic of such ranking approaches, describing 'scales of value' as 'introducing a pecking order to the moral barnyard' which reflects human interests and judgement.

Individual deontological environmental ethics is thus torn between a hierarchical homocentrism, and an egalitarian moral absurdity which is, in reality, unsustainable. Neither seems a very satisfactory basis on which to build an environmental ethic. The philosophers I consider in Chapter 4 attempt to evade this dilemma. How successful they are remains to be seen.

The Problem of Individualism in Environmental Ethics

The individualist focus of these ethical approaches makes them vulnerable to several criticisms, many of which are elaborations of those considered in Chapter 2. These criticisms are often levelled by Callicott and other collectivist ethicists, on whom I will focus in Chapter 4. Their critique is, however, relevant here.

The first and most obvious criticism is the inability of individualist environmental ethics to come to terms with ecological groupings such as species or ecosystems, which individualist ethicists perceive to be collections of individuals, rather than a whole. The good of an ecosystem is purely the good of the individuals who compose it. Thus, an individual member of an endangered species can be of no more value than an individual of a common or prolific species. A domestic cat, a Scottish wildcat, and a leopard are each of identical worth. What gives them value is their lives, their own capacities or interests, their own well-being. Rarity is not a quality which they can experience or which forms part of their well-being. Of course humans might assign value to members of endangered species, hence adding value to that which they already have in themselves. But the difficulties with this are demonstrated by the example above: it is, after all, possible that a domestic cat would be ascribed more value than a Scottish wildcat.

Further, with such an individualist approach, the preservation of species becomes no more than the preservation of individuals within species. This is a position which some individualist philosophers seem happy to accept. Regan (1984*a*: 359) argues, for instance, 'That an individual is among the last remaining members of a species confers no further right upon that animal, and its right not to be harmed must be weighed equitably with the right of any others who have this right.' Indeed, in this instance, since Regan (1984*a*) only accepts that 'subjects-of-a-life' (adult mammals) have rights at all, and he here conflates value with possession of rights, plants and non-mammalian species of whatever scarcity have no value whatsoever, except inasmuch as they are of instrumental value to those who are subjects-of-a-life.

Individualist environmental ethics is unable to cope with diversity as well as scarcity. Diversity cannot be experienced or contribute to the well-being of an individual organism (other than instrumentally). Thus it is impossible for individualist ethicists to prefer complex flora and fauna to monoculture, without the presence of a human valuer. A wildflower meadow cannot have more value than a field of wheat; each individual plant has its own well-being, and in Taylor's terms inherent worth; this is equally true of a wildflower and an ear of corn. This inability to take account of diversity or scarcity extends to the inability to differentiate between domestic and wild animals. Domestic pigs and wild boar, domestic cows and wild buffalo, domestic chickens and wild grouse all have identical moral standing. Even in a hierarchical ethical system where pigs might rate above cows and cows above birds, no distinction between wild and domestic status can be maintained. Yet many environmental ethicists do wish to make a distinction here. Midgley (1983), Callicott (1988), and Shrader-Frechette (1990*a* and *b*), for instance, all differentiate between 'mixed' and 'wild' communities, to which humans have different ethical obligations, as we shall see in Chapter 4. If one accepts the existence of domestic animals at all it seems likely that humans have duties of protection and provision for them which may not apply to wild organisms.[15] While there may be no obligation for humans to feed wild animals in the winter (indeed, some environmental ethicists would argue that there is in fact an obligation not to); to neglect hungry domestic animals in the winter is to fail in duty. Individualist environmental ethics are unable to make such a distinction between communities (although, with his principle of non-interference, Paul Taylor attempts to) and must maintain that the same duties apply to all animals of similar capacities, whether domestic or wild.

That individualist environmental ethics may entail life or well-being duties towards individual wild organisms generates a significant number of problems for environmental ethics. The question of 'interference' becomes a pressing one: should humans ever intervene in wild nature to protect individual organisms?

We have already seen that Paul Taylor includes non-interference as a primary duty towards wild nature, even if by interfering one improves well-being, *if interference involves the removal of the*

---

[15] See Palmer (1995) for further discussion of this question.

organism from wild nature. To remove an organism from wild nature, he argues, is to restrict its freedom. This claim seems reasonable with regard to wild animals—they would, almost inevitably, have to be confined outside the wild. But it is a difficult argument to uphold for wild plants. Transplanting wild plants into gardens is, Taylor claims, 'an absolute negation of their natural freedom'. This is a very strange assertion. What location freedom do plants have in the wild? Is wildness a value in itself, which remains unaccounted for in Taylor's system? Since Taylor focuses on 'taking the standpoint' of individual organisms, and a wild plant (unlike a wild animal) has no mobility and cannot change its location, being moved into a cultivated garden, especially if its well-being is thereby improved, can surely be of no hardship to the plant. Like diversity, rarity, or domesticity, wildness cannot feature in the inherent worth of a plant. Its *telos* can be pursued perfectly well in a garden, providing its well-being needs are met. Taylor's real, if unacknowledged, concern here seems to be the integrity of the ecological system to which he can attribute no value as a whole. The duty of non-interference does not cohere well with the individualist emphasis on inherent worth in his system.

Indeed, the whole force of individualist environmental ethics would suggest otherwise. Rolston describes an incident where a wild bison fell through an ice-sheet into Yellowstone River, where it struggled for many hours in the freezing water (Rolston 1990: 242). Park officials, following a policy of non-interference, refused to allow the bison to be rescued or mercy-killed; nature should be allowed to take its course; this was part of the procedure of natural selection. Four snowmobilers, following a different ethical prescription and defying park officials tried (unsuccessfully) to rescue the bison. Most individualist environmental ethicists would follow the ethical code of the snowmobilers. Schweitzer, for example, would consider rescue to be a duty. Taylor would also support the rescue of the bison, provided that this did not entail its removal from the wild. For most individualist deontological environmental ethicists, human interference to protect wild animals from inanimate threats would be justified, if not a moral duty.[16] Yet this is

---

[16] This need not be the case for a rights position, like that of Regan (1984*a*), as Jamieson (1990: 349–62) argues. While, on Taylor's account, inherent worth is always lost at death, for Regan only a moral agent can violate rights. While this excuses Regan from objecting to predation (since there is no rights violation) it also

problematic for collectivist environmental ethics, and could be considered to disturb natural evolutionary processes, preventing nature from taking its course.

Behind this whole issue there seems to hang a greater, more difficult question about how non-human nature is regarded. If value or worth is located in individuals, then their killing is a loss of value, however essential or good it may be for the system. Predation is thus generally seen as an evil (albeit a necessary one) although few go so far as to suggest interference with it.[17] For this reason, Callicott (1984: 301) accuses 'bioconativists' such as Schweitzer and Taylor, of being 'fundamentally life-denying'. They fail to accept the suffering and death which is crucial to natural biotic processes and which is, in fact, essential for evolutionary and ecological processes to continue: 'Nature notoriously appears indifferent to individual life and/or individual suffering. Struggle and death lie at the very heart of natural biotic processes, both ecological and evolutionary. An adequate biocentric axiology could hardly condemn the very processes which it is intended to foster and protect.'

At the heart of this critique is the conviction that, within the non-human world, concentration on the individual organism is an inappropriate focus. This critique finds its expression in various ways within environmental ethics. Goodpaster (1979: 25) comments that individualist environmental ethics are 'formed from the rib of egoism', and that 'the last thing we need is simply another "liberation movement" for animals, trees, flora, fauna, rivers . . .'. It is, he suggests the 'larger whole' to which we should attribute value (thus developing the possibilities which he left open in 'On Being Morally Considerable'). Many environmental ethicists argue that generalizing from egoism produces an ethics 'made in man's likeness'.

Individualist Deontological Positions and Process Thinking

The comparison between process thinking and the ethical positions considered earlier in this chapter is a complex and interesting

means that no duty of assistance is required morally when any subject-of-a-life is threatened by any non-moral agent. In other words, since the Yellowstone River was not a moral agent, the rights of the bison were not being violated, and hence no duty of assistance ensued.

[17] The exception being Sapontzis (1984: 27–36).

one, with some significant similarities as well as some notable differences. This comparison will be approached first by elaborating on the process concept of 'society'. With this structure in mind, I will consider how process thinkers regard the natural objects and organisms which have been discussed in the first half of this chapter and what their value status might be. This will enable a consideration of process responses to the problems raised by the ethical positions which were put forward in the previous section.

Whitehead's Understanding of Society

The concept of the society is of central importance for Whitehead's metaphysics. It is one of his fundamental categories for understanding the natural world, and links together his concepts of 'nexus' and 'actual occasion'. Actual occasions are never isolated in Whitehead's system: in their own actualization, they positively or negatively prehend the multiplicity of actual occasions which temporally precede them; and they are all members of at least one society—the universe. However, apart from this inevitable membership in the universe, actual occasions can belong to a variety of different nexus and societies. The term '*nexus*' is understood by Whitehead (1948: 234) to mean that its members share a certain '*mutual immanence*'. That is to say, the actual occasions which compose it empty themselves into, or positively prehend, one another. This may happen in two ways. A later occasion may positively prehend a preceding occasion and hence incorporate its content, making a temporal nexus. Alternatively, two contemporary occasions may positively prehend the same preceding occasion thus making them part of a contemporary nexus.[18] Whitehead does not intend the nexus to be a strong form of connection: it does not presuppose any particular kind of order. A society, then, is a specially ordered nexus or collection of nexus:

A society is a nexus with social order . . . a nexus enjoys social order where i) there is a common element of form in the definiteness in each of its included actual entities and ii) this common element of form arises in each member of the nexus by reason of the conditions imposed on it by its prehensions of some other members of the nexus, and iii) these prehensions impose that condition of reproduction by reason of their inclusion of positive feelings of

[18] This presupposes Whitehead's doctrine of asymmetrical internal relations; the significance of this will be discussed in Ch. 5.

that common form. Such a nexus is called a society, and a common form is the defining characteristic of the society. (Whitehead 1978: 34)

Whitehead moves on to explain that the 'common element of form' is simply a 'complex eternal object exemplified in each member of the nexus' and the reproduction of this form is due to the genetic relations between the members of the nexus and the inclusion in the genetic relations of the feelings of the common form.

This complex explanation of the constitution of a society must first be understood within its temporal framework. The cohesion of a society depends on what it inherits from its predecessors. In order to be part of a society, each actual occasion must inherit something common from its predecessors, possessed by all who form part of that society, i.e. a complex eternal object. This inheritance is assured by the positive feelings about that complex eternal object which pass on to each successive actual occasion. The positive feelings mean that each successive occasion in the society will positively prehend the same complex eternal object. This sameness holds the society together and constitutes a 'defining characteristic'.

The cohesive strength of different societies depends on the centrality of the element held in common by all its members. It may be the defining characteristic of the society, but it need not be the most important element in the occasion. The membership of an occasion in any particular society may be peripheral, or it may be definitive. Any one occasion can belong to several overlapping societies at once. An occasion actualizing in a human body, for instance, may be part of the individual organ of the body and the whole human being; or perhaps of three societies, being in the societies of blood, the organ, and the body. The body itself may be a member of a larger society; or the actual occasion may be in undigested food and part of the food society by which it entered the body. In other words, although the criteria for being a member of a society sound complex, they are in fact rather vague.

Much more can be said about Whitehead's understanding of the society, and I will develop further arguments about it in Chapter 4. Here I wish to concentrate on Whitehead's perception of 'individuals'[19] within the natural world: non-living natural objects, plants, animals, and human beings.

[19] 'Individuals' is in quotation marks here because only actual occasions (including God) are true individuals in Whitehead's system. To call rocks, plants, or animals 'individuals' is to speak, as Whitehead says, abstractly; they are in fact societies.

The simplest kind of society is that which Whitehead calls an 'enduring object', such as a molecule or a crystal, which exhibits what he calls 'personal order'. This is a particularly important term for Whitehead. A personal society is one which displays the characteristic of 'serial ordering'—one occasion positively prehends another, which positively prehends another, and so on—creating a single sequence, an enduring connective thread through time. Whitehead (1978: 34) describes this as 'forming a single line of inheritance of its defining characteristic'. 'Personal' has no other sense; no suggestion of personality, life, or consciousness. It merely refers to the persisting sequence. In the case of the enduring object, its persistence is due to repetition. Each of the succeeding actual occasions which compose an enduring object 'exhibit a massive and complete sameness' (Whitehead 1938*a*: 233). This is a sign of a very low-grade society. There is little aim at novelty or an increase in the harmony and intensity of experience.

However, these enduring objects form the building blocks of everything that is around us. At the simplest level, they combine to form what we perceive to be inanimate objects, such as rocks, or tables and chairs. Whitehead names these 'corpuscular societies' or 'nonliving aggregations'. They appear to us to be 'inert and passive' (Cobb 1966: 45). Like the enduring objects of which they are made, they have personal order; and, like them too, this is because of their repetitious nature.

Enduring objects and corpuscular societies both exhibit what Whitehead calls 'structure'. Structured societies contain smaller societies and nexus within them, which Whitehead calls 'sub-societies' and 'sub-nexus'. A table, for instance, contains a structure of 'sub-societies' in the form of molecules. A table, however, is a very simple kind of structured society. The repetitious nature of the actual occasions which compose it mean that it persists through time, and through changing environments, by failing to absorb any of the changes which go on around it. This repetition in the face of change may enable the corpuscular society to persist, but it prevents it from generating novel and deeper experience. 'Its parts merely transmit average expression, and hence the structure survives. For the average is always there, stifling individuality' (Whitehead 1938*b*: 38).

Much more complex are living societies, which are also composed from enduring objects but which produce a higher degree of novel experience. These societies respond to changes in their environment. They receive 'the novel elements of the environment into explicit feelings with such subjective forms as conciliate them with the complex experiences proper to the members of the structured society. Thus in each concrescent occasion its subjective aim originates novelty to match the novelty of the environment' (Whitehead 1978: 102). Thus, Whitehead presents a picture of two kinds of society. One remains obtuse to all changes in circumstance or environment. A mountain would fall into this category; it would persist in the face of enormous external upheaval, such as climatic change; it is what Whitehead describes as an 'unspecialized society'. It does not need specialized conditions to persist.

The second kind of society, however, the living society, responds to a changing environment, and attempts to absorb it into itself. Living societies are flexible, and can generate novel and enriched experiences by positively prehending new data from outside themselves. This responsiveness to environmental change allows them to persist in a different way from the immutability of a society such as a mountain. Living organisms, for instance, might respond to climatic change by colonizing new locations, building different kinds of shelters, and ultimately evolving, adapted to new conditions. Despite this, living organisms are more vulnerable than non-living structured societies. They are more specialized societies than rocks and need more specialized conditions in which to survive, although their ability to adapt makes them reasonably resilient.

The vital difference between living and non-living societies is that a living society produces greater 'conceptual novelty' or 'novelty of appetition'. 'In some measure, its reactions are inexplicable by any tradition of pure physical inheritance' (ibid. 104). This is not necessarily a clear-cut differentiation, but provides for a broad distinction.

Living societies are by no means uniform; Whitehead makes a number of distinctions within them. Lower organisms, he comments, do not think. They 'thoughtlessly adjust aesthetic emphasis in obedience to an ideal of harmony'. It is an automatic, rather than a reflective, response to a change in external circumstances. In higher organisms, thinking is introduced and determines the flexible response to changing circumstances. For both kinds of living organism, those which think and those which act automatically, the response to external variation is 'self-preservative' (Whitehead 1978: 102). Living organisms adapt themselves to changing circumstances in order to survive. Failure to adapt ultimately means failure to survive. Successful adaptation means both survival and the generation of novel experience by the prehension and incorporation of new actual occasions.

The simplest kind of living society is the living cell, whether within a plant or an animal. It is a structured whole, with personal order, and is composed from smaller subsocieties and subnexus of molecules and electrons, which are not in themselves living. (Indeed, it is characteristic of living societies that they incorporate a degree of non-living material, as I shall consider further in Chapter 4.) However, the non-living molecules, or enduring objects, within the living society behave differently from those outside it. The society operates a kind of 'field' within which the molecules behave according to the pattern of the society: 'An electron within a living body is different from an electron outside it, by reason of the plan of the body. The electron blindly runs, whether within or without the body; but it runs within the body in accordance with the general plan of the body, and this plan includes the mental state' (Whitehead 1938a: 98). This control is most developed in the society of the human body; but Whitehead points out that it is found throughout nature, not just within living societies. The 'plan' of the society creates a kind of boundary, differentiating those occasions which are part of the society and those which are not. Non-living enduring objects within a living cell follow a pattern governed by the cell as a whole.

Since a cell is a *living* society, it cannot only be composed from non-living actual occasions. Life, according to Whitehead (1978: 105), is found in the 'interstices of each living cell, rather than space occupied by any corpuscular society'. Cobb (1966: 43) explains this more clearly:

Now there is far more life in the cell than in the molecules found within it. Therefore, this life must be found in the space not occupied by those molecules and specifically in the occasions located there. These occasions must be characterized by much more novelty and much less continuity than the molecular occasions. The cell as a whole, then, combines the stability of the enduring objects and the life of the primarily mental and therefore not physically detectable occasions within it.

This passage highlights an important feature of Whitehead's understanding of the natural world. Life, for Whitehead, is characterized by novel responses generated by actual occasions. Occasions which are capable of such responses are, primarily,*mental*. All actual occasions, while in the process of becoming, are subjective; they are tiny flickers of experience or feeling. Subjectivity is a complete description of them; it is not merely an attribute or a quality that they possess. Thus it is not possible to grade their subjectivity; all actual occasions are equally subjective. All occasions also, as we have seen, have a physical and a mental pole, of varying strengths. Those with strong physical poles largely repeat the actualization of the perished occasions which they prehend. Those with a strong mental pole can generate novel experience. Even here, Whitehead does not identify 'mentality' and 'consciousness', a point which Lewis Ford (1984: 38) makes with great cogency: 'In his later theory, Whitehead carefully distinguishes between subjectivity (ascribed equally to all actual occasions in the immediacy of their own becoming), mentality (ascribed to them by degrees, according to their complexity and capacity for originating novelty) and consciousness (ascribed only to a very specific class of highly mental actual entities, capable of enjoying intellectual feelings).' While a living actual occasion within a cell may have some mental capacity, it is not conscious mental activity, but rather the 'thoughtless adjustment' of a living cell to changing external situations, brought about by mental poles of the living actual occasions in the cell's interstices.

After the individual cell, the least complex living societies are plants. Whitehead (1928: 49) describes these as low-grade organisms. This means that the degree of novel experience that they produce, while greater than a corpuscular society, is minimal. Their responses to stimuli are very predictable; they lack originality of reaction: 'The conformation of present fact to immediate past is more apparent, both in apparent behaviour and in consciousness, when the organism is low-grade. A flower turns to the light with much greater certainty than a human being, and a stone conforms to the conditions set by its external environment with much greater certainty than a flower.' Here Whitehead sets up the hierarchy which dominates his view of the natural world. Plants fall between the utter unresponsiveness of a stone and the profound and unpredictable sensitivity of a human being; they demonstrate some response to their surroundings, but much of this response is predictable.

Whitehead (1938*b*: 33) expresses the low-grade nature of plants by his statement that a plant is a *democracy*, composed from numerous actual occasions which are all of equal status. No occasion is in a powerful or controlling position; no occasion is more essential to the plant than any other. There is no 'one centre of experience' which is dominant. Again, in this, the plant falls between the categories of a rock and an animal. A rock, in Whitehead's system, lacks any real cohesion at all; it is merely a collection of actual occasions. An animal, in contrast, has a unified centre of experience which can have a single purpose and a certain degree of control. The actual occasions which compose a plant do work together with a common purpose, but, according to Whitehead, the plant has no centralized control. It 'can be subdivided into minor democracies which easily survive, without much apparent loss of functional expression' (ibid. 34). That cuttings can be taken from a plant in a way impossible with higher organisms demonstrates its lack of centralization. No particular part of the plant is essential for its survival.

It is thus plant cells which are of particular significance, rather than the complete plant. The cells have greater unity in themselves than the plant as a whole (a point which Hartshorne develops, as we shall see). This lack of inner unity in a plant means that it does not have 'personal order'; there is no single inherited sequence which persists through the plant as a whole. The cells which compose it do have personal order; but the plant as a whole does not. Plants none the less, 'exhibit modes of behaviour directed towards self preservation' (Whitehead 1978: 176). They grow, absorb food, resist disease, and ultimately evolve methods of defence against attack. They demonstrate some 'coordinated organic individuality' (Whitehead 1938*b*: 38). But the co-ordination is secondary to the plurality. Plants are first and foremost societies, lacking even the personal order of the cells that compose them.

Animals and humans can form far more complex and unified societies than plants. Unlike plants, however, distinctions in levels can be made here. While all plants are democracies and produce similar experience, different animals have significantly differing levels of complexity. At the lowest end are the jellyfish and worms, which are like plants in that they can be divided and still survive. However as we saw in Chapter 1, 'higher' animals have one single centre of experience, the 'presiding actual occasion'. This means that 'an animal body, in its highest examples is more analogous to a feudal society, with its overlord' (Whitehead 1938*b*: 35). Some animals fall between democracies and dominance, behaving most of the time like democracies, and failing to produce novel experience, but on some occasions behaving in a co-ordinated or unpredictable way. This suggests that they have a discontinuous dominant actual occasion.

Of what does the dominant or presiding actual occasion consist? Whitehead describes it as a 'living person'. Again, it is important to be careful about his use of 'person' here; he means by this a persisting series of high-grade actual occasions, that is to say, occasions with a dominant mental pole. Their persistence gives them a recognizable form, and can be called 'personality'. The higher the mental grade—and, more particularly, when it reaches consciousness or self-consciousness in humans and other 'higher' animals—the closer it is to our usual use of the term 'personality' with its implications of original traits and individual idiosyncrasies. 'The enduring personality', Whitehead (1978: 118) remarks, 'is the historic route of living occasions which are severally dominant in the body at successive instants.' The enduring nature of the personality means that an animal or a human being can be accurately described as an 'enduring object'. Unlike the molecules and crystals that were described as enduring objects before, this is not because of their repetitive nature, but rather because of the way in which the societies that comprise the enduring object are bound into a whole by their dominant actual occasion.

The dominant occasion is, in fact, more accurately called a 'series of dominant occasions' since it is a constantly changing thread of high-grade actual occasions positively prehending those which preceded them. It is thus a linear society. Indeed, the presence of a dominant occasion is not intended in any way to deny the nature of the animal body as a society. It is, of course, composed from subsocieties and subnexus, which are constantly changing. The dominant actual occasion is an agent of a 'complex process of massive simplification' (ibid. 314), allowing the multitude of different changes going on in the body to be filtered into a single perceived experience. The astonishing thing about the animal body, for Whitehead (ibid. 108), is its unification: 'What needs to be explained is not dissociation of personality, but unifying control, by reason of which we not only have unified behaviour, which can be observed by others, but also consciousness of a unified experience.'

Most animals, then, have dominant actual occasions, are 'regnant' societies, which Hartshorne calls 'monarchies'. However, they lack certain human qualities: 'In animals, we can see emotional feeling dominantly derived from bodily functions and yet tinged with purposes, hopes and expression derived from conceptual functioning. The distinction between men and animals is, in one sense, only a difference of degree. But the extent of the degree makes all the difference. The Rubicon has been crossed' (Whitehead 1938*b*: 37). Animals thus have some conceptual ability; they entertain notions, hopes, and fears. They may have 'flashes of aesthetic insight, of technological attainment, of sociological organization, of affectionate feeling' (Whitehead 1948: 66). But they lack the developed conceptual ability of an adult human. Their 'mental functionings' are deficient (Whitehead 1938*b*: 8). They may have some semblance of morality, but they lack religion (ibid.) and they lack civilization. Humans have a much greater capacity to introduce novelty, and they have a much higher emphasis on abstraction. Although this difference is seemingly only a difference of degree, language such as 'crossing the Rubicon' and nature 'bursting through another of its boundaries' (ibid. 36) suggests that Whitehead believes human capacities to be immensely greater than those of animals.

Whitehead's understanding, then, produces a series of nested societies from the smallest, such as electrons and other enduring objects, through the corpuscular societies, to the living societies: the cell, plants, non-human and human animals. Indeed, societies do not stop with the single human being, as will become clear in Chapter 4: 'An army is a society of regiments, and regiments are societies of men, and men are societies of cells, of blood and of bones, together with the dominant society of personal human experience, and cells are societies of smaller physical entities such as protons, and so on, (Whitehead 1948: 239).

Whitehead's understanding of all that exists as being composed from graded societies of actual occasions forms the basic insight of all process thinking in the Whiteheadian tradition. However, different process thinkers, in particular Hartshorne, have different interpretations of the status of societies which are worth considering briefly, since they have some important implications both here and in Chapter 4.

The Concept of Society in Hartshorne and Other Process Thinkers

Hartshorne accepts Whitehead's fundamental premiss that everything is composed from graded societies of actual occasions, from the electron to the universe (although he prefers to use the language of organisms rather than that of societies). In his essay 'A World of Organisms' (1962), Hartshorne introduces a distinction significantly absent from Whitehead's categories which lends a different emphasis to his ethical concerns. Whitehead's societies exhibit differing degrees of closeness; but he introduces no clearcut distinction between different types of society. Hartshorne, however, using his preferred organismic language, discriminates between what he calls the organism and the quasi-organism (although both are societies). He explains this distinction: 'My suggestion is that any whole which has less unity than its most unified parts is not an organism in the pregnant sense here in question' (ibid. 192). Thus an electron, or a human being, which are both more unified than their most unified parts, are true organisms; while a plant, which is less unified than its most unified parts (its cells) is a quasi-organism.

This intensifies the individuality that Hartshorne attributes to true organisms, and the plurality that he attributes to quasi-organisms. An electron, for example, is a true organism, an individual (Hartshorne 1975: 190–1). Thus it is easier for us to identify with it than for us to identify with a plant, which is a plurality, a quasi-organism. A plant, in contrast, is compared by Hartshorne with the population of a city. It has no feelings as a whole; it is a collocation of cells, which Hartshorne (1987: 10) lists alongside tables and crystals. It is like a flock of birds or a swarm of bees (Hartshorne 1970: 142). Indeed, he goes so far as to say that to 'ask how a plant feels' is like 'asking how America feels, except that America is in some ways much more unified' (Hartshorne 1936: 215).

Two other process thinkers have contributed detailed descriptions of their understanding of the 'grades of being': Jay McDaniel, most prominently in *Of God and Pelicans* (1989) and John Cobb with Charles Birch in *The Liberation of Life* (1981). Since, based on this interpretation, the conclusions they draw about values are interesting, their perspectives will be briefly considered.

McDaniel puts forward, essentially, a simplified Hartshornian position. There are, he suggests, 'at least two basic organizational types', monarchies and democracies (McDaniel 1989: 77). The monarchy, McDaniel says, has a 'psyche' and this is 'the organism's spirit, its soul'. He identifies this with the dominant actual occasion. In organisms with 'complex nervous systems' it is found in the brain. Different kinds of organism have different degrees of 'soul':

Strength of soul is a measure of (1) the extent to which a given occasion of experience in a psychic stream is able to learn from previous experiences, thereby contributing to an ongoing identity over time and (2) the extent to which, as it occurs, the subjective unity of a presiding experience has greater richness of experience than those of its component parts.   (ibid. 79)

Here McDaniel is clearly influenced by Hartshorne, appropriating Hartshorne's basic theme that, in a true organism, the whole is more unified than its most unified parts, and shifting the emphasis from greater unity to greater richness of experience. This emphasis on richness of experience is also a subtle change from the Whiteheadian position where the production of novel rather than rich experience is emphasized. There are, of course, strong links between unity, novelty, and richness of experience in process thought, although it is by no means obvious that a novel experience need be richer than a repeated one.

The democracy, however, McDaniel argues, lacks a psyche; it is 'an aggregate of energy events'. Building on Hartshorne's metaphor of the city, he comments, 'While this city may be more than the sum of its individual constituencies, it is not a "more" with experiences and interests of its own. A democracy *is* the totality of its parts in relation' (ibid. 78). The explicit denial that a democracy (such as a plant) has interests of its own, other than the interests of its parts (such as its cells) is a significant one, maintained implicitly by Hartshorne.

Birch and Cobb approach the description of the 'grades of being' from a more biological perspective (although many biologists might have difficulty with their approach). In addition, they largely eschew technical Whiteheadian language, rarely speaking of societies or actual occasions, but predominantly of organisms and experience. Unlike Hartshorne, no distinction is made between true and quasi-organisms as the full title of their book bears out: *The Libera-tion of Life: From the Cell to the Community* (1981). This suggests that they understand the human community to be the same kind of thing as a cell; for Hartshorne, of course, the human community would be a quasi-organism, rather than a true organism such as the cell.

In accordance with all process thinking, Birch and Cobb stress the 'internality' of an atom; it has subjective, if unconscious, experience. However, their real concern is with living organisms. As with all process thinkers, plants are described as societies of cells. However, Birch and Cobb are slightly more positive about the cohesion of such a society. They do not adopt Hartshorne's 'city' imagery. 'Plants are not mere aggregates of cells. They per-form numerous functions which the cells outside of the societies cannot perform. Nevertheless, we do not attribute to plants the sort of unity we think we discern in the cell' (Birch and Cobb 1981: 153). It is not clear from their description whether Birch and Cobb think that plants as a whole have interests. The most likely inter-pretation of their position is that the survival of the plant is instru-mental for the survival of its constituent cells: after all, 'the life of the plant is the life of the cells which compose it'.

The consideration that Birch and Cobb give to other organisms does not differ significantly from that of Whitehead. Rather than using the language of dominant occasions or monarchies they refer to 'centralized co-ordination' and the 'emergence of conscious experience' as the characteristics of such organisms. However, their value position is very thoroughly developed.

Value in Individual Natural Objects and Organisms

The question of value in individual natural objects and organisms in process thinking is a complex one, and will be approached in the following way. After a brief general discussion, this investigation will be divided into three sections, corresponding to those in the earlier part of this chapter; that is, *moral considerability and significance, non-consequentialism and restitution* and, finally, *indi-vidualism*.

Value: A General Consideration

As we saw in Chapter 1, every actual occasion in Whitehead's sys-tem (including God) is the bearer of intrinsic (non-instrumental) value. More particularly, every actual entity subjectively values its own realization. Such self-valuation, in process thinking, is not restricted to consciousness: this would be, for process thinkers, an unwarranted conflation of subjectivity and self-valuation with consciousness. Birch and Cobb (ibid. 123), for instance, claim that they 'can speak comfortably of "non-conscious experience"'. Valuable experience is not confined to sentient organisms, or indeed, to living organisms at all; it is found everywhere. This approach to value immediately highlights significant contrasts between process thinking and the environmental ethicists considered earlier in this chapter. This contrast is primarily focused around the relationship between value and experience, and the presence, in process thinking, of intrinsic value throughout the universe.

For example, Taylor, as we have seen, affirms that all living organisms, including plants and bacteria, have inherent worth. They all have a good of their own, a *telos*; this is necessary and sufficient for the possession of inherent worth. Only things with inherent worth (in Taylor's sense) have intrinsic (non-instrumental) value in Taylor's system.[20] A rock, with no good of its own, and with no *telos*, has no intrinsic value; a plant, which has both a *telos* and a good of its own, does have intrinsic value. Thus, for Taylor, non-instrumental value is detached from experience and attached to 'having a good'. In his terms, only and all living organisms have non-instrumental value.

This position contrasts with that of process thinkers. Process thinkers hold intrinsic value and experience tightly together. However, they then argue that experience can be found throughout the universe. This leads to the apparently odd position that an ethicist such as Taylor who decouples non-instrumental value from experience may consider fewer kinds of things to be ethically relevant than a process ethicist who argues that value and experience are inseparable.

The breaking of the link between value and experience is, as we have seen, widespread in environmental ethics and is essential for most of the environmental ethicists earlier in this chapter. Since they do not accept that experience extends into the non-human world further than animals, were they to affirm a necessary link

[20] It is worth remembering here that Taylor himself uses '*intrinsic value*' to mean *value that is consciously experienced.*

between experience and value, they would be unable to value such living organisms as plants and bacteria (the route taken by Singer 1976, 1979*a* and *b*, and Regan 1984*a*). By severing the necessary link between experience and value, and suggesting criteria such as (unexperienced) well-being, capacities, having a good, and interests, philosophers such as Taylor have been able to affirm the moral considerability of a variety of individual living organisms. How then might process thinking respond to such claims for moral consideration?

Moral Consideration and Significance in Process Thinking about the Individual

Since the locus of intrinsic value in process thinking is the actual occasion, and the universe is constituted from actual occasions, it might seem as if the entire universe has, or could have, moral considerability. All occasions, after all, contribute to the consequent nature of God. It is for this reason that it is impossible to disentangle moral considerability and moral significance in process thinking. In contrast with Regan (1982) and Feinberg (1974) this is not because the threshold of moral considerability gives very high moral significance. In fact the reverse is the case. The threshold of moral considerability in process thinking is so low that even though something may be morally considerable, its moral significance is negligible. Thus, although technically all actual occasions could be morally considerable, in actuality their significance is so slight, so trivial, that they are not worth consideration. The best approach is to look for the boundary of practical, rather than theoretical, moral considerability; that is to say, where moral considerability becomes moral significance and thus makes a difference in moral decisions.

The Moral Significance of the Non-Living

How, then, would process thinking respond to Regan's (1982) suggestion that non-living natural objects should be treated with 'admiring respect'? It is not self-evident that process thinking would dismiss value claims for the non-living. Life in a process system (like sentience for Goodpaster) is merely an indicator of something beyond itself—the experiencing actual occasion.[21] Life is a particularly specialized form of a universal phenomenon.

---

[21] A similar attempt to push Goodpaster further is made by Hunt (1980: 59–65).

Undoubtedly, then, process thinkers would agree with Regan in 'The Nature and Possibility of an Environmental Ethic' that to draw a line of moral considerability at life is arbitrary.

In addition, process thinking affirms the general goodness of 'what is'. To exist is good (however much better it could have been) in that every actual occasion contributes something to the consequent nature of God. Thus it would not be inaccurate for process thinkers to speak, as Regan does, about 'the inherent goodness of things'—or rather, the inherent good of the actual occasions which compose them. However, beyond this point, despite the metaphysical structure offered by a process system, no unambiguous support is given to Regan's suggestion. 'Natural objects' so-called, such as the Colorado River or Grand Canyon, are, first, from a process perspective, societies lacking cohesion; they are collocations of atoms, or, in Hartshorne's terms, quasi-organisms, since the whole is less unified than the most unified parts. What this lack of cohesion means for value generation is unclear. Hartshorne (1970: 194) suggests that quasi-organisms, are 'valuable not directly, but for the sake of their members, or of some larger whole'. In other words, quasi-organisms do not generate value directly but rather indirectly—for true organisms which compose the quasi-organism (primarily actual occasions); for onlooking organisms (primarily human beings), and God, the cosmic organism. This increased value generated by God is reflected back into the world by the prehension of the consequent nature of God by the newly concrescing actual occasions. Thus the existence of quasi-organisms such as natural objects clearly does increase total value generated in the world. But this value is not intrinsic value generated by the quasi-organisms themselves, as wholes, but rather indirectly, by other, true organisms. (This will be explored in more detail in Chapter 4.)

If we look at the value of natural objects as societies of actual occasions rather than as wholes, we find that the value generated within them is negligible. Having a very strong physical pole, and a weak mental pole, they generate little novel or rich experience; they exhibit only the trivial value of 'narrowness'. Thus, although they may create value, it is not worth practical moral consideration:

The intrinsic value that can be attributed to the subjective experience of events at the sub-atomic, atomic and molecular levels, is so slight that for practical, and therefore ethical purposes, it can be safely ignored. The same is true of mere aggregates of events such as rocks... the effects of most human activities upon such events is trivial. Entities of these types may reasonably be treated as means, or in terms of their instrumental values only. (Birch and Cobb 1981: 152)

As I have already suggested, this does not mean that a non-living object cannot be responsible for generating extremely intense and harmonious experience in higher-grade organisms. In this respect, a process thinker may regard non-living natural organisms rather like artistic masterpieces. One does not judge a great painting by the inconsequential amount of intrinsic value generated by the atoms and molecules which compose the paint and canvas. (In this respect, in any case, all paintings are of virtually identical intrinsic value, whatever their artistic merit.) It is the intrinsic value generated in those who view it which is significant. To destroy the painting is immoral, not because of the value lost to the actual occasions which compose the painting, but because of the potential richness of experience lost through its no longer being viewed and producing value which would have contributed to the consequent nature of God. Thus, inanimate objects, natural or otherwise, are primarily instrumentally valuable for the intrinsic value that they generate in human high-grade valuers (including humans) and for God. Process thinking thus demonstrates a practical, if not a theoretical, concurrence of views with those of the majority of individualist environmental ethicists. This harmony is, however, a fragile one, and significant differences are revealed when the moral significance of plants is considered.

Moral Significance of Plants

Plants in process thinking are primarily societies, or, in Hartshorne's terms quasi-organisms. 'The life of the plant is the life of the cells which compose it... its intrinsic value is the sum of the cells' (Birch and Cobb 1981: 153). The degree of coherence thought to be exhibited by plants varies between process thinkers, McDaniel and Hartshorne suggesting less unity than Cobb and Whitehead. Cobb seems to accept, unlike Hartshorne and McDaniel, that a plant, as a whole, has a *telos*. The situation is less clear in Whitehead, who might argue that since a plant can have cuttings taken to make new plants, it can have no *telos* other than that of its individual cells. However, even if process thinkers were to concede that a plant possessed a unified *telos*, this would not necessarily affect its value status, since it is not having a *telos* or being alive which bestows value. According to all process thinkers, plant *cells* are responsible for generation of intrinsic value. Of course, practically, it would be very difficult to separate the value of the plant from that of its cells, or to protect the cells without protecting the plant. Without the environment of the plant, the cells could not survive. This is, however, assigning the plant as a whole instrumental value for its cells.

The value generated by plant cells gives them practical moral considerability in a process system:

> If a choice were to be made between a completely inorganic universe and a universe in which there was cellular life, there is no question that the latter should be chosen. The value of such a universe would be incomparably the greater of the two. The intrinsic value of cells is not entirely negligible from an ethical point of view.[22]

However, in any situation, other than that of a comparison with non-living material, the moral significance of plants, even plant cells, is extremely low. Indeed, Birch and Cobb conclude that one would not be wrong to ascribe to plants purely instrumental value. They produce little rich experience, largely repeating that of preceding occasions; one also cannot distinguish between experiences of cells in different kinds of plant. Thus, their moral significance is trifling. In assigning moral considerability to the plant world, process thinking is in harmony with the individualist deontological environmental ethicists considered earlier. In focusing on the cells rather than the whole plant, however, process thinking is in serious disagreement with them; and in the degree of value ascribed to them is at odds with Schweitzer and Taylor at least. The position of process thinkers here, in particular their conception of plants as societies, would be vehemently rejected by these environmental ethicists.

That this should be so is unsurprising, since the argument of these ethicists for the moral considerability of plants depends, at root, on the conception of a plant as an individual pursuing its own end, with a good, a will-to-live, and interests of its own, however unconscious they may be. The integrity of the plant is vital to

---

[22] Although Birch and Cobb (1981: 152–3) give no reference here, this comparison between a barren and a plant-laden world is strongly reminiscent of the 'last man' and 'last people' examples used by Richard and Val Routley (1980), drawn from a development of arguments by G. E. Moore.

sustain such a view; and thus the plant as a whole is valuable for these ethicists, rather than the experiences of its cells. If a plant is conceived to be a society, this teleological understanding of the whole plant is weakened.

A number of attacks have been made on this aspect of process thinking, both by biologists and environmental ethicists. Karen Davis (1989: 242), for example, argues:

Not only do cells and other microscopic entities show signs of sensitivity to the environment; so do whole plants as any lay observer can note... I don't understand how Hartshorne can logically ascribe sentience to cells based on the argument that they show signs of sensitivity to the environment, even though they do not indicate the presence of a nervous system, yet deny sentience to whole plants using the nervous system criterion, while ignoring the fact that they too can be seen responding to the environment as individuals.

A similar view is expressed by Jay Kantor (1980: 169), citing the self-regulatory and homeostatic functions of plants as evidence of their integrity. Rolston develops this concept still further in a review of Ian Barbour's process-oriented Gifford Lectures. Like Davis, he thinks it strange that cells are considered to be more integrated than plants, and that their atoms experience more than the whole plant. He argues that plants are 'unified entities of the biological kind'. They have DNA coding; they 'repair injuries', they 'move water, nutrients and photosynthates from cell to cell'. On this basis, they are 'integrated enough to defend intrinsic value, a good of their own kind' (Rolston 1992: 79).

For egalitarian ethicists, the minimal value ascribed to plants in process thinking is an indication of deep ethical inadequacy. Treating a plant as a collection rather than a whole, and judging its value by its experiences rather than its interests, its aim, or its will-to-live, is a sign of insufficient respect or reverence for life. Even Lombardi and Johnson would argue that to judge a plant by its richness of experience is to use an inappropriate value standard. This difference in attitude towards plant life between process thinking and other ethicists in this chapter illustrates the central contrast between the duty-oriented, individualist basis for ethics in systems such as Taylor's, and the consequence-oriented, experience-generating approach of process ethics. This differentiation is even clearer when we consider the value of animal and human life.

Moral Significance of Animals and Humans

Some implications of a process understanding of humans and animals have been considered in the preceding chapter, and will not be repeated here. It will already be clear that the moral considerability of animals and human beings is assumed in process thinking; the questions remaining concern their degree of moral significance.

To recap: all animals, human and non-human, are societies composed from subsocieties and subnexus, and ultimately from experiencing actual occasions. Value is generated by the harmony and intensity of the experiencing actual occasions. Animals and humans have a 'dominant actual occasion', which allows the perception of unified experience. In addition, the mental pole of the dominant actual occasion is very strong—in humans and possibly some animals it is conscious—which generates considerable complex and novel experience. A large number of contrasting (but compatible) eternal objects generating harmony and intensity of experience can be incorporated into the dominant actual occasion, which ultimately contributes to the consequent nature of God.

The generation of such intense and harmonious experience among animals and humans gives them high value in the process system; significantly greater than plants, whose experience is largely repetitious. The degree of value, however, varies considerably between different species of animals, and different human individuals, according to the strength of the mental pole of the dominant actual occasion and the harmony and intensity of experience produced.

This underlines the inegalitarian nature of process ethics. Here, then, process thinking parts company with the ostensible egalitarianism of Schweitzer and Taylor. Indeed, Cobb is strikingly sceptical of Schweitzer for precisely these egalitarian reasons. He argues that Schweitzer has failed to think through the ethical implications of his environmental system, and in practice makes ad hoc decisions without justifiable theoretical grounds for his behaviour. Cobb and Griffin (1977: 79) comment, like Singer, that Schweitzer 'refused to work out a theoretical justification for choosing the life of human beings over the lives of the lower organisms which as a doctor, he sought to destroy'. An attack such as this on Schweitzer for his lack of system could not, however, be sustained against Taylor, who has, as we have seen, attempted (albeit unsuccessfully) to develop a systematic approach to egalitarian ecological ethics, including dealing with disease organisms. However, Cobb would have little more time for Taylor's egalitarianism than Schweitzer's, since this was the real root of his objection to Schweitzer. In this respect, at least, process thinking is closer to that of Lombardi or Johnson than Taylor.

How, then, do process thinkers 'grade' the value of animal life? Broadly speaking, value is dependent on the strength of the mentality built up within the society of actual occasions, governed by the mental pole of the dominant actual occasion. Whitehead himself says little about the relative values of different animals and humans, although he does clearly perceive there to be a gulf between humans and other animals. Hartshorne (1979: 50) is more detailed here. In humans 'the positive characteristics of animals generally, and for all we know, of creatures at large, are present in highest degree and therefore in most unmistakable form'. Among these characteristics are mental and conceptual capacity, sentience, morality, and religion, characteristics which, according to Hartshorne, allow humans to generate substantially richer experiences than those available to animals.

A second interesting observation made by Hartshorne is that while we recognize the individuality of other humans, we see animals as representatives of their species, rather than as individuals with their own personalities. We came across this idea with reference to 'chickenness' in Chapter 2. Hartshorne (ibid. 56) says, for example, 'We tend to think that humanity is important because of the values in each individual person; but we tend to think that one nightingale or one hermit thrush is significant chiefly as a specimen of its species.' This reaction is, in Hartshorne's view, justified. The added complexity and novelty of human experience, generated by our intellectual, moral, and religious capacities, means that each human has recognizably different experiences. Birds and animals, however, lack these human capacities; they have, according to Hartshorne 'no concept of self', they make no plans for the future, they do not fear death. Their experience is correspondingly less complex, less intense, and less valuable.

'Rights' in Process Thinking

Hartshorne, rather surprisingly, entitles his key paper in this area, 'The Rights of the Subhuman World'. The use of the concept of rights would be, one might think, uncharacteristic of a process consequentialist position. However, McDaniel, Dombrowski, and Cobb all adopt the same rights terminology in their expositions of the relative values of humans and animals in process thinking. In addition, all three develop structurally similar accounts of the value of animals, although this is far from saying that they in fact adopt the same conclusion.

McDaniel's account is the least sophisticated. As we have seen, he distinguishes between democracies and monarchies, and between more and less sophisticated monarchies, with more or less complex nervous systems. As an example of this, he comments 'The first assumption implies that a dog has a greater intrinsic value than a fungus, the second that a dog has greater intrinsic value than a tick.'[23] Which of these organisms, then, has rights for McDaniel? The dog, the fungus, or the tick?

It must first be commented that McDaniel's use of the term 'rights' is very loose. This is illustrated by his inclusion of Peter Singer as an 'animal rights advocate'. Although Singer himself carelessly spoke of 'rights' in *Animal Liberation*, he has since dissociated himself from the term. However, since, as a process thinker, McDaniel's position is close to that of Singer, and Singer is perceived to be advocating rights, it is not surprising to see McDaniel accepting the terminology too. But for McDaniel, as for any process thinker, the possession of a right guarantees nothing absolutely, not even a right to life. Indeed, having a right seems to mean little more for McDaniel than 'deserving of respect'. As one would expect, all rights in McDaniel's system are overridden if greater richness of experience may be generated by doing so.

None the less, McDaniel certainly employs the language with the intention of securing greater respect towards those to whom it is applicable. Which animals then do have rights? Those who,

---

[23] McDaniel (1989: 84) does not deny that from the point of view of the creature being ranked, its life is as important to itself as that of a higher-ranked creature to itself. This is the only time I have read such a comment (with which, of course, Taylor and Schweitzer would wholeheartedly concur) in process writing. Since it makes no actual difference to McDaniel's system, and reappears nowhere else in process thinking that I am aware of, I shall not dwell on it here.

(1) 'have discernible interests in living with some degree of satisfaction'; and (2) 'whose interests can be respected or violated by human moral agents' (McDaniel 1989: 67). These criteria, although sufficiently vague to include all living organisms (since he is talking about 'having interests' rather than 'being interested in') is presumably meant only to refer to those animals with more complex nervous systems (it is cows, sheep, chickens, and fish to which he later refers). For McDaniel, these higher, sentient organisms are of greatest value and deserving of greatest respect—next, of course, to human beings who have highest value of all because of the greater richness of experience which they generate.

McDaniel's conclusions are very similar to those of Birch and Cobb in *The Liberation of Life*. Since the values of Birch and Cobb were considered extensively in Chapter 2, I shall not dwell on them here, other than to comment that they do have a slightly more sophisticated understanding of rights:

we would be prepared to consider the question of rights to be a terminological one if those who denied rights to animals were nevertheless willing to speak in some other way of their ethical claim upon us and our duties towards them. But this is very rare. On the whole the denial is taken as also entailing that we have no obligations towards them, that we are free to exploit them to our private pleasure or advantage without limit.   (Birch and Cobb 1981: 154)

This view of rights need not guarantee the rights-holder very much—as, indeed, it does not. For Birch and Cobb, rights may be overridden, wherever the consequences judged by maximizing total richness of experience demand it. The idea that not only may rights be overridden, but that organisms (understood as clusters of experience) may be replaced, providing that equivalent experience is produced, weakens their understanding of rights still further.

The weakness of this understanding of rights, and the ease with which they may be overridden, for McDaniel and Birch and Cobb, contrasts sharply with Dombrowski, who intends rights to be understood in a much stronger sense. His book *Hartshorne and the Metaphysics of Animal Rights* (1988) is less an exposition of Hartshorne (who, like McDaniel and Cobb, understands rights in a weak sense) than a suggestion of how Hartshorne might be interpreted to support a strong rights position.

Dombrowski identifies two kinds of 'sentiency' in the process system. The first is the experience of actual occasions and singulars such as molecules and cells, which do not feel pain. These he labels S1. The second is that of whole organisms that can suffer pain: S2. Plants, Dombrowski (ibid. 43) argues are only S1, and consequently 'can be eaten with equanimity'. They have intrinsic value, but this is much less than the value of S2, because of their inability to feel pain. Animals, including humans, are S2— although, Dombrowski comments, when animals or humans 'lapse into dreamless sleep' they become as S1: a 'mere colony of cells'. S2 organisms have high value, because of their ability to feel pleasure and pain and hence to generate rich experience. Thus causing pain to sentient animals (S2) is to 'contribute to vicarious divine suffering'; generating rich experience for them is to contribute to divine pleasure (ibid. 69).

Animals which are S2 have rights; and Dombrowski intends these rights to have a high degree of inviolability. He rejects Cobb's replaceability hypothesis outright: 'Cobb's utilitarian reasoning whereby one quantity of value can be sacrificed if another replaces it is precisely the sort of reasoning that Cobb himself (as well as Hartshorne) has spent a good deal of time criticizing' (ibid. 82). Certainly, Cobb has criticized utilitarianism; and, certainly, his position is utilitarian in form. Dombrowski here seems to be suggesting that the experiences of all animals which are S2 are unique and irreplaceable (as Cobb argues for humans). He supports this idea by arguing first that in Cobb's version of the replaceability argument it 'is really only the (supposedly Platonic form) of chickenness which is reverenced, not the particular chicken killed', and secondly that 'the negative experiences of slaughter end up contributing to the divine life', and do not add to the richness of God's experience.

Dombrowski seems confused here. First, he is objecting to the painful experiences generated by the slaughter of animals (his particular aim is to justify vegetarianism on process grounds). Such negative experiences hurt God as well as the sentient animal, and consequently should not be continued. This argument from painful experience is, of course, a standard utilitarian one; the effect which such experiences have on God, a standard process one. By arguing this case, Dombrowski is hardly opposing Cobb's replaceability argument. It is not painful experiences which are in question here. Killing can be done without inflicting painful experience, and a new organism generated; how does Dombrowski respond to this?

Dombrowski's own position here is highly ambiguous, partly due to his categories S1 and S2. By his own admission, organisms that are S1 are not morally considerable, and can be eaten with impunity. In addition, organisms which are S2 when awake are S1 when in dreamless sleep. Does this mean that if they are killed when they are asleep, that is, in an S1 state, their killing is morally acceptable? Killing an organism in an S1 state would avoid inflicting the negative experiences on the organisms and God. If one were to generate a similar amount and kind of S2 experience which would not otherwise have existed, and no negative S2 experience had resulted from the killing, would this not be acceptable? (This approximates the position of Birch and Cobb.)

Dombrowski wants to reject this by arguing that each S2 organism has unique and irreplaceable experience—and, as a corollary, that their rights are generally inviolable. To support this point, Dombrowski would have to contest (1) that the experiences of S2 organisms are unique; (2) that uniqueness is in itself valuable; and (3) that being valuable in this sense would generally render an organism inviolable, all points which were touched on in Chapter 2.

If Dombrowski is maintaining the first of these contentions— that the experiences of all S2 organisms, human or non-human, are unique—then he is certainly the most radical of process thinkers. More precisely, he would be maintaining that the kind of experience produced by one S2 organism is sufficiently different from that of another S2 organism (say, the difference between the experiences of two mice) to be primarily described as that individual's experience, rather than a 'mousey experience'. This contrasts, as we have already seen, with Birch and Cobb's understanding of 'chickenness', where the difference between the feelings of one chicken and another is negligible, and the view of Hartshorne that animals are primarily representatives of their species.

Assuming that this is what Dombrowski intends, for his argument to succeed he must also maintain that uniqueness is valuable, and that this value confers inviolability. As we have already seen in Chapters 1 and 2, there are problems with this idea in process thinking. First, for the actual occasion itself, uniqueness does not necessarily lead to greater satisfaction. Uniqueness in an actual occasion is due to a high degree of novelty. It is certainly true that the more novelty there is in a new actual occasion, the more likely it is to be valuable, because of the incorporation of new, contrasting eternal objects. But it is not the novelty itself that is of value. In a crucial remark on this subject, Whitehead says, 'In the foundations of his being, God is indifferent alike to preservation and to novelty. He cares not whether an immediate occasion be old or new, so far as concerns derivation from its ancestry. His aim for it is depth of satisfaction as an intermediate step towards the fulfilment of his own being' (Whitehead 1978: 105). Secondly, whilst uniqueness of experience may lead to contrasts, and contrasts may deepen God's satisfaction in the world, this does not make any one unique experience, or kind of experience, inviolable. Thus, even if Dombrowski's argument that the experiences of each S2 organism is unique are accepted, they are not guaranteed inviolability. If an S2 organism was killed whilst in an S1 state, and a new organism produced in its place, then not only would there be no overall loss of rich experience in the world, but there would be no loss of contrast in the world to add to God's experience. The new S2 organism would be equally as unique as the old. The replaceability position championed by Cobb still seems to be the logical position for process thinking. The real aim is to maximize total richness of experience for the consequent nature of God.

This suggests that the rights language of process thinkers in general, and of Dombrowski in particular, is largely redundant, having at best only rhetorical value. Whereas many animals are of high value and have S2 status, they do not have inviolable rights, since it is not they, but their experiences and contrasts between them, that are of value.

Process Thinking and Taylor's Duty and Priority Principles

Having examined ways in which different kinds of organism are graded in process thinking, it is now interesting for us to consider how process thinking might respond to Taylor's duty and priority principles. While process thinkers would, for instance, broadly adhere to Taylor's principles of non-maleficence and fidelity, this is not because they are, in themselves, binding duties, but because they generally produce the best consequences. Maleficent and untrustworthy behaviour are unlikely to promote rich experience.

This having been said, one of Taylor's main examples of infidelity is hunting or trapping, where an animal is lured by deceit into a fatal situation. The attitude of process thinkers to both hunting and trapping is ambiguous, and very much context-dependent. Theodore Vitali (1990: 74) attacks Taylor vigorously over his use of fidelity as a duty principle with which to oppose hunting. Vitali cites Whitehead and Hartshorne as providing a metaphysical foundation for environmental ethics—and his own, favourable views on sport hunting. Is process thinking positive about sport hunting? For this to be the case, total richness of experience within the universe would have to be increased by hunting, outweighing both the negative experiences of the hunt and the loss of the future experiences of the hunted animal (assuming it was caught). This kind of calculus is, of course, very difficult to carry out—a problem with which utilitarians are familiar. Certainly (as indicated in Chapter 2) where the human value of preserving an ancient culture is concerned, hunting even of very high-grade experiencers such as whales may be justified.

This again raises the problem of the 'gap' between human and non-human experience. Within process thinking, non-basic human interests (which generate rich human experience) can win over basic non-human interests (where experience is not as rich). Thus it is at least possible that a non-basic human interest, such as the pleasurable experiences generated by hunting, could outweigh the suffering and death of an animal for sport. Gamwell (1981: 48), for instance, would certainly think so. In what he considers to be a defence of the ecological awareness of process thinking, he comments, 'Far from condoning every destruction that is executed upon nature in the name of human purposes, the maximal happiness principle prescribes such sacrifice only when human possibilities are thereby greater than they would otherwise be.' One is tempted to ask whether in fact this criterion would prevent any destructive action at all, since virtually any human act towards the non-human world could be said in some way to further human possibilities. For Gamwell, if any kind of increase in the harmony and intensity of human experience can result, then destroying a living organism is acceptable. Other process thinkers, such as Dombrowski, narrow the human/non-human gap considerably and would argue that only a significant human gain could outweigh a high-grade non-human loss. Perhaps the only firm conclusions which can be drawn here is that fidelity and non-maleficence cannot be ultimate duties for process thinkers, although they may be instrumentally useful in increasing the richness of experience for the consequent nature of God.

A comparison of process thinking with Taylor's priority principles is also interesting. Taking Taylor's priority principle of self-defence as an example: generally speaking, human self-defence against attack by non-humans would be perfectly acceptable in a process system; in fact it would normally be a moral requirement. In addition, one would also normally have a moral obligation to rescue other humans from similar situations of threat. No individual non-human could outweigh the life of a human being (unless the human was categorized as a marginal human: a foetus or baby, in a coma or with a mental handicap, and the attacker was a high-grade experiencer attacking for survival). An individual human being would also produce substantially richer experience than millions of disease bacteria, since the actual occasions from which they are composed lack strong mental poles. Thus process thinking has no problems of the sort created by Taylor, of maintaining each bacterium to be of equal inherent worth to a human being.

However, it is just conceivable that there may be circumstances in which self-defence might not be the ethically correct choice in process thinking. If a human being were to be threatened by an animal which was one of the last breeding individuals of its species—a tiger perhaps—its death would threaten the continuance of the species. Replacement would not be possible. Whilst the experiences of that individual tiger would not outweigh those of the human, the loss of the tiger species would impoverish God's experience, reducing the potential contrasts of kinds of feeling in the world. At issue here is a dilemma hinted at in Chapter 1, which will recur in later chapters of this book. Which is of more significance for enriching God's experience, feeling the rich experiences of high-grade societies such as human beings, or feeling the contrasts between different kinds of experience? If the former, then despite the rarity of the tiger, the human being should engage in self-defence. If the latter, then the tiger, by virtue of its tigery experiences, should be allowed to live even at the cost of human life. Questions are also suggested about how many tigers are enough to preserve the existence of tigery feelings in the world: one? a breeding population, to ensure that these kinds of feeling will continue in the future? This has a number of practical implications for the ways in which endangered species might be treated (e.g. in the instigation of captive breeding programmes).

Moving on, Taylor's principles of proportionality and minimal wrong would meet with a mixed response from process thinkers. It is most unlikely that they would support the practices listed by Taylor as directly incompatible with the attitude of respect for nature (such as fur trapping). The traumatic nature of the experience to the animals, and the loss of total experience from their deaths, would outweigh the relatively trivial human pleasures to be gained. It is just possible that Gamwell might advocate such practices on a process platform; but most would find it unacceptable.

Taylor's principle of minimum wrong, however, is a far more interesting comparison. Taylor himself, as we have seen, cannot logically sustain such a position, because violation of basic non-human interests for human cultural and political ones is involved. However, the 'maximum right' position of process thinking *could* produce the ethical response sought by Taylor. The building of a concert hall, say, on a wild area would generate significant richness of human experience. The cost would be the lives, or the habitat, of native flora and fauna. How might these be balanced? It would certainly be possible for process thinkers to argue that the human gain outweighed the non-human loss. Provided that the wild area was not especially rare or packed with endangered species, it is unlikely that there would be a great loss of contrasts in the world. Indeed, on the side of contrasts, the elevated feelings of the human beings at the concert halls might provide richer contrasts for God.

Taylor's last principle, that of distributive justice—where human and non-human basic interests conflict—raises a number of questions, most particularly that of vegetarianism. For ethical egalitarians, killing animals and plants for food is, at first sight, an equal violation. One may as well eat animals (or indeed humans) if all have equal worth. For Schweitzer, this problem remains unresolved. Taylor, as I indicated, first (illegitimately) adds the criterion of pain, and secondly comments that less land is used and hence fewer lives are lost by the use of plant food rather than animal food.

Thus, by his principle of minimum wrong, vegetarianism should be adopted. For Johnson and Lombardi, vegetarianism should also be obligatory; animals have greater capacities (or more interests) than plants to be taken into moral consideration; hence they are worth more. Process thinkers, as we have seen, consider animals to be of more value than plants, and thus one might think that they would advocate vegetarianism. However, as we have also seen, their focus on experience means that animals, if killed painlessly, are replaceable. The replaceability argument destroys any case for vegetarianism on this basis. Could a process thinker, such as Dombrowski, who wishes to endorse vegetarianism have recourse to Taylor's land-use argument? It would at first sight seem possible to argue, on a process basis, that if less land overall is used by adoption of a vegetarian diet, maximum value would be produced. This argument is, however, difficult to sustain in a process system. Since food animals, such as pigs, cattle, sheep, are high-grade experiencers, generally speaking their presence makes land more rather than less valuable. (Exceptions might be if the land had been previously settled by humans or a particularly rare ecosystem or a forest with a high primate population—which will be explored further in the next section.) Rather than Taylor's principle of minimum wrong, the process principle of maximum rich experience comes into play, and vegetarianism becomes difficult to maintain in process thinking. Here, then, there is a divergence between process thinking and that of individualist environmental ethicists. This divergence is continued into the next section, that concerning restitution in process environmental ethics.

Restitution in Process Thinking

Since process thinking, as described in the previous chapter, is clearly consequentialist in form, one would expect it to avoid difficulties associated specifically with the deontological nature of the ethicists considered in this chapter, in particular the inability to affirm restitution. It can, after all, accept the substitution of one organism for another which would not otherwise have lived. Whereas substitution suggests temporal replacement (one animal bred to replace another), restitution suggests spatial replacement (often, though not exclusively, one place to replace another). The possibility of affirming restitution on a larger scale in a process system is interesting but rather complex. The overall principle must be to replace the rich experience lost to God by the destruction of an organism or a group of organisms. Either new organisms generating equal or greater experience must be brought into being or already existing organisms which are threatened should be protected. Such restitution would seem entirely possible within a process system. After all, it is not organisms themselves which are valuable in process thinking; it is their experiences and contrasts between them. A case study may clarify the situation.

Let us say that an ancient wildflower meadow is ploughed up in order to plant a grass ley for the grazing of cattle. The wildflower meadow is lost forever. What would count as restitution for such an act in a process system? To answer this question we need to examine closely what has been lost by the destruction of the wildflower meadow. First, and most obviously, the experiences of the wildflowers, as societies of cells and experiencing actual entities, have been lost. In addition, the organisms supported by the wildflower meadow may have been lost or displaced: for instance insects and small mammals. Thirdly, some human beings may regret the loss of the meadow, because they enjoyed looking at it, or walking in it, or even knowing it to be there. Fourthly, the field was composed from a group of diverse and contrasting organisms which would have added to the richness of God's experience and would be reflected back into the world in subsequent prehension of God's consequent nature.

What restitution might suffice for these losses? The initially surprising response is that the planting of the grass ley itself goes some way towards restitution. Most process thinkers would argue that the experiences of wildflowers and grass plants are essentially indistinguishable. Both are quasi-organisms, producing low-grade, non-sentient experience and it would be difficult to argue that the actual occasions composing a wildflower produced significantly more intense and harmonious experience than those of a grass plant.[24] The subsidiary organisms would also be more than compensated for: some wild organisms would persist in the field, and

---

[24] However, Sprigge (in a personal communication to the author, 1993) has suggested that since 'each finite actual occasion can appreciate variety in its own synthesising activity', wildflowers may produce richer experiences than grass because of their prehension of the greater variety around them. This contrasts with the Birch and Cobb position that plant experiences are indistinguishable from one another, and is an interesting subtlety which would strengthen the need for restitution.

the addition of cattle—high-grade experiencers—would produce much richer experience than the former meadow inhabitants of lower-grade experience. So far the destruction of the wildflower meadow might seem a gain rather than a loss needing restitution!

What about the loss of human experience? The destruction of a cherished wild place for agricultural expansion may cause considerable disharmonious (if intense) experiences to a large number of people. On the other hand, some humans might derive richer experience from observing a field of cattle than a wildflower meadow—and not only the farmer! (For instance, the recent expansion of land under set-aside schemes in the United Kingdom has led to some public concern about the messy appearance of uncultivated fields.) In addition, the new productivity of the field could also generate rich human experience, which might compensate for the loss of the wildflower meadow. So, at this point, it is not at all clear that any restitution needs to be made for the loss of the wildflower meadow.

A fourth factor is the loss of rich experience for God, previously generated by the contrasts between the experiences of the many different species in the field. It certainly is not likely that the cattlefield will produce anything like the same variety of *kinds* of experience as the wildflower meadow, although the cattle will produce higher-grade, rich experience. This raises a key question about the generation of value in process thinking, relevant of course to the question of restitution, but also of broader significance in process ethics.

As described in Chapter 1, the ultimate aim of process ethics is to generate rich experience for God. Such rich experience comes about in two ways: God's feeling of the feelings of actual occasions; and God's feeling about the feelings of actual occasions by enjoyment of the patterned contrasts between them. But commonly in questions of environmental ethics, these two sources of rich experience are in conflict with one another. The ploughing up of a wildflower meadow for a cattlefield is one example of this. The existence of cattle, producing high-grade experience which would not otherwise have existed in the world, *increases* the richness of God's experience. However, the loss of the variety of organisms in the field detracts from the richness of God's experience, since God can no longer experience the contrasts between the different kinds of actual occasions. Does the former cancel out the latter, such that no restitution is needed? Does the latter outweigh the former, suggesting that restitution, in some form, should be made?

How can such decisions be made within the context of process thinking? How should the two different sources of value be weighed against one another? Resolution of this difficulty is central if process philosophy is to provide a workable environmental ethic, because such conflicts lie at the heart of environmental decision-making. However, this problem does not seem to have been recognized by process ethicists, including those working on environmental ethics, which means that currently, as far as I am aware, no attempts at resolution exist. In the rest of this book, I will be examining this conflict further, and in my conclusions will suggest some ways in which process thinking might address it.

Individualism in Process Environmental Ethics

A number of criticisms were levelled at the individualist approaches of the environmental ethicists considered earlier in this chapter: that they were unable to give reasons for protecting ecosystems and endangered species beyond the protection of individual members; that they could not distinguish between wild and domestic animals; and that they would encourage actions in nature to protect wild animals from inanimate threats. Some of these questions have been touched on above; others will be explored in the next chapter. Here I wish to focus on process thinking and the question of rescuing wild animals from inanimate threats—an important question in wildlife management. What actions, for instance, would process thinkers consider appropriate with regard to the trapped bison which fell through the ice of Yellowstone River?

The bison, as a mammal, is a high-grade experiencer. Its sojourn in the icy water must produce negative experiences. Its death means the end of its own high-grade experiences, as well as those of its possible future offspring. These are all powerful positive reasons why a process philosopher might wish to rescue the bison. But process thinkers—unlike the other environmental ethicists in this chapter—would also take into account the potentially negative consequences of rescuing the bison, such the future negative experiences which might be generated by, perhaps, the weakening of genetic lineage, overgrazing, and the consequent loss of some species, thus reducing species variety.

It is surely the case here, though, that the experiences of the bison are of overwhelming significance. Negative consequences from rescuing the bison are diffuse and uncertain; the positive consequences are significant and definite. Almost unquestionably in such a case a process thinker would recommend the rescue of the bison; or, if there were overwhelming reasons why it should not be rescued (a massive overpopulation of bisons, for instance) a process thinker would advocate that it should be mercifully killed to prevent the continuance of its negative experiences.

It is difficult to know how far to generalize from this instance about the degree to which process thinkers might feel an obligation to act in wild nature to protect suffering high-grade experiences from an inanimate threat. It would seem likely that the direct, certain gains of doing so would outweigh the indirect and uncertain negative consequences. Would this extend to providing medical treatment for individual diseased or injured wild animals? The answer to this question again depends on the relative weighting of rich organismic experience and contrasts between different kinds of experience, both in the short and in the long run—an issue to which I will return.

In conclusion then, this chapter has examined egalitarian and inegalitarian deontological approaches to environmental ethics, both of which generated their own difficulties. These approaches were contrasted with the consequentialist, experience-centred approach of process thinking. Substantial theoretical differences in approach were discussed, and these, unsurprisingly, led to some differences in practice—although also some concurrence. Because contrasts between different *kinds* of experience are valuable in a process system as well as intensity and harmony of the experiences themselves, it seems likely that, in some instances at least, process thinking will be more amenable to collectivist ethical views than the individualist philosophers considered here. This issue will be discussed in the following chapter. Finally, an important difficulty within the process ethical system was encountered—how can process thinking reconcile the possible conflicts generated by two different ways of value creation? This question will also be examined in more detail in Chapter 4 and in the Conclusions.

4

Process Thinking and Collectivist Environmental Ethics

Collectivist Consequentialist Positions

In contrast with the individualist approaches to environmental ethics discussed in Chapters 2 and 3, some environmental ethicists have adopted a collectivist approach.[1] This is not to say that the two approaches are necessarily exclusive; several attempts have been made to reconcile them.[2] It is none the less true to say that there is tension, if not hostility, between individualist and collectivist approaches.[3]

Collectivist approaches to environmental ethics tend to be consequentialist, aiming at the good of the whole, although the scale of the whole and what constitutes good for such a whole is disputed. A variety of scales and putative goods are suggested by different philosophers, influenced by different uses of scientific ecology and Darwinian evolution. Similarly a variety of models are used to describe this whole—community, organism, and energy field being some of the most popular—each with different nuances of interdependence and interconnectedness. This multitude of differing collectivist approaches to environmental ethics makes it a complex maze, impossible to explore in its entirety. The focus here will be on Aldo Leopold and J. Baird Callicott, perhaps the most prominent advocates of a collectivist approach. An examination of their work, and the concerns that have been raised about it, will be followed by a consideration of process thinking in the light of their thinking.

---

[1] I have chosen to use the word '*collectivist*' rather than '*systemic*', since systems are not necessarily the basis of such approaches, and because 'systemic value' is the name given by Rolston (1988*a*: 216) to a specific kind of collectivist value.

[2] e.g. Warren (1983); L. Johnson (1991).

[3] See Hargrove (1992: ix–xxvi) for further discussion of this.

Leopold: The Land Ethic and Ecological Models of the Land

Callicott claims that Leopold is the 'father or founding genius of recent environmental ethics', primarily for his collection of essays *A Sand County Almanac* (first published 1949).[4] Here Leopold espouses a land ethic that 'enlarges the boundaries of the community to include soils, waters, plants, and animals, or collectively, the land' (Leopold 1968: 204). His guiding principle is famously expressed: 'A thing is right when it tends to preserve the integrity, stability and beauty of the land community. It is wrong when it tends otherwise' (ibid. 224). This compact expression of 'the land ethic' hints at several important features of Leopold's thought. The consequentialist nature of his ethic is immediately evident; particularly striking is its similarity in form to that of Mill's Greatest Happiness Principle.[5] Mill (1979: 257) states that 'actions are right in proportion as they tend to promote happiness, wrong if they tend to produce the reverse of happiness'. That Mill might be an influence on Leopold is hardly surprising. The utilitarian principle had been the focus of the United States Forest Service (in which Leopold worked) since its foundation under Pinchot in the first decade of this century, albeit directed purely towards human benefit. Characteristically consequentialist, Leopold aims at achieving the best 'state of affairs'—it is not the individual members of the land community, nor the community as a whole that is valued, but rather the state of affairs within that community: its integrity, stability, beauty.

This concise statement of the land ethic immediately raises questions about how human beings might relate to the 'biotic community'. Does Leopold consider humans to be part of the biotic community? How might human activities such as agriculture relate to the land ethic? It would at first sight, for instance, seem possible that Leopold would advocate the abandonment of agriculture as having a negative effect on the integrity, stability, and beauty of the land community. Answering such questions uncovers difficulties and ambiguities in Leopold's approach. For instance, he does on some occasions clearly state that human beings are members—and humble members—of the biotic community: 'In short, a land ethic changes the role of homo sapiens from

[4] Callicott in Nash (1989: 65).
[5] Also noted by Merchant (1990: 57).

conqueror of the land community to plain member and citizen of
it. It implies respect for his fellow-members and also respect for the
community as such' (Leopold 1968: 204). However, Leopold's
attitude towards the relationship of human beings to the land
community is more ambiguous than this would suggest. For
instance, in his essay 'On A Monument to the Pigeon', Leopold
tells us both that humans are 'fellow voyagers with other creatures
in the odyssey of evolution' and that humans are now 'captain of
the adventuring ship'—the first image suggesting plain citizenship,
the second navigational control (ibid. 109–10). The superiority
that Leopold sometimes ascribes to human beings causes Fritzell
(1987: 147) to suggest that Leopold can speak of humans as if they
were 'a stranger to nature, a questing perceiver of outside processes'. Whilst there is little doubt that Leopold regarded humans
as fundamentally part of the land community, his perception of
their role within it is certainly ambiguous.

The persistence of this ambiguity is revealed if *community* is
considered alongside two other models of the natural world
which are both found in *A Sand County Almanac*, namely the
land as *organism* and the land as a *fountain of energy*. These different
models imply different philosophical conceptions of the ecological
system. The use of the community model in his crucial statement
of the land ethic suggests that Leopold ultimately preferred it to
either of the others. An examination of the *organism* and *energy flow*
models may help to indicate why.

'The most important characteristic of an organism is that capacity for internal self-renewal known as health. There are two
organisms whose processes of self-renewal have been subjected to
human interference or control. One of these is man himself (medicine and public health). The other is land (agriculture and conservation)' (Leopold 1968: 194). This passage begins Leopold's
extensive metaphor of the land and the (individual) human body.
This is not a new metaphor in Leopold's work, as Callicott points
out. In his much earlier essay 'Some Fundamentals of Conservation in the Southwest', Leopold uses this concept more extensively,
claiming as a source the Russian philosopher Ouspensky. Leopold
suggests that the entire Earth could be seen as an organism 'which
we do not now realize because it is too big and its life processes too
slow' (Leopold 1979: 139). He even wonders, in Stoic vein, if there
might be a world soul or consciousness.

Little of this metaphysical approach filters through into the later *A Sand County Almanac*, where Leopold seems to have moved away from the picture of Earth as organism. His use of the term 'organism' is much more consciously metaphorical and he has changed his emphasis from seeing the whole Earth as an organism to speaking of the *land* as an organism (perhaps reinforcing the shift from metaphysics to metaphor). Use of the term organism in comparison with the human body allows Leopold to speak of 'sick' and 'healthy' land. Soil erosion and loss of fertility, pestilential levels of certain species, species extinctions, slowness and insubstantiality of tree growth are all examples of land sickness. In contrast, healthy land is only found in wildernesses which are the 'most perfect norm', or where humans have not disturbed the 'land physiology'. Human activity has caused the sicknesses of the land; and humans must learn, not only to 'doctor' the land, but the 'science of land health'. To extend Leopold's metaphor further, he is advocating preventative medicine for the land, in order to avoid sickness in the first place.

What is interesting about the metaphor of the land as organism in Leopold's writing is the suggestion that human beings are excluded from this organism. Humans are outside, acting on the land organism, rather than part of it and acting from within. Furthermore, human behaviour can have the effect of damaging the land organism, which is most perfect when it is pristine. This contrasts with Leopold's understanding of human beings as *part of* the land *community*. Why might Leopold include human beings when discussing the land as community, but exclude them when discussing the land as organism? It is of course impossible to provide definitive answers to this question, but one approach might be to consider the different nature of the two metaphors. The metaphor of land as organism emphasizes a strong sense of interdependence, and of the parts as functioning for the benefit of the whole. The metaphor of land as community suggests a stronger sense of independence, individuality, and equality. Katz (1985: 251) makes a similar point about the greater independence ascribed to individuals in a community than to organs in an organism. The organs of an organism cannot survive outside the organism (except in exceptional circumstances); they have no autonomy. The only aim of their existence is the well-being of the whole. Within a community, however, it is still appropriate to refer to the individual's autonomy, and even individual worth; individuals have their own ends, as well as the aim of the well-being of the whole. The wholeness of an organism is indivisible; the wholeness of a community is not.

Why might this difference be significant for Leopold? Katz (ibid.) moves on to indicate a problem for environmental philosophies which use the metaphor of land as organism. Both species and individuals can have only instrumental value, that is, to the extent that they fulfil their function of maintaining the whole organism: 'If an entity in a system is valued for its instrumental function, and not its intrinsic value, then it can be replaced by a substitute entity, as long as the function it performs remains undisturbed.' If human beings were to be considered as part of the land organism, this might suggest that their interests should be subordinated to the overall health of the land. This is a conclusion with which, given his comments on human superiority, Leopold was unlikely to be comfortable. The metaphor of land as community, however, need not entail the same subordination of the parts to the whole; perhaps this is why Leopold, in his more mature writing, preferred the metaphor of land community to that of land organism. It is also interesting to note Katz's point that this metaphor of land as organism raises the possibility of replaceability—also discussed in the context of utilitarianism in Chapter 2. There it was argued that utilitarianism allows for replacement of organisms provided that a similar amount of positive experience, or preference satisfaction, is generated in the world. Here, in the language of the land organism, replacement is possible provided that the function of the individual in the biotic organism can be carried out by a different individual, or even an individual of a different species. It is possible that Leopold was aware of this implication, which also stimulated his move away from the metaphor of land as organism. For instance, he was not compensated for the loss of the last passenger pigeon by knowledge that worms and weevils would take its place in the ecosystem (Leopold 1968: 111). Perhaps he wished to affirm the 'right to continued existence' of species of plants and animals, aside from their role in the maintenance of the land (ibid. 204).

Of course, these suggestions about Leopold's move towards the use of the metaphor of community rather than organism may be mistaken. Callicott, in contrast, suggests that Leopold de-emphasized

the metaphor of land as an organism because it had been abandoned by the ecologists of Leopold's time, and Leopold adopted
their preference for the language of community. But whether or not
Leopold was aware of the implications of using these metaphors,
the questions they raise are more generally important for collectivist environmental ethics, as will shortly become clear.

Leopold (ibid. 216) also uses a third metaphor for land—land as
a 'fountain of energy'. Here he describes the passage of energy
from the sun through different ecological levels—the biotic pyr-
amid: 'Land, then, is not merely soil; it is a fountain of energy,
flowing through a circuit of soils, plants and animals. Food chains
are the living channels which conduct energy upward; death and
decay return it to the soil.' The image of the land as a flow of
energy is one which has become increasingly common since Leopold's time, in particular by those making metaphysical interpretations of quantum physics. Callicott (1985) has championed this
approach and it is common among deep ecologists, who will be
considered in Chapter 5. Although Leopold himself does not draw
any metaphysical conclusions of this sort, I will delay discussion of
this metaphor until the next chapter.

Preservation of Integrity, Stability, and Beauty

The key injunction of the land ethic concerns preservation of the
integrity, stability, and beauty of the land community. No direct
explanation of these terms is suggested in *A Sand County Almanac*;
but it is possible to glean some general guidance. Although Leopold does say that land without humans is the 'most perfect norm',
it would be misleading to draw from this the conclusion that all
human activity is bad. Leopold's land ethic states that human
action which tends to preserve integrity, stability, and beauty is
good. His acceptance of active land management and agriculture,
and his own, amply described, activities of hunting and forestry,
witness to this. As Flader (1974) and Thompson (1995: 119) point
out, for Leopold the biotic community includes human agriculture
(albeit agriculture of only particular kinds). Where stability, integrity, and beauty are retained or enhanced, human action is desirable; presumably this is so even in wilderness areas.

Leopold seems to understand the stability of a biotic community
to mean its ability to remain at some kind of equilibrium, or to

return to an equilibrium if disturbed. Thompson (ibid. 138) suggests that in using this term Leopold was probably drawing on the then current understanding of climax plant communities as represented in forest ecology. Leopold's understanding of stability thus seems to correspond closely to his organic model of land health. 'Health', he tells us 'is the capacity of the land for self-renewal' (Leopold 1968: 221). Stable communities, despite extensive human action, have retained their ability to keep going, to 'persist'. Unstable communities, however, show signs of 'disorganization', operating 'at some reduced level of complexity and with a reduced carrying capacity for people, plants and animals' (ibid. 219).

This reduced ability to support a variety of species illustrates the conceptual closeness of stability and integrity. The stability of the land community seems to depend on its integrity. A land community which retains integrity retains wholeness. This seems to mean, for Leopold, primarily that it retains its full quota of species. In wilderness, he contends, 'component species were rarely lost' and neither was the soil (ibid. 196). Humans damage the integrity of an ecosystem when, for instance, they remove the top predators, such as wolves. This damage to integrity has an effect on stability, since deer (for instance) may increase in population, overgraze the land, cause soil erosion and thus damage the integrity of the land community still further. The land will become disorganized and, if it settles to a new equilibrium (i.e. regains some stability), it will be at a less complex, less diverse level than before. Although complexity and diversity are not mentioned alongside stability and integrity in Leopold's statement of the land ethic, both are important, and in need of preservation (ibid. 209). Complexity, stability, integrity, and diversity all seem linked together in Leopold's understanding of the land community. Ethical action is action which preserves this. By preservation, Leopold does not mean immutability—as if without human intervention, the land community would remain exactly the same; the land is dynamic, a fountain of energy. Preservation would be best interpreted here not as the protection of any particular state of the land, but rather as allowing the land to pursue its own dynamic states unimpeded.

Whilst what Leopold may have meant by stability and integrity is not difficult to imagine, his inclusion of beauty is more difficult to interpret. He insists that the *aesthetically* right should be considered alongside the *ethically* right, and preservation of beauty, for Leopold, obviously corresponds to the aesthetically right. The land can contribute an 'aesthetic harvest' to human culture, a harvest at present not being reaped (indeed, actually being destroyed with the destruction of the land). This seems to divide beauty from stability and integrity. Stability and integrity are part of the land ethic; beauty is part of the land aesthetic. The land community can be stable, and can have integrity, on Leopold's terms, with no human presence at all. (This is not to say that integrity and stability are necessarily *valuable* without human presence.) But beauty is a human harvest, a cultural benefit. To act to preserve beauty is to act for the enrichment of human culture.

What, then, is beauty for Leopold? Callicott (1987: 157–71) offers some helpful directions in his essay, 'The Land Aesthetic'. He argues that Leopold advocates a natural aesthetic which stands in contrast to the Western landscape-art tradition, a tradition which is 'conventionalized, not well informed by the ecological and evolutionary revolutions in natural history; it is sensational and self-referential, not genuinely oriented to nature on nature's own terms; in other words, it is trivial' (ibid. 160). This kind of aesthetic appreciation of scenery requires huge panoramic vistas and is primarily visual and dramatic, labelled by Leopold (1968: 191) as an 'under-aged brand of aesthetics'. In contrast, Leopold urges aesthetic appreciation of the small, the local, and the undramatic parts of the land community, which, as yet, are not widely accepted as beautiful. Greater aesthetic appreciation of the land will, according to Leopold, result in 'enlightened . . . landuse decisions'. This sounds as if aesthetics is being used ultimately for an ethical purpose. If people change, or rather extend, their views of what is beautiful, from the sublime and dramatic to the small and local, then it will be easier to preserve them.[6] There seems to be a close link for Leopold between that which is ethically right and that which is aesthetically right: that which is ethically right (the promotion of stability and integrity in biotic communities) also provides positive aesthetic experience; and positive aesthetic experience leads to more ethical behaviour.

---

[6] Thus contrasting with Hargrove (1989: 109) who suggests that the landscape-art tradition led to appreciation for and preservation of wild countryside—and ultimately (rather than the science of ecology) led to the development of environmental ethics.

Human aesthetic experience from the biotic community is particularly important for Leopold because of his interpretation of the origin and nature of human ethics: ethics is, he suggests, biological in origin, and has its basis in human feelings (rather than in God or human reason). According to Callicott, both these ideas about ethics came from Leopold's understanding of Darwin, the second reflecting Darwin's own use of Hume. Leopold certainly argues that ethics evolved out of a process of co-operation within the land community. Primitive humans were part of such a co-operative community, unconsciously operating for the benefit of all. As humans developed in consciousness and correspondingly developed ethical systems, they understood their ethical obligations to apply only to humans—indeed, for a long time, only to some humans. Now, Leopold urges, human ethics should evolve still further to include the land community once more, self-consciously this time. This would extend rather than change existing ethics; as Moline (1986: 102) points out, 'To extend or enlarge is to render more capacious the structure one is extending; it is not to evict that structure's present inhabitants.' Since ethical attitudes here are based on sentiment, this means developing sentiments about the land: 'We can be ethical only in relation to something we can see, feel, understand, love, or otherwise have faith in' (Leopold 1968: 214).

The main features of Leopold's ethics—the ethical priority of promoting stability, integrity, and beauty in the land community; the biological origin of ethics and the basis of ethics in feeling are developed in the more recent work of Baird Callicott, and it is his work on which I will now concentrate.

Callicott and Collectivist Environmental Ethics

Callicott, as a key interpreter of Leopold, has produced work in environmental ethics which, while more rigorous in presentation, in many respects is inspired by Leopold. This is not to say that all Callicott's work is in a Leopoldian tradition—he has produced a small body of work that more closely resembles the approach of some deep ecologists.[7] Consequently this approach will be

---

[7] Callicott (1985, 1989). He describes these papers as his attempt to construct a post-modern ethics, as opposed to the modernist approach in his Leopoldian ethics (personal communication to the author, 1994).

examined in more detail in Chapter 5. Here I will focus on the main body of Callicott's work in environmental ethics; that which is broadly Leopoldian in approach.

Even here, it is important to note that, although Callicott's understanding of the origin and basis of ethics is largely unchanged, the way that he has worked this out has changed over time—in particular between his influential early paper, 'Animal Liberation: A Triangular Affair' (1980), and more recent reconsiderations of this position, such as 'Animal Liberation and Environmental Ethics—Back Together Again' (1988), and 'Can a Theory of Moral Sentiments Support a Genuinely Normative Environmental Ethic?' (1992). Thus I will begin by outlining some of the basic elements of Callicott's position, common to all these papers, before considering the different ways in which he has worked this out.

Callicott's ethics has several crucial interwoven strands. The first indicates a strongly Darwinian background. Our ethical sense has evolved with us, biologically; it was essential for human survival that humans learned to co-operate;altruism in the sense of co-operation was biologically selected for. One important implication of this biological evolution of ethics is Callicott's contention that, to some extent at least, our ethical sense is 'standardized' or 'universalized': it is based around the well-being of the community or communities with which we identify: 'the human capacity for moral sentiments . . . is fairly uniform (because this category is a genetically fixed psychological category like sexual appetites) and roughly equally distributed throughout the human population' (Callicott 1989: 151). Understanding evolution, Callicott argues, also develops human awareness of kinship with the rest of the natural world. This combines with the second strand of Callicott's ethics, again as with Leopold: the grounding of ethics in feelings, a basis which Callicott ascribes to Hume. Callicott contends that, according to Darwinian theory, when any human recognizes another being as having kinship or community membership an instinctive positive emotional response is triggered. Hence the realization that we are members not only of a human community but also of an ecological community should extend our affectional base and thus our range of ethical awareness into the ecological community: 'The biotic community is the proper object of that passion actuated by the contemplation of the complexity, integrity and stability of the community to which we belong' (ibid. 117). In basing morality on human sentiment, Callicott is consciously opposing the ethical approaches both of utilitarians such as Mill and deontologists such as Kant. He argues that these ethical theories—and positions in environmental ethics based on them—'cannot be adapted to accommodate natural wholes' (Callicott 1992: 187). Essentially, he contends, both traditional forms of utilitarianism and deontology are based on universalized egoism, which works well enough for sentient or even conative individual organisms, but which cannot be applied to ecosystems or species which have 'no capacity comparable or analogous to reason, sentiency or conation' (ibid. 187). Callicott proposes that a Darwin/Hume approach to ethics 'which openly affirms the role of feeling in moral deliberation, motivation and judgment' is the important undergirding of the land ethic.

Three main elements, then, emerge from this consideration of Callicott's ethic. It is affectional; it is centred on wholes or communities rather than individuals; and it extends beyond human communities into the biological world of species and ecosystems. Beyond this point, a dichotomy emerges between Callicott's earlier and later views. Although Callicott himself now rejects his earlier paper, 'Animal Liberation: A Triangular Affair' (1980), I will consider it briefly here, as it has been influential in the development of environmental ethics, and also provides an interesting point of comparison for process thinking.

Callicott's intention in 1980 was to differentiate environmental ethics not only from standard anthropocentric ethics, but also from animal liberation approaches. Animal liberation, whether based on rights (as Regan) or interests and suffering (as Singer) was, according to Callicott, an extension of ethical humanism to humane moralism, only capable of valuing ecosystems and species in as much as they are useful to the well-being of sentient mammals. But environmental ethics, Callicott argued, was not about sentience nor about individuals, but rather about the 'integrity, stability and beauty of the biotic community'. The biotic community, he contended, was a 'third order organic whole', the preservation of which was the 'summum bonum, the ultimate good in environmental ethics', by reference to which 'competing claims may be adjudicated and relative values and priorities assigned to the myriad components of the biotic community'. The good of the biotic community, he argued, is the 'ultimate measure of moral value, the rightness or wrongness of actions'. The primary value of all organisms can be judged by their contribution to the *summum bonum*. Anything which threatens this ultimate good, the biotic community, should be removed, and this includes human beings. It is in this context that Callicott made his now infamous remark that the human population should be roughly twice that of bears. Any species whose population growth or resource consumption threatens the good of the whole requires restraint.

Thus, in 1980, Callicott maintained the primary human duty to be that of support for the biotic community, even where this required human sacrifice. Other human duties were acknowledged; Callicott spoke of duties of self-preservation (maintaining one's own organic unity) and societal preservation (maintaining the fabric of human society). But land preservation, the duty to the biotic community, trumped all these; all ethical decisions should be taken in the light of the effects which they would have on the integrity, stability, and beauty of this community. One might present his 1980 view as a series of concentric circles of value intensity. Value is concentrated within the inner circles and becomes more diffuse at the periphery. The inner circle, where value is at its most intense, is the biotic community; the second circle human society, the third circle the human individual. Beyond that, it seems likely that one might place domestic animals or plants, which are not part of the human or biotic community, yet are not of the same value as individual human beings. Indeed, Callicott recommended a shrinkage in the size of the domestic community; the logic of his 1980 position drives towards the elimination of domestic plants and animals in favour of hunter-gatherer lifestyles, with a substantially reduced human population.

By 1988, however, Callicott had substantially reformed his position. Whilst the underlying principles remained the same (affectional, community-focused, and extending into the biotic community) the outworking of these principles had changed substantially. The *summum bonum* was no longer the integrity, stability, and beauty of the biotic community. Humans, Callicott suggested, live in a series of 'nested communities'. Ethical obligation should be measured by the intensity (or otherwise) of valuational feelings within these nested communities. And one's most intense feelings will be for the human community in which one lives, most specifically for one's family and immediate community, then, perhaps, for one's nation, and then humanity in general. Human beings, and specifically those who are emotionally and hence valuationally closest, will thus have ethical priority.

Beyond the human community, Callicott inserted the mixed community where domestic animals mix with human beings (an idea derived from Midgley 1983). These animals, he suggested, have a special relationship with human beings and thus are affectively closer than wild animals. They are entitled to protection from outside threats, and from the exploitation of over-mechanization. They may, however, be killed for food. Beyond the human and the mixed community, Callicott argued, lies the biotic community, of wild ecosystems and species. While ecological education engenders the realization in human beings that the wild ecosystem is a community of which one is a member, and hence triggers valuational feelings, these are weaker than the feelings for either human beings or the mixed community. Thus the biotic community has been displaced from its position of ethical priority to a position of ethical subordination. Claims of human beings trump the claims of the biotic community and the mixed community of domestic animals. Now 'duties and obligations to human beings (and to humanity as a whole) . . . supersede the land ethic, although I have by no means abandoned the land ethic' (Callicott 1990). However, Callicott does add two qualifications to this position. First, he comments that 'the outer orbits of our moral spheres tug on our inner ones—inclining us to act on behalf of those communities more distant from us. Secondly, he suggests that 'one may well make sacrifices for the sake of ecological integrity'—such as fencing cows out of wild areas, despite the farmer's (and the cows') preferences. The strength of these qualifications will be examined in the next section. What is clear is that in this later writing, the 'moral heartwood' (as Callicott puts it) is not the biotic community but human families and communities. The biotic community becomes an add-on outer ring, remote from the centre (ibid. 123).

These different outworkings of a fundamentally affectional, consequentialist, and community-focused ethic bear some resemblance to the differences illustrated in Chapter 3 between egalitarian and hierarchical individualist deontologists. In this case, ethical priority can be given to the human community over the biotic community, or the biotic community over the human community (inverting the hierarchy). Of course, on occasions where the goods of the different communities conflict, these different priorities will result in very different behaviour. However, the community-focused nature of these ethical approaches still distinguish them clearly from both individualist consequentialists such as Singer and individualist deontologists such as Regan and Taylor. Their inability to ascribe value to plants or collective wholes such as communities or species 'fails to articulate our considered moral intuitions regarding collective and holistic entities' (Callicott 1984: 300). Such individualist views, Callicott contends, are fundamentally 'life denying'. They fail to accept the suffering and death which is at the very heart of natural biotic processes and are, in fact, essential for evolutionary and ecological processes to continue (ibid. 301).

In summary, then, Callicott's ethics is deeply influenced by Aldo Leopold. He combines a Darwinian evolutionary perspective on the origin and scope of ethics with a Humean 'sentimentalism' and a neo-Platonic emphasis on the priority of the whole over the parts. Like Leopold, he speaks of the land in terms of both 'organism' and 'community'. Humans have ethical obligations to the communities in which they belong; in his earlier work, Callicott emphasized the ethical priority of the biological community; in his later work, the ethical priority of the human community. In either case, a sharp distinction is made between human obligations to wild animals and to domestic animals. From this perspective, Callicott attacks individualist ethics, especially that of animal liberationists, describing them as 'effete' and 'against nature'.

Critical Responses to Collective Consequentialist Positions

Criticism of Leopold's and Callicott's approaches to ethics has been diverse, but clusters around several themes. First, the biological basis of these ethical positions, and their ethical implications, have been questioned. Secondly, broader criticism has been aimed at the emphasis on the integrity and priority of the whole over and against its parts. Thirdly, the subjective basis of Callicott's axiology has been attacked. All these questions are deeply entrenched problems of moral philosophy in general and are not confined to the environmental ethics debate. For the purposes of this book, however, I shall primarily be considering their bearing on questions of environmental ethics, rather than ethics in general.

Critical Biological and Ecological Responses

A biological, evolutionary foundation for ethics is essential to Callicott, in describing both the origin of his ethic, and its manifestation in a community. Ecological considerations are also crucial in both his and Leopold's statements on what constitutes 'land health' and hence what behaviour is ethical within the land community. The idea that ethics might have a biological origin is not, of course, original to Leopold and Callicott. As Callicott (1992: 184) notes, there is a body of moral theory in biology developed from Darwin by T. H. Huxley and E. O. Wilson amongst others. Callicott thus sees his own contribution as falling within this moral tradition—an appropriate one, after all, for the development of an environmental ethic.

Ethical theories which claim a biological evolutionary origin are concerned fundamentally with inherited altruistic tendencies. They accept that some kinds of altruistic behaviour—taking altruism to mean 'benefiting others at some cost to oneself' (Singer 1981: 5)—are of evolutionary advantage and have been selected for. The most obvious and commonly suggested form of inherited altruism is that of *kin* altruism. Offspring to whom parents exhibit altruistic behaviour are more likely to survive; thus this characteristic is selected for. Other kinds of altruism which have been suggested as conferring evolutionary advantage are *reciprocal* altruism between members of the same species, and *group* altruism, where the survival of the group is put ahead of that of the individual. The last, for which there appears to be least evidence, is that adopted by Callicott, quoting Darwin as his source (who was, of course, writing before genes had been discovered).[8]

In adopting this group or community interpretation of inherited altruism, Callicott is in a minority position. Even Singer, who has no sociobiological axe to grind, suggests that group altruism could have played only a small part in conferring evolutionary advantage, although it may have a cultural role. If Callicott is wrong about the significance of group altruism, even if he is right about the basis of ethics in evolution and sentiment, it is difficult to see how his

[8] For further comment on this see J. L. Mackie (1978: 455–65).

argument could be maintained. Recognition of community or group membership would not spark an instinctive affective feeling which would lead to an ethical response.

Secondly, Callicott's interpretation of Darwin himself is contestable, as is illustrated by the number of competing ethical accounts which claim to be based on Darwinism. James Rachels for instance, in *Created from Animals: The Moral Implications of Darwinism* (1991), fails to mention Callicott's interpretation of Darwin at all (or that of Singer 1981). Rachels, like Callicott, considers that realizing the implications of Darwinism undermines belief in the differentiation of humans from the non-human world, and hence ends the exclusion of animals from moral consideration. However, Rachels develops an ethical system, 'moral individualism', based on Darwin, where individual organisms and their characteristics are of primary ethical consideration. There is no trace of the community concept championed by Callicott, despite the fact that Rachels and Callicott quote the same passages to support their differing positions.

I am not intending to claim that Rachels is right and Callicott wrong; or even that kin altruism is correct and group altruism is wrong—although in the latter case the evidence seems to be against Callicott. However, at the very least, the possibility of such plural interpretations of altruism and evolution in general, and of Darwin in particular, must raise a question mark over the foundations of such ethical positions. It is, perhaps, possible that Darwinian evolutionary theory is being used to support a position which the author already holds (a practice which will be discussed in Chapter 5). Callicott's interpretation is surely, as Anthony Weston (1991: 286) suggests, 'context-dependent and culturally specific'. Indeed, it is difficult to escape Weston's conclusion that 'evolutionary arguments are too ideologically promiscuous to be trusted at all'.

This is not the only difficulty with the idea of an evolutionary ethic based on affection; a second debate concerning the kind of 'normative force' such an ethic might have has also taken place. However, this debate has been amply discussed elsewhere (Shrader-Frechette 1990b; Callicott 1992) and I will not develop it here. More interesting for this study, perhaps, are the directly ecological problems raised by Leopold's and Callicott's approaches to ethics, in particular, what is meant ecologically by the 'land community' or the 'land organism', and by the conditions which are best for promoting 'land health'. Are Leopold and Callicott 'wishfully imposing patterns on what is chance aggregation' (Shrader-Frechette 1990*b*: 196)? Are there, ecologically, groupings either with sufficient coherence or sufficient definition to be called 'communities' or 'organisms'?

Scientific ecologists dispute both appellations: in particular that of the land organism. There is even doubt whether the term 'ecosystem' is appropriate. As early as 1952, the biologist Gleason (1952: 8) rejected the concept of the land organism in no uncertain terms: 'Far from being an organism, an association is merely the fortuitous juxtaposition of plants. What plants? Those that can live together under the physical environment and under their interlocking spheres of influence and which are already located within migrating distance.' The rejection of the concept of the land as an organism has been reinforced more recently by Brennan. The term 'land organism', according to Brennan, suggests that it is in some sense an 'individual' with parts co-ordinating for the whole. But, he concludes, 'current research in ecology does little to support the claim that natural systems are individuals in the required sense' (Brennan 1986: 79). There are also problems with the concept of the 'land community', although Brennan remains more sympathetic to this less integrated, less systemic image. One key problem is 'the difficulty finding any structural properties that would enable us to set individuals composing some ecosystems aside from all the others'. It is easier, Brennan argues, to accept some kind of coherence and definition in species—which reproduce and share much common genetic material—than the 'land community' which does neither. By 1988, Brennan seems even less sure that coherence and definition can be attributed to the 'land community': 'Because of the complex nature of ecology it is hard to be sure that the proposed [ecological] laws ever apply in an explanatory way to any real situation' (Brennan 1988: 49). Despite this, he is still prepared to use the term 'community' in a very loose sense to describe human relations with the non-human natural world. Other critics of Callicott and Leopold reject both models completely. Harlan Miller (1988: 171), for instance, argues that the 'land' is hardly an affectional community, as Callicott portrays it, but rather 'bound by collocation and mutual exploitation'.

Problems with accepting that there is sufficient ecological coherence or definition to speak of the land as community are

compounded by unease over Leopold's and Callicott's definitions
of 'land health'. Callicott (1991: 27) claims that 'clear objective
criteria of biotic health should be specifiable in principle' and that
the objective criteria are those of 'species diversity, ecological
health and integrity'. 'Active invasive management of the land'
can be adopted in order to achieve these ends. But is Callicott
imposing his own criteria for land health onto the land? This point
is picked up by Shrader-Frechette (1990a: 188). She asks, 'What
pattern of excellence is it which an ecosystem maximizes? From a
biological point of view there is a clear notion neither of balance,
integrity, stability nor of community.' The constantly changing,
dynamic nature of ecological processes makes it impossible to
establish 'objective criteria' of land health. One example of this is
the foremost position accorded to species diversity by Callicott,
among others. Yet ecological studies have demonstrated that wide
species diversity does not necessarily mean greater ecosystemic
stability; nor is the climax state of an ecosystem necessarily its
most diverse point. (Indeed, more recent studies have suggested
that the idea of a stable climax ecosystem is in itself questionable:
e.g. Botkin 1991.) Thus, contrary to Callicott, species diversity is
not necessarily an objective criterion of land health. Species can
become extinct without human intervention; mature ecosystems
may have fewer species than younger ecosystems. A particularly
potent illustration of this is found in Horn's study of forest succes-
sion, quoted by Brennan (1984: 85). Here, over time, one species
becomes dominant, driving another to extinction, reducing natural
diversity. In such circumstances, adherence to the 'objective criterion' of species diversity would clash with the criterion of integrity or stability, which entail a non-anthropogenic loss of diversity.
This suggests that Callicott's criteria for land health bear no necessary relationship to what is 'good for the land community'—if there
can be such a good—at all.

   A further question is also raised here about the indistinctness of
the boundaries between different communities for constructing an
ethic based on ecological communities. Is the only really definitive
community the biosphere? Or can different communities be separated from one another, and the diversity, integrity, and stability
of all be aimed at? What if they conflict? As Shrader-Frechette
(1990a: 188) comments, 'Optimizing the wellbeing of a particular community leads neither to the optimization of another

community, nor to that of the biosphere, nor to that of a particular association.'

Parts and Parts, Wholes and Wholes in the Land Ethic

> If the welfare of the biotic community is the sole standard of right and wrong, then if I beat my wife, cheat on my income tax, torture kittens, ax-murder my neighbour and burn down the local schoolhouse, my actions are morally neutral so long as I do not allow the sparks to start a bushfire.
>
> (L. Johnson 1991: 239)

Johnson's mocking comments on Leopold's land ethic are both an acknowledged caricature and an incisive critique. Leopold does not, in fact, suggest that the land ethic should stand alone as the only ethical guideline for all behaviour. If this were so, then virtually all that is now legally or ethically unacceptable would immediately become permissible, and conversely, that which is at present legally or ethically neutral, such as the introduction of exotic species into unfamiliar ecosystems, would become ethically unacceptable. Leopold and Callicott want to say something about the latter concerns without eliminating the former. For Leopold, the land ethic should be incorporated into already existing ethical structures. A similar position is now held by Callicott, whose more recent theory of nested communities gives both human and biotic communities moral considerability. Yet Johnson's remark raises two important issues for Leopold and Callicott: the place of the individual in a community-based ethics, and ways of balancing the well-being of different wholes or communities against one another.

This issue was previously touched on by addressing the question of whether ecological groupings were the kind of things that could be considered to be 'wholes', and if so what kind of whole: is the model of 'community' more accurate than that of 'organism'?[9] Ecological evidence suggested very strongly that the model of 'organism' posited a much greater cohesion than was in fact present in ecological groups, but a cautious use of 'community' might be acceptable. For the purposes of this section, it will be assumed that the expression 'land community' makes some sense and is not scientifically unacceptable. The question, then, concerns the

---

[9] I will address the metaphysical question concerning holism in the next chapter.

consequences of attributing moral standing to such a community: both with regard to the effect on the individual, and the balancing of communities against one another.

The relation of the individual to the community, and the problems raised by assignation of priorities, are at the heart of all moral and political philosophy. The focus here will be on the implications of including the mixed and biotic communities, rather than just the human community, in ethical systems based on a community concept.

The implications of this view [Leopold's land ethic] include the clear prospect that the individual may be sacrificed for the greater biotic good, in the name of the 'integrity, stability and beauty of the land community'. It is difficult to see how the notion of the rights of the individual could find a home within a view that, emotive connotations to one side, might fairly be dubbed environmental fascism. (Regan 1984a: 361)

Coming from a rights perspective, where moral standing is assigned to those who are subjects-of-a-life, Regan is understandably horrified by the seeming implication of the land ethic for the individual. As with any political system where individuals are sacrificed for the supposed good of the whole, this can be labelled a kind of fascism, here based around the environment rather than the state.

Regan (ibid. 362) suggests an example of such fascism, which will serve as a useful test case:

If, to take an extreme, fanciful, but, it is hoped, not unfair example, the situation was either to kill a rare wildflower or a (plentiful) human being, and the wildflower, as a 'team member' could contribute more to the 'integrity, stability and beauty of the land community' than the human, presumably we would not be doing wrong if we killed the human and saved the wildflower.

The wildflower is an insentient (but alive) individual within the land community which is both rare (hence its loss would affect species diversity) and important to the functioning of the community (hence its loss would upset stability and integrity, and probably beauty as well). The human is conscious and sentient—for Regan, subject-of-a-life, unlike the wildflower; a member of a common species; and not important to the function of the land community. For Regan (at least in so far as his rights argument is concerned) the human has rights and the plant does not.

It is important to note that part of Regan's objection to Leopold's position, as he perceives it, is the standard deontological objection to the utilitarian: insufficient consideration for the individual. This objection was considered in Chapters 2 and 3. The substantial and interesting part of Regan's objection here is specifically ecological. According to the land ethic, he contends, a human being could be sacrified for a wildflower. That a human being might be sacrificed for the best interests of humanity is one thing. That a human might be sacrificed for a flower is quite another.

Of course, if the land ethic were the *only* moral guideline, Regan would be right. Indeed, if this were so, it would seem reasonable to urge the destruction of the entire human species (except, perhaps, for a handful, to retain species diversity) on the grounds that humans damage the integrity, stability, and beauty of the land community far more than they contribute to it. But we have already seen that Leopold claims to be 'enlarging the boundaries of the moral community' not excluding everything but the land community from moral consideration. There is no doubt that Leopold, particularly with the ambiguity of his attitude towards humans, would choose the human over the wildflower.

Callicott's work, however, has a more complex relationship to Regan's test case. In his earlier writing, primarily in 'Animal Liberation: A Triangular Affair', Callicott seems to be close to the 'environmental fascist' position characterized by Regan; an impression reinforced by statements such as: 'In every case, the effect upon ecological systems is the decisive factor in the determination of the ethical quality of actions' (Callicott 1990: 61). In his more recent work, where he envisages humans to be living within a nested series of moral communities, his position is less straightforward. As with any consequentialist ethical theory, where ethical action is aimed at achieving some kind of *summum bonum*, the individual can have no ultimate recourse to rights or absolute obligations (which is in itself objectionable to Regan). Where the *summum bonum* is the well-being of different nested communities, the situation becomes extremely complex. If the only *summum bonum* were to be the well-being of the biotic community, then Regan's human could be sacrificed for the wildflower. If the well-being of the human community or of the mixed community is given priority, then the wildflower would be lost.

Not all ethical decisions, of course, will generate such problems. There are plenty of cases where several *summa bona* coincide: where for instance the good of the human community coincides with the good of the biotic community. More interestingly, and perhaps more controversially, the nested community model also provides for a resolution of conflict within any one nest of a community. Culling a population explosion, for instance, among any one species, where to leave them to multiply would damage the biotic community, is unquestionably ethically correct for Callicott. Neither the human nor the mixed community is threatened by the cull; and it is for the well-being of the biotic community to act.[10] This kind of culling, especially of mammals, is anathema both to an individual consequentialist (because of the suffering inflicted, unless ultimately more suffering would be caused by allowing continued population expansion and hence starvation) and to an individualist deontologist.

The real problems begin where the good of one community clashes with another, as in Regan's wildflower example, of in a more generalized version of it, where the *summum bonum* of the human community is in direct conflict with that of the biotic community. Yet Callicott's later work seems to give a clear answer to this; the human community wins. The human community is the inner circle, with closer affective and hence ethical ties, and is thus of ultimate ethical significance. 'Human rights and human welfare generally come first; they are not challenged or undermined by an ecocentric ethic' (Callicott 1986: 420). One of Callicott's critics, Varner (1991: 176), concludes at this point, 'obligations to family members and human beings trump our obligations to non-human animals and ecosystems'. However, this conclusion seems to rob the land ethic of any practical force. Rather than choosing the wildflower over the human in a life-and-death situation, such an ethic would presumably allow a child that wanted to please her parents (and hence add to the well-being of the family *qua* community) to pick an entire bunch of rare wildflowers in order to give them to her parents.

As I suggested in the previous section, in 1988 Callicott proposed several 'qualifications' intended to mitigate the seemingly

---

[10] Better still, from an ecological collectivist perspective, would be the reintroduction of top predators such as wolves, if their absence was ultimately responsible for growing populations.

human-centred conclusions I have outlined above: these qualifications being that the 'outer orbits of our moral spheres tug on our
inner ones' and that one may make sacrifices for ecological integrity. More recently he has suggested that a kind of weighting (other
than intimacy) may be used to influence moral decision-making
amongst competing claims.[11] As an example, Callicott refers to a
test case raised by Varner (1991) who suggests that Callicott's 1988
position would support the continued logging of old-growth forests
in the Pacific Northwest as the logging was providing jobs for local
people (the human community trumping the biotic community).
But Callicott (1994: 53) suggests that the human community
would only trump the biotic community if the choice was between
'cutting down all the trees, and cutting down all the local people'.
But the choice is, in reality, between 'temporarily preserving a
human lifestyle that is doomed in any event and preserving in
perpetuity an ecosystem and the species which depend on it'.
Here, Callicott is introducing something like a discriminatory
principle of basic/non-basic claims, where a non-basic claim of
the human community would lose out to a basic claim of the
land community. Such discriminatory principles allow Callicott
to escape the accusation both of environmental fascism, and that
he is robbing the land ethic of any significance.[12]

It would be interesting to speculate further about the implications of Callicott's approach for a thoroughgoing system of
discriminatory principles. What, for instance, would it mean for
the mixed community of domestic animals? If the basic claims of
the mixed community are given priority over the non-basic claims
of the human community, it seems likely that vegetarianism would
be entailed, at least as far as domestic animals are concerned. (This
would not, of course, rule against wild hunting in the biotic community.) This is certainly a significant change from Callicott's
earlier position.

As a consequentialist, and a collectivist who extends ethical
concerns into the biological community, it is not surprising that
Callicott's position (and that of Leopold, on which it is built) raises
difficulties where the well-being of individuals clashes with that of

---

[11] A weighting which he describes as being 'in something of VanDe Veerian
fashion' (personal communication, 1994).

[12] Wenz (1988) constructs a similar system, but it is pluralist, and hence would be
rejected by Callicott.

communities, and the well-being of one community clashes with that of another. The introduction of discriminatory principles has helped to resolve some of these difficulties. But further questions have been raised about Callicott's basing of ethics on affection.

Critical Responses to the Basis of Ethics on Feeling

Callicott's argument that ethical behaviour is primarily based on feeling has been widely disputed by environmental ethicists (and is, of course, controversial in traditional Western ethical thinking more generally).[13] A number of practical dangers of such a position have been raised by critics of a 'sentiment-based' approach to ethics. Singer's argument in *The Expanding Circle* (1981) makes this point particularly clear.

As we have seen, Callicott bases his ethics on affectional nested communities, the sense of community having an evolutionary basis in inherited community altruism. Singer, in contrast, argues that the altruistic predispositions humans may have inherited, whether kin, reciprocal, or group, are not the last word in ethics. Humans do, after all, possess rationality which allows consideration of, and movement beyond, inherited feelings. It is rationality that enables generalization from our limited altruistic feelings to all humans and indeed, for Singer, all sentient animals. Singer (1972: 232) makes this point with particular clarity: 'if we accept any principle of impartiality, universalizability, equality or whatever, we cannot discriminate against someone merely because he is far away from us (or we are far away from him)'. Attfield (1987: 6) similarly points out that tribalists and racists could—and indeed do—endorse an ethical philosophy where being related or being similar to someone else is ethically significant.[14] Singer's approach here directly conflicts with Callicott's nested communities, where reason plays no universalizing part, and different ethical relations pertain between any individual and different humans and non-humans, according to their emotional closeness. But this may lead Callicott to some difficult ethical conclusions. Is it ethical, to use one of Singer's examples, to have an expensive family holiday

---

[13] Kant, of course, maintained that actions prompted by feeling could not be ethical at all. However, more recently feminist ethicists have developed ethical positions not dissimilar to Callicott's here.

[14] Rawles (1990) raises this same point when discussing Callicott's work.

while thousands starve in Africa? An unmodified version of Callicott's 'nested communities' could justify this ethically, since one's
obligations to one's family would outweigh one's obligations to
Africans. Callicott (1988: 169) certainly says that 'in general,
obligations to family come before obligations to remotely related
fellow humans'.

The case of family comfort (non-basic claim) versus starving
strangers (basic claim) is a special case of the conflict between
communities which we considered in the preceding section. The
recent introduction of weighting principles on top of the affectional
communities allows Callicott to handle difficult questions about
giving priority to the wants of family over the needs of strangers. In
fact, his revised position here starts to look rather like that of
Singer, above. Discriminatory principles mean that ethical behaviour is not based solely on affection, but also on reason. This
seems to be a fundamental change to an ethical theory flagged as
being based wholly on sentiment, but it enables Callicott to suggest
that someone holding his views can 'weigh duties on a single scale,
calibrated in a single metric, and attempt to balance them fairly'.

Callicott also provides a separate response to the question that
his position might offer support to racism (since it suggests humans
have greater moral obligations towards those to whom they feel
closest). He contends that racism (as well as, for example, sexism
and speciesism) is based on a faulty understanding of biological
fact (Callicott 1992: 195). In the same way as with environmental
education (for instance), people may come to acknowledge that
they are part of the biological community and hence begin to value
it, so also when individuals realize the factual inaccuracy on which
racism is based, their feelings may correspondingly alter. Thus,
Callicott (ibid. 196) argues that 'the normative dimension of a
sentiment-based environmental ethic depends, surprisingly, on
matters of fact and scientific revelation'. Thus the affective basis
of ethics for Callicott is doubly qualified: feelings should be
based on accurate knowledge of the facts; and the enactment of
sentiment-based ethics is regulated by discriminatory weighting.

Callicott is a far more systematic writer than Leopold; he has
attempted to reply to questions raised by his critics about the
difficulties associated with the adoption of a collective land ethic,
but with, perhaps, varying degrees of success. This discussion of
Leopold and Callicott, and of criticisms of their work, has set the

agenda for a study of process ethics in this sphere. Questions concerning biological origins, parts and wholes, and associated ethical priorities, different communities and their relationships are also raised in process thinking about the environment.

Process Thinking and Collectivist Environmental Ethics

This section will be divided into three parts. First, the status of ecological collectives in process thinking will be examined. How do process thinkers regard ecological collectives, and do they think of ecological collectives as having internal integrity and a good of their own? Could one speak of them in Leopold's or Callicott's terms as organisms or communities? Secondly, the interpretation of such collectives within process thinking will be considered. This will, of course, build on the conclusion of the first section. Thirdly, the ethical implications of process thinking in this context will be developed and compared with the conclusions of Leopold and Callicott.

The Status of the Ecological Collective in Process Thinking

As Christian (1967: 158) points out, since Whitehead designated his philosophy the 'philosophy of organism' it is remarkable that he makes so little use of the term otherwise. Although one would expect 'organism' to be Whitehead's primary metaphor in this context, in fact he uses it comparatively rarely. Whitehead speaks of 'organic relations' between the prehensions which make up an actual occasion, and between perishing and concrescing actual occasions, but he rarely describes anything as an organism in itself. This reflects what might be described as his emphasis on time over space. 'Organic', for Whitehead, is a relationship which has primary reference to the interconnection of *past* and *present*. This contrasts with the spatial reference of the metaphor of organism for Leopold and Callicott.

Whitehead's preferred term (although this is not to say that it also does not primarily have temporal rather than spatial reference) is, as we have seen, that of 'society', a concept which was investigated in Chapter 3. Are ecosystems, or species, societies in the Whiteheadian sense? Whitehead explicitly touches this issue only in passing, so any conclusion is bound to exhibit some creative application of his principles.

It is easier to begin with species, because they more obviously display the property which one would associate with a Whiteheadian society: inheritance of a common characteristic, a common element of form (Whitehead 1978: 34). There is a direct genetic[15] linkage between each of the members of any one species; this is, of course, part of the common definition of being a member of a species.[16] In Whiteheadian terms, all the members of the species actualize a complex eternal object (the genetic identification of the species, the ability to interbreed) and all the actual occasions that constitute the species' members participate in this actualization. This is enough to make a species a society in Whitehead's system; and indeed, on one occasion Whitehead (1948: 335) does in fact call a species a society.[17]

It is more difficult to establish whether Whitehead would call *ecosystems* societies. When he wrote the bulk of his philosophical work in the 1920s, the science of ecology as we now know it was in its infancy. The term 'ecosystem' was first used by the British ecologist Arthur George Tansley in 1935 (although the concept itself is much earlier, associated with Marsh's book *Man and Nature* in 1864). Thus Whitehead would not have been aware of the term 'ecosystem' itself, although on several occasions, as we shall shortly see, he refers to what might be regarded as an ecosystem in current terminology.

However, it is still possible to ask the question whether an ecosystem fits Whitehead's criterion for a society, that is, the inheritance of a common characteristic, the possession of a common factor. That ecosystems should be societies is clearly not as obvious as that an animal is a society (with personal order) or even that a species is a society. However, we should not rule out the possibility that Whitehead might consider an ecosystem to be a society.

[15] I do not mean 'genetic' in the general Whiteheadian sense of having inherited (although this is, of course, also true), but rather in the biological sense of the inheritance of genetic material.

[16] The definition of a species is, however, problematic in itself. See Marlene-Russow (1981).

[17] 'Beyond the soul there are other societies, and societies of societies. There is the animal body ministering to the soul: there are families, groups of families, nations, species...'

In the most general of terms Whitehead (1978: 148) comments, 'Every item in the Universe, including all other actual entities, is a constituent in the constitution of any one actual entity.'[18] However, there are different degrees of closeness between different actual entities. Such differences are, as Whitehead comments, necessary to 'rescue actual entities from becoming undifferentiated repetitions, each of the other'. He calls this 'the principle of intensive relevance': 'Any item of the Universe, however preposterous as an abstract thought or however remote as an actual entity, has its own gradation of relevance, as prehended in the constitution of any one actual entity' (ibid.). How might this relate to ecosystems? One could argue that for any actual entity in an ecosystem, the other actual entities within that ecosystem constitute particularly relevant prehensions in each new actualization. Their relevance lies in the fact that they are dependent upon one another for existence in a way that is not true of entities outside the ecosystem. This is not a surprising conclusion; the whole point of designating an ecosystem, as such, is to reflect its inner interconnectedness in a way not shared by those outside the ecosystem. It seems likely that Whitehead would have regarded such an association as a defining or common characteristic, since such a characteristic is not intended to be final or exclusive. Indeed, an ecosystem may have been what Whitehead was intending to suggest by his description of 'groups of different species associated in the joint enterprise of keeping alive' as societies (1948: 335), and by his remark 'Wherever there is a region of nature which is itself the primary field of expression issuing from each of its parts, that region is alive' (1938a: 48). It is probable that Whitehead would have understood both ecosystems and species to be societies.

It is less clear, however, that Hartshorne would have had such a view, since as we have seen, rather than working with the single category of 'society', he distinguishes between organisms and quasi-organisms. From Hartshorne's perspective both species and ecosystems are quasi-organisms—since both 'wholes' here surely have less unity than their parts. This does not necessarily imply that Hartshorne considers ecosystems to be less unified than Whitehead does, since Whitehead's societies can have differing degrees of closeness. What is important is that the classification of an ecosystem as a quasi-society implies that, for Hartshorne, it

---

[18] This idea is examined further in Ch. 5.

has no good of its own: it is of indirect significance only, for its members and 'some larger whole'—the cosmic organism (Hartshorne 1962: 194). Whitehead, however, having no such distinction between quasi- and true societies, considers that all societies have a collective good, which may not be identical with the sum of the individual goods of the parts. The implications of this will be explored later in this chapter.

How, then, do Whitehead's and Hartshorne's models of society and quasi-organism compare with those of organism and community in Leopold and Callicott? Although at first sight Whitehead's term 'society' resembles 'community' more closely than 'organism', in effect the opposite is the case. This is evident from Whitehead's understanding of the common good of a society. Ultimately, although value is registered in individual actual occasions, their role is to generate value for the whole, even if this entails self-sacrifice. Thus they function more as organs in an organism than as members of a community. The parallel is not exact, because the organs of an organism, as Katz suggested, have instrumental not intrinsic value. There is no doubt that, for Whitehead, the actual occasions bear intrinsic value. But the aim of the occasions, in their value generation, should be at the good of the society. Thus, although they themselves are bearers of intrinsic value, to act most valuably, they must act *as if they were* instrumental to the whole. They should play the part of organs to an organism in their actualization, although they could choose to actualize themselves differently. To act for the good of the whole is to act in accordance with the lure of the primordial nature of God. But this is not coercion. Unlike organs in an organism, they have freedom.

Thus, in a perfect Whiteheadian society, be it an ecosystem, a species, or an individual human being, all the concrescing actual occasions should behave as if they were organs in an organism, maximizing value for the whole, although they will be doing this by choice, not by necessity. The same would be true for a perfect Hartshornian organism. However, as I have already pointed out, Whitehead probably would have considered ecosystems to be societies whilst Hartshorne sees them as quasi-organisms and thus only indirectly valuable—for their truly organic parts, and for the cosmic organism beyond. Thus, for Hartshorne, true organisms which form part of an ecosystem should not act for the good of the ecosystem as if it were an organism for which they were organs. Rather, they should only act for the good of true organisms—themselves, organic wholes such as animals of which they are a part, and the cosmic organism, God. This suggests that for Hartshorne a quasi-organism is unlike either a Leopoldian organism or even the land community. While Whitehead could, in principle, endorse the Leopoldian land ethic in that he could accept the priority of the good of a society over its members (although in fact, his perspective in the case of an ecosystem is rather different, as we shall go on to see), Hartshorne could not. The ecosystem is a quasi-organism; it should serve its truly organic members and the cosmic organism beyond.

The Interpretation of Ecological Collectives in Process Thinking

To understand the approach of process thinkers, in particular Whitehead, to collectivist environmental ethics, we must first look at the broader context into which such ethics might fit. As was true of Leopold and Callicott, the concept of evolution provides the vital scaffolding, although the support given by evolutionary theory to Whitehead is of a somewhat different type.

In arguing this, I am putting myself in opposition to George Lucas (1985: 287), who argues that 'evolution and evolutionist theories play no significant part in Whitehead's metaphysics'. While Lucas seems to be correct in his contention that evolutionary cosmologies such as those of Bergson[19] and Alexander did not have a detailed influence on Whitehead because elements of their systems are deeply at variance with Whitehead's own, he omits some of Whitehead's most interesting comments about evolution, particularly in *Science and the Modern World*. While Whitehead's scientific background was not in evolutionary theory, he assumes a basic evolutionary schema, and this schema is a fundamental influence on his philosophical work. That Whitehead does not refer in detail to scientific evolutionary theory (Darwin, Lamarck) or evolutionary cosmology (Bergson, Alexander) is evidence, I will be arguing, more of his appropriation of evolutionary theory to his own ends than the insignificance of it to his work.

[19] This does not discount a more general influence; Ford (1984: 127), for instance, considers that Whitehead's general view on the 'creative advance of nature' in *Religion in the Making* 'is very much like Bergson's elan vital, having the events or actual occasions as its by-products'.

Whitehead (1978: 93) considers himself to have accepted the 'full sweep of the modern doctrine of evolution'. However, this does not prevent him from having reservations about interpretations of Darwin that concentrate on natural selection where 'instead of dwelling on the brotherhood of man, we are now directed to procure the extermination of the unfit'.[20] Despite these reservations, evolution becomes one of the building blocks of Whitehead's metaphysical system, as an example of the self-generative creativity which characterizes nature. But it is important to make clear that Whitehead uses the concept of evolution for his own ends; in Cheney's terminology, he '*colonizes*' evolution for his system, taking it over and imposing his own methodology and conceptuality onto it (Cheney 1989: 293–325).

This colonization primarily, takes the form of a teleologization of evolutionary theory which Darwin and subsequent scientific evolutionary theory explicitly excluded. Whitehead was not, of course, unique in making such a move—teleological evolutionary metaphysics characterizes such works as Alexander's *Space, Time, and Deity* and Bergson's *Élan Vital*. Whitehead's teleology, however, stamps evolutionary theory with his own unmistakable imprint. It is not just this world that is evolving but the entire universe, which is being lured forward by the primordial nature of God towards 'greater evocation of intensities' to provide rich experience for the consequent nature of God.[21]

However, this does not mean that any specific occasion, any particular actualization, will either manifest 'progress' from the preceding occasion (measured in terms of harmony and intensity) or even produce the maximum intensity and harmony that is possible for it, as we saw in Chapter 1. Within contextual constraints, the occasion is free to actualize itself how it chooses. The

[20] There is some suggestion in this passage that Whitehead had sympathy with Lamarckian ideas. This is not surprising, since Darwin himself did not dismiss Lamarck, and Lamarck's idea of the inheritance of acquired characteristics was not decisively refuted until well into the twentieth century (as Rachels 1991: 15). Lamarck's concepts were more congenial to a theological interpretation than Darwinian natural selection, which may explain why many theologians, such as Teilhard de Chardin, clung to Lamarck even after his work had been largely discredited.

[21] Whitehead (1978: 105). Williams (1961: 356) considers that it is this approach that enables Whitehead to avoid relativism: 'He avoids complete relativism through the evolutionary assumption that there is a movement in Man and in the Universe itself towards a more spiritual, valid and adequate expression of the good and the true.'

same openness is true of societies of actual occasions, including the rise and decline of human societies: 'There have been real periods of decadence, and at the present time, as at other epochs, society is decaying' (Whitehead 1948: 237). During times of decline, experience generated is less rich than it might otherwise be, and than that it has been. Indeed, the generality of process thinking—the scope being the entire universe—is such that there is no guarantee that the earth as a whole will ultimately go on generating such rich experience. The future is open; its fate depends on the choices of actual occasions and societies of actual occasions. Birch and Cobb (1981: 4) reinforce this point by commenting, 'The future is open in the sense that the human species may extinguish itself and destroy much of the life on the planet; yet such an outcome is not inevitable.' The only certainty is that whatever happens on, or to, the Earth, the primordial nature of God will continue to lure the actual occasions which constitute the universe on to new harmonies and intensities of experience.

This teleological, cosmological backdrop is of vital significance when considering process views of ecological collectives. The initial aim of all actual occasions is the production of rich experience. In harmony with this, ethical behaviour, as has been repeatedly pointed out, must be behaviour which generates maximum richness of experience for God. This sets the perspectives of process thinkers into a rather different matrix of considerations from those of the environmental ethicists considered earlier in this chapter.

As we have already seen, the term 'ecosystem' (as also 'biological community') was not in currency when Whitehead was writing. In addition, as he was a physicist rather than a biologist, one would not expect Whitehead to have extensive knowledge of developments in ecology. Given these factors, he makes surprisingly detailed comments about ecological relationships, most particularly in his chapter, 'Requisites for Social Progress', in *Science and the Modern World*. Indeed, one passage, to which I shall now turn, prompted Eugene Hargrove to wonder if Whitehead was not in fact a source of some of Aldo Leopold's ideas.[22] This is an extensive passage, and I shall go through it in some detail.

---

[22] 'Most interesting of all is the similarity of some of Whitehead's comments and those of environmentalist Aldo Leopold. Long passages in the last chapter of *Science and the Modern World*, for instance, could easily have served as the source

To a large extent, the environment is fixed, and to this extent, there is a struggle for existence . . . We must admit the struggle. The question is, who is to be eliminated. In so far as we are educators, we have to have clear ideas upon this point; for it settles the type to be produced and the practical ethics to be inculcated. (Whitehead 1938*a*: 238)

Here Whitehead begins his curious, and revealing, interpretation of evolution. Noticeable is his elision of evolution in nature with evolution in culture. There is no division between the two (unlike, for instance, in the work of Rolston); the same processes are exemplified in each. Thus, Whitehead does not question the derivation of norms for society from nature. The frequent portrayal of the nineteenth century as a 'struggle for existence, competition, class warfare and commercial antagonism between nations and military warfare' was understandable as an extrapolation from evolution. But this is an incomplete picture, an inadequate interpretation of evolution. It wrongly emphasizes competition: 'The full conclusion to be drawn from a philosophy of evolution is fortunately of a more balanced character. Successful organisms modify their environment so as to assist one another. This law is exemplified in nature on a vast scale' (ibid.). The key word here is 'successful'. What does Whitehead mean by a successful organism? At first glance, he seems to mean biologically successful—able to survive and to produce offspring which survive. This may mean that the organism must alter the environment to provide best for itself and its offspring. However, an organism that improves conditions such as to assist its competitors for the same biological niche is not going to last very long, or be very biologically successful.

To understand what Whitehead actually means, it is necessary to read on a few paragraphs. An initially puzzling passage casts light on how he understands 'successful':

In the history of the world, the prize has not gone to those species which specialised in violence, or even defensive armour. In fact, nature began with producing animals encased with hard shells for defence against the ills of life. It also experimented in size. But smaller animals, without external armour, warm-blooded, sensitive, and alert, have cleared these monsters off the face of the earth. Also, the lions and tigers are not the successful

of some of Leopold's ideas, and suggest that Leopold's notion of community could be derived from Whitehead's theory of organism without much difficulty' (Hargrove 1989: 103). I do not know to what extent Hargrove intends this to be a serious suggestion.

species. There is something in the ready use of force which defeats its own object. Its main defect is that it bars co-operation.

(Whitehead 1938*a*: 239)

It is surely odd to claim that lions and tigers have not been biologically or evolutionarily successful. The sabre-toothed tiger, after all, co-existed with the mammoths and other long-extinct 'monsters'. What is revealed here is that Whitehead understands evolutionary success to spring from co-operativeness. Lions and tigers, however, behave with 'ready use of force' (by which one can only assume that he means their carnivorousness). Carnivorous species are, then, bound to be 'unsuccessful' because they are not 'co-operative'.

There are several responses which can be made to this. First, Whitehead seems to be mistaken about what co-operation in an ecosystem amounts to. As Callicott repeatedly points out, ecosystems are about killing and feeding on other organisms. Even herbivores are no exception to this. A species which does not subsist on others in some form cannot survive, and would most certainly not be evolutionarily successful. It is this cycle of life, death, and decay that makes an ecosystem co-operative. Without top predators such as lions and tigers—or, to draw a comparison with Leopold, wolves—the ecosystem would collapse. Leopold makes this very clear in his description of the devastation caused by deer when wolves were eliminated.[23] To call top carnivores 'unco-operative' is to misunderstand their vital function in the system.

This mistake, however, raises the question of whether Whitehead is actually imposing metaphysical categories on biological science. Co-operation is crucial to Whitehead's system; organisms should co-operate together to achieve the greatest good: maximum richness of experience for God. The real good of the individual coincides with the good of the whole. The good for the whole is the real good for the individual, even if the individual seems to be achieving less rich experience than it might if it ignored the whole. Further, individuals are lured by the primordial nature of God to make their decision towards the good for the whole, rather than merely their own good. It is a persuasive rather than a coercive action.

[23] 'I thought that because fewer wolves meant more deer, that no wolves would mean hunter's paradise . . . since then, I have seen every bush and seedling browsed, first to anaemic desuetude, then to death' (Leopold 1968: 130).

Predation, however, fits only awkwardly into such interpretative categories. It is not the sacrifice of a little individual gain for the good of the whole in co-operation with the persuasive lure of God. Rather it is the absolute involuntary death of the organism by force. Even though this may ultimately achieve the good of the whole (as well as producing rich experience for the predator, as Sprigge[24] points out)—if as whole here we take the maintenance of the ecosystem—the method of achieving such good is distasteful for Whitehead. He wants to affirm the priority of persuasion over coercion throughout the universe, and as the driving force of the evolutionary process. In *Science and the Modern World*, for instance, he comments: 'Such order as we find in nature is never force—it presents itself as the one harmonious adjustment of complex detail . . . Evil is overruling, retarding, hurting' (Whitehead 1938*a*: 223). Of course, Whitehead acknowledges that predation and conflict do exist in the world. He seems to be referring to this with his comment that 'life is robbery' (1978: 105) and also in his remark 'By reason of the individuality of the many things there are conflicts of finite realisations. Thus the summation of the many with the one and the derivation of the one into the many involves the notion of disorder, of conflict, of frustration' (1938*b*: 70). However, a general reading of Whitehead's work suggests that he is never reconciled to seeing predation as a way of achieving the good. Both Whitehead and Hartshorne perceive conflict, particularly predation, as tragic. (In contrast, most collectivist environmental ethicists would want to urge that predation is *good*, since as Leopold might insist, it ensures continuance of integrity, stability, and beauty in the land community).

Williams, also a process thinker, affirms the continuity of evolutionary processes in both the non-human and the human sphere. However, unlike Whitehead, he also accepts the predation and force within the natural world: 'Granted all the tenderness of life (Whitehead's term) no organism would survive five minutes on the exercise of tenderness alone. Whitehead's doctrine, moreover, leads him to ignore the wide ranges of types of coercion and of mutual interaction' (Williams 1961: 370). Thus Williams concludes that force and coercion 'have their place in the necessities of being and therefore require us to find their place in God's being'. One

---

[24] In a personal communication to the author, 1993.

might say that for Williams, the argument from the struggle for existence acts as an incentive to change his model of God, while Whitehead's understanding of God acts as a model through which to reinterpret the struggle for existence.

Whitehead's comments on what we would surely call an ecosystem provide an illustration:

The trees in a Brazilian forest depend upon the association of various species of organisms, each of which is mutually dependent on the other species . . . In nature, the normal ways in which trees flourish is by their association in a forest. Each tree may lose something in its individual perfection of growth, but they mutually assist each other in preserving the conditions for survival. (Whitehead 1938a: 239)

This describes perfectly the way in which Whitehead envisages all societies working, including human society. Each individual must be prepared to accept some restriction on itself, the 'loss of some individual perfection of growth' in order to preserve the common good. This is ultimately an advantage to the sacrificing organism—who, after all, could not exist without the context. But it is also an aim at the *summum bonum*. Ultimately, the co-operative behaviour of the organisms in such an association will add to richness of experience for God. The loss of small intensities are nothing to the intensities generated by the persistence of the association.

In the benign forest association described above, there is no predation, but rather 'mutual assistance'. It is an 'environment of friends'. Each individual organism complements the others to create a harmonious working whole—harmonious both in the sense of being without conflict, and also in the sense of harmonious contrasts between the experience of a variety of different organisms, thus contributing to God's richness of experience.[25] This is a perfect example of Whitehead's belief that the individual's real interest is the common good (Whitehead 1978: 15).

Not all process thinkers agree: as we have seen, Williams explicitly accepts the presence of force in the natural world and its implications for his metaphysics. Hartshorne's thinking also contrasts interestingly here with Whitehead's. It is unlikely that

[25] Whitehead comments at this point that the sexes also 'exhibit the advantage of differentiation'. One can only assume that he means by this that the two sexes complement one another to make a whole—a position worryingly reminiscent of that of Ruskin in *Of Queen's Gardens* (although unlike Ruskin, Whitehead supported women's suffrage).

Hartshorne would describe a 'forest association' in such terms, since such a forest association would be a quasi-organism, having less unity than its most united parts (which, in a plant-only eco-system such as Whitehead describes, would be the individual cells making up the plants). As a quasi-organism, it does not have its own good in a Whiteheadian sense; its good is the summed goods of its truly organic members, and the contribution which it can make to the true cosmic organism. But since its members have freedom, there is, inevitably, the generation of tragic conflict: 'The tragedy of the world, I conclude, is the price of individuality. The greater the depth of individuality, the greater the possibilities of both good and evil. It is not simply a question of moral evil. The most innocent uses of freedom involve some risk of conflict and suffering . . . every individual is fate for other individuals' (Hartshorne 1962: 314). The ecosystem is no exception to this. Within the natural world, 'every individual is fate for other individuals'. The fulfilment of one individual, the expression of its freedom, may well be at the expense of another individual. Predation is one example of this. Further, the ecosystem, as a quasi-organism, does not represent the kind of common good to which each individual should subordinate itself. The only relevant *summum bonum* in Hartshorne's approach is the cosmic organism.

The Ethical Significance of Ecological Collectives in Process Thinking

> I hold that the ultimate value of human life, or of anything else, consists entirely in the contribution it makes to the divine life.
>
> (Hartshorne 1962: 314)

Transcending ecological collectives and individuals alike, for both Whitehead and Hartshorne, is the divine life. All value generated by actual occasions contributes to the value of the consequent nature of God, the final, greatest, and all-encompassing whole, and is preserved there, where it can be reflected back into the world as concrescing actual occasions prehend it. Every other whole—cells, animals, ecosystems, human societies—are, to use Callicott's terminology, nested within God's consequent nature. Although Whitehead and Hartshorne differ as to which wholes have collective goods—for Whitehead all societies, while for Hartshorne only true organisms—they are united in their conviction that the ultimate aim of ethical behaviour is the maximization of cosmic value by the maximization of rich experience. Thus, for both, the first ethical question to be asked is, 'Does this maximize possible cosmic richness of experience?' The aim at value for the cosmic organism, or for the consequent nature of God, is an ultimate aim which reaches far beyond the land community or the ecosystem. This background must underpin all thinking about the ethical implications of ecological collectives in process thinking.

In Whitehead's system, the ultimately important *summum bonum*is the contribution to the divine life. Thus, there should be no conflict between lesser and greater *summa bona*. The real good for any society coincides with the aim of all other societies. All societies therefore should work together harmoniously to produce the same consequences and should limit their own actions if, ultimately, this generates more rich experience. Hartshorne, acknowledging fewer *summa bona*—the actual occasion, the cell, the animal, and the cosmos—is ultimately in a similar situation. Although there may be conflict between true organisms, conflict resolution is achieved by application of the principle of maximizing rich experience for the cosmic organism. To make ethical decisions, then, Hartshorne and Whitehead look beyond the land community, and even the global community, to the cosmic and divine. Any other principle of ethical action is subordinated to the overarching principle of generating rich experience for the divine life.

How is this rich experience for the divine life generated? As we have seen in previous chapters, intensity of feeling within actual occasions, or a greater degree of harmonious contrast between actual occasions enriches experience for the divine life. Ecosystems (or ecological communities) therefore are significant in process thinking inasmuch as they contribute to the enhancement of the divine life. They can do this in several ways. First, the organisms within an ecological community produce experience. In particular, the ecological community provides life-support for many high-grade experiencers, whose intensity of feeling contributes to the richness of God's experience. Without the ecological community, such high-grade experiencers could not exist. From this perspective, the low-grade experiencers in an ecological community— actual occasions in inanimate objects such as rocks and rivers, and organisms such as bacteria and plants—provide the supportive context out of which those who can generate rich experience arise.

The simplest members act as a kind of raft, bearing up the high-grade experiencers. This approach is taken, for instance, by Mc-Daniel (1989: 82): 'We respect the integrity, beauty and stability of ecosystems not because these systems are [moral] agents or patients in their own right, but rather, because they include complex networks of living beings who are moral patients in their own right.'[26] Armstrong-Buck (1986: 246) develops this argument further by suggesting that a good ecosystem is one in which high-grade experience is promoted: 'We can rate ecosystems on relative importance according to their success in promoting intense experiences in their members, and we can rate individuals partly on their promotion of higher grade order in the ecosystem.'

Were this Whitehead's only way of measuring value produced by an ecosystem, as the above two writers seem to suggest, the ecological implications would be profound. Returning to the example considered at the end of Chapter 3, this would justify the destruction of an ecological community such as a wildflower meadow for the grazing of high-grade experiences, such as cows. But as I argued there, an ecological community is composed of a variety of kinds of organism, all producing different types of experience. The feeling of contrast between these different kinds of experience adds to the richness of the divine life, and means that even the lowest-grade experiencer, in conjunction with other kinds of experience, can produce intensity of divine experience. Thus 'blue-bottleness' can enrich God's experience because it contrasts with other kinds of feelings (like dragonfly experience or toad experience) even though it is not in itself high grade. Indeed for low-grade organisms, this species-representative experience is of central importance since the harmony and intensity of experience produced by them is so low that their non-instrumental value otherwise in process thinking would be negligible. Even for higher-grade organisms—wild mammals in ecosystems for instance—whilst they may produce considerable harmony and intensity of experience as individuals, in terms of generating contrasts, process thinkers such as Cobb and Hartshorne regard them primarily as representative of a species rather than as individuals. Thus one fox's or badger's experience is much the same as another's.

[26] In fact, McDaniel is being a little inaccurate here; it is the experiences of living beings that are morally relevant, not the beings themselves (although they do not exist outside their experiences).

Birch and Cobb (1981: 174), in an unusual and brief discussion of the value of ecosystems, introduce another dimension—the contrast which results from different kinds of ecosystem (presupposing that an ecosystem is a 'whole'): 'The elimination of a unique desert ecosystem is not to be favoured, even if this were to be replaced by one that had a larger quantity of high grades of life.' They seem to be suggesting that the unique nature of the ecosystem (as a whole) provides for unusual contrast with other ecosystems; and that thus a rare ecosystem can enrich the divine life more than a few more high-grade experiencers (presumably of a similar kind to those already existing). However, it is not clear quite what they find valuable about the unique ecosystem here. Is it that it provides a place in which rare kinds of experience can be produced, and without the ecosystem, those experience-producing species would be lost? Or do they think that the system as a whole produces its own kind of patterned experience (as a society) which contrasts as a whole with other ecosystems? If we were to take the latter suggestion seriously, it would raise many of the problems suggested earlier about the nature of ecosystems and whether they are the kind of things which can be defined or bounded.

However one might interpret this last point, it seems clear that in process thinking ecological communities can contribute value to the divine life in different ways: in the experiences, especially the high-grade experiences, of community members; in the contrast between kinds of experiences in the community; and in the contrast of different kinds of ecological communities with one another. How does this relate to the work of Leopold and Callicott which was considered earlier in this chapter?

Process Thinking and the Work of Leopold and Callicott

In common with Leopold and Callicott, process ethics is consequentialist; ethical behaviour is behaviour aimed at achieving certain states of affairs. For Leopold and Callicott, this is characterized as the good of the community, albeit the human, mixed, or biotic community. For Whitehead and Hartshorne, the aim is at the cosmic *summum bonum*; all other communities, organisms, or quasi-organisms are servants to the cosmic *summum bonum*; they point beyond themselves; they exist to produce value for the divine life (although this does not mean that they always produce the maximum value possible for them: their freedom of choice about actualization remains). This theological setting of ethics in process thinking is an important contrast to the biological setting of ethics in Leopold or Callicott. It means that process thinking can escape some of the criticisms levelled at the biological foundations of Leopold's and Callicott's position (although, of course, the metaphysical basis of process thinking is at least as controversial as the sociobiology of these collectivist environmental philosophers!)

This theological framework means that process thinkers understand ecosystems and species in a very different context from that of Leopold and Callicott. Process thinkers do not seek 'objective criteria of land health' and elevate these into moral norms. Unlike Leopold, their particular concerns are not—directly at least—with stability or integrity. The relevant criterion for process thinking is what maximizes rich experience in the divine life: the production of high-grade experience, and contrasts between different kinds of experience.

However, this emphasis amongst process thinkers on the value of high-grade experiencers in ecological communities and species contrasts strikingly with the emphases of collectivist environmental ethicists. The production of experience (let alone high-grade experience) is not, according to these philosophers, of significance in the biotic community—except as a practical mechanism to avoid danger and promote survival. Most of the key members of a biotic community probably do not have experiences at all, and thus from the perspective of Callicott, for instance, such a focus is inappropriate. Whitehead's negativity about predation is a further sign of an inappropriate focus on high-grade experience, and the resulting capacity for suffering. As Callicott points out, 'nature is notoriously indifferent to suffering'.

In contrast, *variety* is important both to process thinkers and collectivist environmental ethicists. Leopold explicitly discusses the need to preserve complexity and diversity; similarly, Callicott (1991: 27) contends that species diversity, ecological health, and integrity are the main criteria for land health. Whilst the purpose of the preservation of variety is very different in process thinking (due to its theological *summum bonum*) it would appear, at first sight at least, that in practice the two approaches would, in this respect, result in the same ethical understanding of ecological communities. To this extent, process thinking is open to the same criticisms as were made of this element of Leopold's and Callicott's work. Does this mean, for instance, that human beings should intervene in ecosystems to protect species which are becoming extinct without human intervention (where one native species is driving another to extinction, for instance)? Or that humans should attempt to keep ecosystems in a less mature condition when this means that there is greater species diversity? Both of these are problematic implications of an emphasis on variety in ecosystems faced by both groups of thinkers.

It is also possible, however, to imagine circumstances where, despite the importance of variety to both groups of thinkers, a divergence of practice might emerge. This is due to the different part which variety plays in the two approaches. For process thinkers, the contrast between different *kinds* is valuable for the divine life. For collectivist environmental ethicists, it is the ecological community that is valuable; variety is important in the context of supporting an ecological community. Thus, process thinkers might countenance the introduction of exotic species into an ecosystem to increase its diversity (provided that this would not harm or destroy other species and hence reduce overall diversity) because their focus is on increasing contrasts between different kinds. Genetically engineered species might also be welcomed in particular contexts. It is improbable that such actions would be acceptable to collectivist environmental ethicists because their concern is with protecting the variety already present within an ecological community rather than in the pure multiplication of kinds.

In order to make any meaningful judgement about how Whitehead's ethics would compare, in practice, with those of Leopold and Callicott, it would be necessary (as was noted in Chapter 3) to decide whether maximizing high-grade experience or maximizing variety would have priority in process ethics. Obviously there would be some instances where these two ethical aims would coincide. But equally, there are occasions where the aims are not only in tension (as Birch and Cobb admit in passing) but also where they conflict. In addition, the apparently special status given to human beings, where individual humans are not just representatives of their species (i.e. providing God with 'humany' experiences) but also individuals whose differences from one another contrast in their own right, creates a further difficulty in making ethical decisions about the environment. This provides another distinction from Leopold and Callicott, as we shall see in the next section.

Some Practical Implications of Process Thinking about Ethical Collectives

In Chapter 3 I considered the possible ethical responses of process thinkers to the destruction of a wildflower meadow in order to introduce a grass ley and cattle-grazing. I suggested that this was a case where the 'Maximize high-grade experience!' element of process thinking conflicted with the 'Maximize contrast!' element. Suppose we now propose a revision to this case. The same wildflower meadow is near to a small rural community, where a number of recently married couples, unable to find local housing but unwilling to move out of the area, live with their parents. Many of them would like to start families but will not do so in the cramped conditions in which they live. Proposals are brought forward to build a housing estate on the wildflower meadow in order to accommodate these local people, provide them with space to have families, and so on. What might a process ethicist make of this proposal?

As with the previous case of the dairy cattle, the introduction of human beings to the area would mean that it would be inhabited by high-grade experiencers. Their experience would be enriched by the move, producing an increase in their happiness compared with their previous location. They would produce children which it is probable would not otherwise have existed—i.e. new centres of rich experience in the world. It is thus likely that the development would increase the amount of rich experience in the world. But what of the loss of contrasts between all the species currently in the wildflower meadow? Can the housing compensate for that?

This raises a number of questions about the rarity of the species of wildflower in the meadow, and hence how unusual the contrasts between them are. This ultimately leads to the more general question of how the value generated by individual human beings in process thinking compares with the value generated by contrasts between species, a question first raised in Chapter 2. If we put this in a rather stark and practically unlikely fashion: in a choice between a human being and a species, which would process thinkers consider to generate more value?

A number of issues are, of course, raised here, because the loss of a species means the loss of all the future individuals of that species, with all the richness of experience that they might generate, as well as the lost of that unique *kind* of experience in the world, with the potential rich contrasts it might produce. Does a single human being outweigh all that value? But what of the future offspring of that human being—assuming that the choice in this instance is between the existence of a human being at all, rather than one human being instead of another? And how does the unique kind of experience generated by an individual human being compare with the unique kind of experience generated by a species? Which contrast generates the greatest value for God?

Hartshorne is the only process writer I can find who explicitly addresses this question in his work (Hartshorne 1974*a*: 72; 1979: 57). On the first occasion he comments 'To risk a man's or woman's life for a subhuman individual is, I believe, unwarranted. But to do so to save a species, say of whale or of elephant, would this be unwarranted? I'm not so sure.' On the second occasion he enquires: 'Which would be a greater loss to the universe, the disappearance of all birds, or the premature deaths of nine thousand human beings? I could perhaps seriously consider giving up the remainder of my life if it would definitely save a threatened species for millenia.' We cannot deduce anything very clearly from this. Obviously Hartshorne is unsure. His 1974 remark speaks only of *risking* life, refers to very high-grade species, and expresses no certainty about the choice. His 1979 comment, given that he was 82 when he wrote it, is equally uncertain on the following points: the species at issue (probably a bird, i.e. a fairly high-grade species); that the species would definitely be saved, and for a timescale of thousands of years; and that he should only 'perhaps seriously consider' the sacrifice of the rest of his life. It seems unlikely, then, that Hartshorne would rank the existence of a species as being clearly of more value than the life of a human being.

The case of the ancient wildflower meadow is, however, less extreme than either of the examples Hartshorne considers above. The wildflowers are not the last of their species, so that *kind* of experience would still exist elsewhere in the world. They are not high-grade experiencers such as birds or whales. Furthermore, we have seen in earlier chapters that within process thinking the contrast between different human individuals can be felt by God in a way that is not the case for most non-human individuals, which are species representatives. Given what Hartshorne has said above, and the fact that the wildflower species are not threatened with immediate extinction, it is likely that contrasts between the humans (in particular the new humans who would not otherwise have existed) would compensate for the loss of the contrasts previously present between different species in the wildflower meadow. If this is so, both the 'Maximize rich experience!' and the 'Maximize contrast!' principles of process ethics can be met by carrying out the development. Thus the presence of human beings introduces a new element to the case, which was not present when the proposal was to introduce cattle-grazing. The cattle are only species-representative; humans are individual-representative. The introduction of new human beings seems to create a strong reason in favour of development in wild areas. Indeed, it perhaps suggests a general principle that where total richness of experience for the divine life would seem to be increased by development on wild areas, then the development would be desirable for process thinkers.

But what would the implications be of this conclusion for the protection of ecosystems in a world with growing human populations? What would process thinkers make of the idea that human population growth should be limited in order to leave room for the flourishing of wild areas (as championed, for instance, in the *Basic Principles of Deep Ecology* (Devall and Sessions 1985))?

Birch and Cobb (1981: 314, 328) explicitly address questions about human population growth, arguing that it should be limited. But this does not seem to be the logic of a process position—which is, in this respect, in a similar position to that of some utilitarians.[27] From a process perspective, extra human beings add rich experience to the world and provide contrasts between their own feelings and those of other humans. Thus it would seem important to keep on adding humans until the point where the addition of an extra human would reduce total richness of experience in the world (by increasing human misery so much that it would be better that they had never been born) and/or result in the death of other humans (thus leading to the loss of contrasts in the world). This point (rather like Parfit's Repugnant Conclusion)—would presumably

---

[27] See the discussion in Parfit (1984: 351–441).

be at a very high level of human population indeed. It would seem to follow from this that unless the human population had reached a point of collapse, an increase in human population might, in every instance, be said to equal or outweigh the value generated by wild ecosystems.

This conclusion seems rather different from that which one would expect from most collectivist environmental ethicists. A development of housing on a wildflower meadow would, from the perspective at least of 'Animal Liberation: A Triangular Affair' be unacceptable. If the biotic community has priority over the human community in ethical decision-making, then a wild-flower meadow would not be sacrificed for a housing development, however great the needs of the humans concerned (especially since the development would encourage an increase in human population). From a nested community perspective, where the human community has priority over the biotic community, it might be argued that the development should go ahead, since human needs trump the needs of the biotic community. However, if (as in Callicott's more recent work) weighting principles are introduced, this situation can be understood as one where the basic needs of the biotic community are in conflict with the serious needs of the human community. In such circumstances, depending upon how the weighting worked, whilst some justification for the development could be given (since the reason for the development is not a trivial or unimportant one) it seems more likely that the development would be rejected on the grounds that the human interest is not basic (rather like the example of employment versus logging of old-growth forests, considered earlier in this chapter).

However a collectivist environmental philosopher might construe the above case, it is unlikely that he or she would adopt the attitude to human population growth which appears to follow from process thinking. Collectivist environmental philosophers have no overall aim at total richness of experience, but rather an aim at well-being in human and biotic communities. The well-being of human communities is surely not essentially linked to an increase in their size (although there may be a few instances where population increase for a particular community would be beneficial). The well-being of biotic communities, however, *is* linked to a decrease in the size of human populations—to a degree, at least. Thus, even a collectivist philosopher who argues that the interests of human communities always trump the interests of biotic communities is *not* likely to maintain the importance of population growth. There is no sense, as in process thinking, that human population growth is a good in itself.

Thus, despite the value that process thinkers can attribute to ecological communities, it seems difficult within process thinking for these ecological communities to be assigned protection against the expansion of human populations. In part, this is because of the elevated status given to human experience: both because it has greater harmonious intensity than non-human experience, and because each human individual's experience provides unique contrasts with the experiences of other human individuals, rather than experience representative of the species. It may also, in part, be due to a variation of a problem raised earlier—the difficulty of maintaining integrity in a process system. The ecological community, like a human individual, is a society of experiencing actual occasions. It is not, primarily, a 'whole' in the strong sense that some ecological collectivists might argue. Rather, an ecological community is a flow of experiences with different degrees of richness and contrast—experiences that might be 'traded off' for those produced by human beings (or domestic animals). Thus, provided that total richness of experience produced remains constant or increases, 'substitution' of human beings for ecosystems remains possible.

Thus, in conclusion, although there are some similarities between collectivist environmental ethicists and process thinkers, there are also substantial differences. These include the way in which ecological communities are conceived and the ethical behaviour due to them. Whilst Whitehead, at least, probably thought of ecological communities as *summa bona* (although not the ultimate *summum bonum*), where ecological communities conflict with expanding human populations process thinkers can offer little protection to ecological communities. It thus seems likely that collectivist environmental ethicists, like the individualists of Chapter 3, would find process approaches to environmental ethics unsatisfactory.

So far in this book, I have compared process thinking with three different approaches to environmental ethics. With one of these approaches, individualist consequentialism, process thinking shared substantial methodological affinity. With two approaches, individualist deontology and collectivist consequentialism, whilst some points of similarity were identified, similarities were largely overwhelmed by differences of method and content. In contrast, in Chapter 5, I will be comparing process thinking with an approach to environmental philosophy which actually claims to share common ground with process thinking, and to have been influenced by Whitehead's work: deep ecology.

5

Whitehead's Philosophy and the Deep Ecology Movement

The focus of this chapter differs in several respects from those that precede it. Process thinking has, until now, been compared with environmental ethical approaches which, generally speaking, have themselves made little comment on process thought. Here however, process thinking will be laid alongside an approach whose promoters actively claim support from it: deep ecology. In addition, deep ecology does not only concern environmental ethics; it also emphasizes metaphysics. The relationship between ethics and metaphysics in deep ecology is a complex one, as I will go on to explain. This chapter will compare process thinking (primarily that of Whitehead, the process thinker to whom most deep ecologists refer) with the metaphysics of deep ecology, a comparison which is interesting in its own right, but which also has important ethical implications.

Introduction to Deep Ecology and Process Thinking

Deep Ecological Claims about Process Thinking

A variety of claims are made by different deep ecologists concerning process thinking. Fox (1984*b*: 149), for instance, claims that Spinoza, Whitehead, and Heidegger 'articulate the vision' of deep ecology, while Shepard (1969: 3) argues that 'the wisdom of deep ecology' is manifest in 'current Whiteheadian philosophy'. One would expect to find a substantial number of articles elaborating such claims; after all, a small and frequently controversial new philosophical school could only gain by revealing conceptual closeness to relatively illustrious philosophical ancestors. Such articles do exist in the case of Heidegger and Spinoza. Both Arne Naess (1977: 418–26) and George Sessions (1977: 481) have written reasonably substantial pieces on Spinoza; and Sessions (Devall and Sessions 1985: 98–100) and Zimmerman (1983: 99) on

Heidegger. However, there is a marked void where Whitehead is concerned. In a tightly packed 7-page appendix to *Deep Ecology* (ibid. app.) entitled 'Western Process Metaphysics: Heraclitus, Whitehead and Spinoza', Sessions manages only two meagre paragraphs on Whitehead. If Whitehead really is 'one of the patron saints of deep ecology' as Sylvan (1985: 10) suggests, why is so little evidence cited to support this view? Why is Whitehead's name so frequently used as a reassuring philosophical tag, with no explanatory philosophical baggage? There are several possible explanations. First, perhaps the Whiteheadian system is so self-enclosed that, without concentrated study, a detailed consideration is impossible. Deep ecologists thus simply appropriate popular conceptions of the system as supportive of their own ideas. There is certainly some truth in this, but Whitehead's approach is not markedly more self-enclosed or difficult than that of Spinoza or Heidegger. Perhaps it is just historical chance that those writing about deep ecology have focused on other philosophers whilst acknowledging that a Whiteheadian perspective shares some common ground. This is also a possible explanation, although not a very satisfying one. A third possibility is that the relation of Whitehead's process philosophy to the conceptual world of deep ecology is profoundly ambiguous and complex. It is this complexity which renders an approach such as that of Naess to Spinoza, where he 'invites the reader to consider a set of [sixteen] hypothetical connections between Spinozist and ecological thought' infeasible (Naess 1977: 418). This ambiguity becomes obvious even on a brief study. Sessions, for example, in the two paragraphs mentioned above, expresses some doubts about the compatibility of Whitehead's system with his own view of deep ecology (Devall and Sessions 1985: 236). It is this complex relationship that will be examined in this chapter.

Deep Ecology: An Attempt at Delimitation

The mere use of the expression 'deep ecology' suggests—misleadingly—that there is some clear definition, or that there are, at least, defining characteristics to which those who call themselves deep ecologists adhere. This is far from the truth. Deep ecology is an amorphous cluster of ideas, not all of which are held by all who call themselves deep ecologists, and some of which are held by those who definitely would not. These concepts are frequently prioritized differently and are sometimes in tension with one another. To complicate matters still further, over time individuals (in particular Arne Naess) have altered the presentation of their views. The first priority, then, is to clarify this situation, so that it is plain which individuals, and which of their ideas, are being considered, in order to find some sort of path through what Sylvan (1985: 2) describes as a 'conceptual bog'.

The systematic use of the expression 'deep ecology' is usually traced back to Arne Naess in his 1973 *Inquiry* article, 'The Shallow and the Deep, Long-range Ecology Movement'. Here, Naess drew a distinction between the movements for 'shallow ecology' and 'deep ecology', putting forward what he called the fundamental tenets of a deep-ecological position. Shallow ecologists, he argued, 'fight against pollution and resource depletion', their central objective being the 'health and affluence of people in the developed countries'. Deep ecologists, however, have deeper concerns: 'principles of diversity, complexity, autonomy, decentralization, symbiosis, egalitarianism and classlessness'. He states that the tenets of the deep ecology movement are 'clearly and forcefully normative'.

This was the beginning of a long series of attempts to describe the basis of deep ecology, attempts already catalogued by Sylvan (1985). These attempts often divide deep ecology into two categories: the principally *metaphysical* and the principally *ethical*. However, the one does not preclude the other; indeed, ethics and metaphysics stand in such close, if controversial, relationship in deep ecology that it is impossible to consider the one without reference to the other. Thus, although the explicit focus of this chapter is on the metaphysics of deep ecology, it is impossible to disentangle metaphysics from its ethical foundation and conclusions, as I will shortly indicate.

Before doing this, I must add one further delimitation. Recently, the adjective 'deep' has been applied to any philosopher who 'believes that nature . . . must be respected as valuable in itself' (Sprigge 1991: 108)—thus encompassing most of the ethicists I have considered in previous chapters. I will not be using the term 'deep ecology' as widely as this; rather I shall be restricting this study to those philosophers who actively call themselves deep ecologists or who are associated with the deep ecology movement.

I am thus confining myself to a smaller group than does, for instance, Merchant (1992).

The Metaphysical and the Ethical in Deep Ecology

The relative significance of the metaphysical and the ethical in deep ecology is much disputed. In his 'Critique of Deep Ecology', for example, Sylvan argues that it was originally, and is fundamentally, a normative or value system. The metaphysics, he suggests, came later, being introduced by other deep ecologists such as Seed and Sessions: 'Although Deep Ecology was in origin part of value theory, and basically concerned with environmental values, it has been presented as a metaphysics, as a consciousness movement (and as primarily psychological) and even as a sort of (pantheistic) religion' (Sylvan 1985: 2). Sylvan later suggests that deep ecology has been hijacked by 'metaphysicalists'. While he accepts Naess's deep ecology as 'authentic' (because of its ethical emphasis), Sylvan (1990) calls other deep ecologists, especially Fox, 'Western Deep Ecologists' (stemming from the West Coast of Australia and the USA). Their form of deep ecology, he implies, is inauthentic.

Fox's own interpretation of deep ecology is diametrically opposed to that of Sylvan. For Fox (1990: 225), deep ecology 'renders ethics superfluous'. He rejects 'intrinsic value approaches', claiming concern with ontology rather than ethics, and quotes supporting passages from other deep ecologists such as George Sessions: 'The search for an environmental *ethics*, in the conventional modern sense (which Routley wants to endorse) seems wrongheaded and fruitless . . . the search, as I understand it, is not for environmental ethics but for ecological consciousness' (Sessions cited in Fox ibid.). The situation is thus unclear. Is deep ecology a value system, proposing a new ethics of the natural world, or is it a metaphysical system which goes 'deeper' than ethics, and regards ethical reform not only as insufficiently radical but as wrong in approach?

Naess (1973) speaks of deep ecology both as 'clearly and forcefully normative' and as metaphysical, with metaphysical principles, such as 'rejection of the man-in-environment image in favour of the relational, total field image'. This suggests that, at this point at least, Naess considered the ethical and the metaphysical to coexist.

This impression is reinforced in Naess's subsequent work: in 1974 (30–7) he explained his plainly metaphysical system to A. J. Ayer; his article 'Intuition, Intrinsic Value and Deep Ecology' (1984*b*), and his book *Ecology, Community and Lifestyle* (1989) confirm the importance of metaphysics. He speaks of a four-level discussion, beginning with 'verbalized fundamental philosophical and religious ideas and intuitions' moving through the Deep Ecology Platform to general consequences and finally concrete situations. Everything is derived from the fundamental metaphysics. Naess's 'authentic' deep ecology is, in fact, strongly metaphysical and cannot be separated from 'Western' deep ecology in the way which Sylvan suggests.

However, Sylvan's case is not without justification. While deep ecology was always perceived by Naess to be a metaphysical system, there is no doubt that he also repeatedly expressed its normative nature—as is true of his 1973 article. The exact role he considers ethics to play is somewhat obscure and contradictory. In the same article in which he remarks 'I have the feeling that moralizing is not a great force in the world' (Naess 1988*a*: 4–7), he includes what has become known as the Eight-Point Platform of Deep Ecology apparently agreed by Naess and Sessions in 1984 (Devall and Sessions 1985: 69–76). These principles (to which I shall return) are clearly value-oriented.[1] Variations of these eight points appear throughout discussions of deep ecology and are restated as recently as late 1990 in Naess's work (1990: 87–97). There is no doubt of their centrality. Certainly, Naess sometimes claims that they represent the second level of deep-ecological thinking which, as we have seen, follows from fundamental religious ideas and intuitions. But even if we accept that Naess has always thought of the deep ecology platform as in this sense derivative, it need not imply secondary importance. After all, Naess insists on the need for pluralism at the primary level, while commenting that all who call themselves deep ecologists must accept something approximating the Eight-Point Platform. This may make ethics more rather than less significant than the underlying pluralist metaphysics.

---

[1] Fox denies this value orientation, claiming that the deep ecology platform is colloquial and 'not a formal philosophical position'. Sylvan is correct to say that this defence is 'ridiculous': the deep ecology platform can surely be interpreted in no other way than as a series of value statements (Fox 1986: 49; Sylvan 1990: 48).

In addition—a point that Sylvan does not make—there seems to be a hidden ethical imperative at work behind the metaphysics of deep ecology. Naess repeatedly affirms the importance of a pluralist metaphysics; both he and Fox guide others by suggesting ways in which they might construct their own ecosophical system. But the word 'guide' is significant here. This is pluralism within very tight restraint—that of ecosophy. Neither Naess nor Fox could accept truly pluralist metaphysics in case they issued in the wrong conclusions. A metaphysics of the supremacy of humanity, for instance, would not be welcomed by either. Is this the re-emergence of an ethical imperative? The whole purpose of the deep ecology enterprise is to 'guide'—to achieve a change in outlook. Fox's fundamental argument seems to be that a change of world-view to 'transpersonal ecology' will issue in a symbiotic approach to the natural world. In these circumstances, ethics becomes superfluous, because the flourishing of others would instinctively be regarded as the flourishing of ourselves (as will be illustrated). However, concealed within this denial of ethics is a clear ethical imperative: that one ought to change in attitude to the natural world, and that changing metaphysics is the most successful way to do so. Thus, at the most fundamental level, the urge within deep ecology is an ethical one—the urge to change, and still more, the urge to make others change. Without this imperative, what point would there be in such extensive publication and propagation of the deep-ecological view?

This would suggest that ethics is, in this sense at least, fundamental to deep ecology. It is the ethical imperative for change that produces the pluralist metaphysics that, according to Fox, render ethics superfluous. This does not mean that metaphysics is superfluous, but that it is founded on an ethical imperative and issues in ethical conclusions.

Thus Sylvan is right to cavil at Fox's attempt to drop the normative side to deep ecology; an attempt which reaches its climax in *Towards a Transpersonal Ecology* (1990). Here Fox, by a remarkable sleight of hand, argues that the concept of the *extended self* is in fact the defining characteristic of deep ecology, which should, therefore, more accurately be called transpersonal ecology. Indeed, Fox employs a number of deceptive and even contradictory arguments to make this point. He argues that deep ecology is popular because it is misunderstood to be a value theory; whilst simultaneously arguing that deep ecology is popular because those that use it perceive that there is *more* to it than a value theory, that is, a metaphysics. He also operates a *distinctiveness criterion*: what is *authentic* to deep ecology must be what is *distinct* or *unique*. Since ecological value theories are found elsewhere in environmental philosophy, they are not distinct to deep ecology, and are therefore not authentic; the theory of the extended self is not found elsewhere in environmental philosophy and is therefore distinct, authentic, and in fact the defining characteristic of deep ecology. The fallacy involved in this argument is clear. The fact that a concept is or is not distinctive bears no necessary relation either to its authenticity or its centrality.

None the less, Sylvan certainly has an agenda of his own. Since his primary interest is environmental ethics, it is the ethical side of deep ecology with which he wishes to engage. Thus he accepts the parts of deep ecology of which he approves (that is, the Eight-Point Platform) as 'authentic' while dismissing the rest as 'inauthentic'— Fox in reverse. These positions are unbalanced. Both ethics and metaphysics are of central importance to deep ecology, and to attempt to strip either of them away is to present deep ecology only half-clad. Hence this comparison between the metaphysics of deep ecology and the metaphysics of process thinking is carried out very much within an ethical context.

Holism and the Extension and Realization of the Self

As we have already seen, Naess repeatedly affirms that metaphysical pluralism must lie at the root of deep ecology: his own system is but one path amongst many (Naess 1990: 88). Despite this, there is significant agreement between the views of those who call themselves deep ecologists. Two closely related metaphysical themes are particularly prominent: *holism* and *the extension and realization of the self*. It is these two themes upon which I will be focusing.

Holism in Deep Ecology

Holism can be and has been defined in different ways, and as several writers suggest, can be held with varying degrees of intensity. For the sake of clarity, I will begin by using the classification of Phillips in his book *Holistic Thought in Social Science* (1976). Phillips divides holism into three types, which he calls Holism 1, 2, and 3. He focuses primarily on Holism 1, which he claims is composed from five interrelated ideas, namely (*a*) Rejection of the 'analytical' or 'reductionist' approach of much science; (*b*) Argument that the whole is more than the sum of its parts; (*c*) Argument that the whole determines the nature of its parts; (*d*) Argument that the parts cannot be understood in isolation from the whole; (*e*) Argument that the parts are dynamically related, or interdependent.

To distinguish Holism 2 from Holism 1, it is important to understand 'emergent properties'. An emergent property is a property possessed by a whole which is not possessed by its parts: for instance, water having the property of being a clear liquid at 5°C which is not a property of its constituents, hydrogen or oxygen. In Phillips' classification, in Holism 1, emergent properties *cannot be predicted from investigation of the parts*; but this does not mean that after one has the whole, one cannot explain it by examining the parts and their interactions. This is a weaker contention than Holism 2, which claims that even after one has the whole, *it still cannot be explained by studying the parts*. Holism 3, in contrast, is a much simpler hypothesis; merely that new terminology is needed to explain the properties of wholes.

In this chapter, Holism 1 and 2 will be of primary interest. This is not to say that Holism 3 would be refuted by either process thinkers or deep ecologists, who would certainly affirm the need for new terminology to explain the properties of wholes. Indeed, there are very few scientists or philosophers, as Phillips points out, who would refute Holism 3, and it is for this very reason that 1 and 2 are more significant.

Within deep ecology, support for holistic views is often derived from quantum physics or scientific ecology, although the support of neither is necessary; Naess for instance defended a kind of holism against Ayer in 1974 without reference to the physical or biological sciences. Most commonly, however, deep ecologists refer to the work of physicists such as Capra and Bohm as a basis for their views. Capra (1982) argues that the discoveries of modern physics invalidate not only Newtonian physics, but also the whole philosophical view of the world which, he claims, was built on it. This 'Newtonian' view espouses mechanism and reductionism: that is to say, the twin beliefs that everything which exists has a mechanical explanation, and that the best way to understand something is by breaking it down into its components; a view of the world built on atomism—elementary solid particles—and the concept of absolute space and time. However, the new physics, according to Capra, invalidates this view (rejection of analytical approach: Holism 1(a)).

'In contrast to the mechanistic, Cartesian view of the world, the world view emerging from modern physics can be characterized by words like organic, holistic and ecological' (Capra 1982: 66). Central to the new physics, claims Capra (ibid. 69), is the discovery that 'subatomic particles have no meaning as isolated entities, but can be understood only as interconnections' (interdependence: Holism 1(e)). There are no 'isolated building blocks' but only a great 'web of relations': 'Quantum theory has shown that subatomic particles are not isolated grains of matter but are probability patterns, interconnections in an inseparable cosmic web that includes the human observer and her consciousness . . . at the subatomic level, the interrelations and interactions between the parts and the whole are more fundamental than the parts themselves' (ibid. 83). Capra's characterization of quantum physics describes one common interpretation of holism. One can sensibly *consider only the whole* (parts dependent on whole: Holism 1(d)) since, as modern physics has shown, everything is interconnected. Atomism and reductionism fail to recognize this and create artificial divisions between things that cannot be separated. It is not therefore so much that the whole is greater than the sum of its parts, but that there are no clearly defined parts, just one constantly interacting, changing web of energy.

Scientific ecology is also used as a source for the deep ecological holistic view; in particular in the work of Commoner, who defines holism as the belief that a whole is more than the sum of its parts (Holism 1(b))—that is, the whole may have emergent properties very different from the properties of the individual parts which make it up. He uses this concept to attack the work of molecular biologists for concentrating on the molecular structures of cells and failing to look at the complexity of the whole—that is to say, studying the parts as if that would explain the whole (rejection of analytical approach: Holism 1(a); possibly Holism 3). Commoner is at pains to emphasize the complexity and degree of interdependence among ecosystems. Indeed, he describes the principle that everything is interconnected as the first and foremost Law of Ecology (Holism 1(*e*)) (Commoner 1972: 37–41).

Statements of this kind by physicists and ecologists have both *generated* deep ecological views and acted to *reinforce* them. Indeed, many deep ecologists view their relationship to modern physics and scientific ecology as surprisingly close. Both Fox and Naess claim that their systems are *inspired* by ecology (as science) rather than *derived* from it(e.g. Naess 1989: 39). Fox's (1984*b*: 149) position illustrates the centrality of science to his philosophy: 'Not to refer to the parallels between deep ecology . . . and the so-called "new physics" (i.e. post-1920s physics) might well indicate that one had missed the central intuition of deep ecology since, fundamentally, each of these fields of understanding subscribes to a similar structure of reality, a similar cosmology.'

The descriptions of holism in deep ecological writing reflect the influence of such writing by physicists and ecologists. The most extreme statement stems from Fox, who comments that the central intuition of deep ecology is

the idea that there is no firm ontological divide in the field of existence. In other words, the world is simply not divided up into independently existing subjects and objects, nor is there any bifurcation in reality between the human and non human realms. Rather, all realities are constituted by their relationships. To the extent that we perceive boundaries, we fall short of deep ecological consciousness. (Ibid.)

This emphasis on complete interrelationship again falls clearly into the category of Holism 1(e), and is a common feature in most deep-ecological writing. Indeed, although there are some differences of emphasis and degree among deep ecologists about holism, certain common features can be identified. Leaving aside for the present questions about the extension and realization of the self, these features can be presented as follows.

1. The fundamental idea that all is ultimately one, and that the 'whole' or 'total' view is the best. A rejection of reductionism necessarily follows.

2. The description of the world as a metaphor of ecology (the web of life) or a metaphor of physics (the field of energy) which not only interlinks everything, but which actually constitutes all that is. With this as a basis, it is common to describe individual organisms as 'knots in the biospheric web' or 'centres of interaction in one

great field'. This web or field of relations is in a constant state of flux, or as Fox (ibid.) puts it 'characterized by process, dynamism, instability, novelty, creativity, etc.'.

3. Since individuals are 'knots' or 'centres of interaction', their solidity disappears. The 'notion of the world as composed from discrete, compact, separated things' should be abandoned (ibid.).

4. A doctrine of internal or intrinsic relations is proposed. Naess described this in 1973 as 'an intrinsic relation between A and B, so that without the relation, A and B are not the same things'.[2] This is sometimes expressed as 'everything being constituted by its relationships'. Rather than the world being made from objects which are fundamentally independent, but which may touch one another externally and so cause an effect, it is the relationships which fundamentally constitute what is. Relationality is more fundamental than independence.

5. Following from this, there is a rejection of the categorization of 'objects and subjects'. While the subjective and the objective as perspectives still exist, they are not conceived of as properties pertaining to some items and not others.

6. No ontological divide between humans/non-humans, spirit/ matter, soul/body. 'The two aspects of nature, those of extension and thought are both complete aspects of one single reality' (Naess 1977: 419).

7. The world is seamless and cannot be divided into independent parts, neither can parts of the world be analysed in isolation from the whole.

If this analysis is considered in the light of Phillips's categories, all the elements of Holism 1(a)–(e) are represented. In addition, there is a strong suggestion of Holism 2: that even if knowledge of the whole is obtained, it cannot be explained by examining its parts and their interactions.

However, it will be noted that deep ecology also stresses an element not prominent in Phillips's account: the rejection of categorizing subjects and objects. This is not a necessary stress of holistic thought (although it could be said that, by its emphasis on interconnectedness, it leans in such a direction). It is, however, significant to deep ecological thinking.

---

[2] This analysis is virtually identical to that found in Bradley (1946) and McTaggart (1921).

Holism and Process Thinking

Process philosophy is frequently described as holistic and organic, the two terms being closely associated. Whitehead himself, as we have seen, explicitly describes his philosophy as a philosophy of organism. This immediately sounds like Holism 1(e) establishing a similarity between process thinking and deep ecology (which could well be described as an organic philosophy). It is important, however, to note that a coincidence of vocabulary between process thinking and deep ecology does not necessarily mean a coincidence of conceptuality. It is necessary to explore further what Whitehead means by 'organism' in order to see how similar his philosophy might be to deep ecology.

For Whitehead (1938a: 81), the world should be 'founded upon the ultimate concept of organism'. Actual occasions can be described as organisms; indeed, 'Biology is the study of the large organisms, while physics is the study of the small organisms' (ibid. 129). Like deep ecologists, Whitehead supports this organismic view of actuality by reference to his understanding of relativity and quantum physics, both new concepts when Whitehead was writing (indeed, not existing until virtually the conclusion of Whitehead's mathematical and scientific career). He argues that his philosophy of organism is compatible with the discoveries of modern physics, a conviction which frames his methodology in *Science and the Modern World*. As with deep ecologists, Whitehead does not say that he *derives* his conclusions from modern science but, like them, sometimes he is very close to so doing. For Whitehead, as a mathematician/mathematical physicist, this is to some degree inevitable.[3]

Returning to the earlier seven-point summary of holism in deep ecology will assist in a further comparison with holism in process thinking. The fifth point, the question of subjects and objects, provides a good place to begin, since this lies at the heart of the metaphysics of process thinking, as it does in deep ecology.

Both Whitehead and deep ecologists cite Descartes (widely vilified in environmental philosophy) as affirming the centrality of the subject/object distinction. Descartes viewed the human mind,

---

[3] As Emmet (1933: Preface) remarks 'I am constantly conscious that the way in which his mind is working is that of a pure mathematician. I have an uneasy suspicion that [his ideas] probably connote something quite different to someone with a trained understanding of the mathematical ideas involved in them.'

and God, as the only subjects; everything else was perceived to be an object. This perspective raises two problems for process thinking: first that, apart from God, subjectivity is confined to humanity, and secondly that it is seated in the mind, not in feeling. As we have seen, Whitehead attributed subjectivity to all actual occasions; human consciousness is just a peculiarly concentrated form of the experience which is present in all existence, indeed which defines all existence. Further, it is not identified with mind or thinking; there is no mind or thinking in Whitehead which is separable from feeling or emotion. Thus he can say of Descartes:

> [His] structure presupposes that the subject/object pattern is the fundamental structural pattern of existence. I agree with this presupposition, but not in the sense in which subject-object is identified with knower-known. I contend that the notion of mere knowledge is a high abstraction, and that conscious discrimination itself is a variable factor only present in the more elaborate examples of occasions of experience. The basis of experience is emotional. (Whitehead 1948: 171)

As every actual occasion, when coming to be, exercises subjectivity, so, once it is complete, does it become objective—to be 'felt' or prehended by other concrescing actual occasions. There are no longer pieces of matter (*res extensa*) that are purely objects—or anything (*res cogitans*) that is purely subject. Subjective and objective perspectives pertain to all that is actual, at different phases of existence. Thus Whitehead has *reinterpreted* the understanding of subject/object to fit with his philosophy of organism, and, with this reinterpretation, 'the subject-object relation is the fundamental structure of existence' (ibid.).

How far does this interpretation dovetail with that of deep ecology? Deep ecologists also argue that the traditional understanding of subject/object as divisible categories is obsolete. Callicott (wearing his deep ecology rather than his Humean hat), argues, for instance, that quantum physics indicates that we cannot escape from subjectivity: 'to make an observation, energy must be exchanged between the object of observation and the observer' (Callicott 1985: 269). In other words, there are no 'objects' and 'subjects' but only *interactions*.

Both process thinking and deep ecology seek to undercut the mechanistic-science idea of 'subject' and 'object'. In fact, both reject dualism of any sort: of subject/object, mind/matter, extension/thought. This is as clear in Whitehead and other process thinkers as it is in deep ecology. Hartshorne (1970: 112) comments: 'The real difference between mind and matter is not an absolute difference in kind of singulars but a) a relative difference in kind (between high and low forms) of experiencing singulars, this difference falling within Mind in the broadest sense, and b) a difference in kind, not between singular and singular, but between singular and inadequately apprehended group.' There is no divide between mind (meaning subjectivity) and matter. There are merely differing degrees of mind (depending on the strength of the mental poles of the actual occasions) and inanimate objects, which lack mind as a whole, but which are composed from actual occasions with minds. Thus there is no bifurcation in reality. All things have some degree of animation, even if only in the actual occasions which compose them.

This attack on dualism is one which would be strongly defended by deep ecologists, although for differing reasons. (Many would be unhappy with Hartshorne's suggestion of 'grading' subjectivity for instance.) Involved in this denial of dualism, for both deep ecology and process thinking, is the question of interrelatedness and inter-connectedness. This has several important aspects: the idea of the 'web' or 'field'; the tendency to dissolve the individual into the web or field; and the doctrine of internal relations.

Here again, some terminological caution is required. Deep eco-logists, and their scientific sources such as Capra, argue that 'hol-ism' must be seen in opposition to 'atomism'. This opposition even forms part of Phillips's definition of holism. Here, atomism is interpreted as meaning fundamentally composed from independ-ent elementary solid particles. Yet Whitehead (1978: 35) can describe his own philosophy as atomic: 'Thus, the ultimate meta-physical truth is atomism. The creatures are atomic.' Whitehead means by 'atomic' something rather different: not that the world is fundamentally composed from solid, independent particles, but that it is made up from tiny discrete units—the actual occasions.

Every concrescing actual occasion is surrounded by other, per-ishing actual occasions which it can positively or negatively pre-hend. The closeness between past and presently actualizing occasions may be so close as to almost equal identity. Indeed, it is this kind of identity—where a new occasion virtually repeats the content of the old—that creates the enduring objects we recognize.

Enduring objects endure because the new actual occasions composing them are indistinguishable in the short term and recognizable in the long term as what they used to be. The old has emptied itself into the new, the past continues to live in the present. This means that Whitehead (1938*b*: 121) can envisage a strong connection between an actual occasion in the present and the past: 'The data for any one pulsation of actuality consist of the full content of the antecedent universe as it exists in relevance to that pulsation.' This closeness also applies to the future, which, says Whitehead (1948: 187), 'lives entirely in its antecedent world. Each moment of experience confesses itself to be a transition between two worlds, the immediate past and the immediate future . . . Also, this immediate future is immanent in the present with some degree of structural definition.'

Thus, process thinking envisages very close *temporal* interconnectedness: there are no abrupt discontinuities between past and present, present and future (a view common to organic political philosophers, such as Richard Hooker). However, this temporal interconnectedness is not identical with the interconnectedness of deep ecology, where the emphasis is on interconnectedness over space, not time. This distinction echoes that between 'successive' and 'coexistent' laws of society suggested by Mill in *The Philosophy of Scientific Method* (1950: 347–8). Process interconnectedness emphasizes the temporal or successive, while deep ecology envisages interconnectedness as simultaneous or coexistent. One might also call these 'vertical' and 'horizontal' interconnectedness (as Phillips, in another context).[4]

Whitehead (1948: 190) insists that simultaneous actual occasions are independent of one another.[5] Actual occasions can only 'feel' or 'prehend' perished actual entities which are complete or which have reached their satisfaction: 'It is the description of

[4] Although as Sprigge points out (in a personel communication, 1993) this distinction may be more apparent than real as spatial interconnection, if it is causal, must also be temporal.

[5] Hartshorne (1972: 87) considers this lack of contact between simultaneous occasions to be very 'troubling': 'Can it be without qualification true that contemporaries are causally independent? Since they are all immanent in God and he immanent in them, must they not be immanent in one another?' In 1984: 108 while referring to several possible explanations of influence of contemporary actual occasions on one another, he leaves the question open. If influence between contemporaries is accepted—although it is not a Whiteheadian idea—then this would bring process thinking and deep ecology still closer.

contemporary events that they happen in causal independence of each other. 'Thus two contemporary occasions are such that neither belongs to the past of the other.' Temporal interconnectedness cannot apply to simultaneous occasions. This by necessity has an impact on spatial interconnectedness, because at any one instant of time, all the occasions which are actualizing are actualizing independently of one another. There is no connection between them—in other words no immediate spatial connection, as Whitehead continues, 'Indirectly, via the immanence of the past and the immanence in the future, the occasions are connected. But the immediate activity of self-creation is separate and private, so far as contemporaries are concerned.' What form does this immanence take? Two contemporary occasions, A and B, may have prehended the same preceding actual occasion, C, and therefore the occasion is, objectively, within both of them: 'C is objectively immortal in both A and B, thus in this indirect sense, A is immanent in B and B is immanent in A. But the objective immortality of A does not operate in B, nor does that of B operate in A. As individual actual entities, A is shrouded from B, and B is shrouded from A.' It is this indirect immanence that characterizes spatial interconnectedness for Whitehead. At any one instant of time, there is only indirect interconnectedness between concrescing actual occasions.

Whilst in a frozen instant of time it is the discrete nature of actual occasions which is foremost, this is a narrow, if very important perspective. At a broader level, of longer time-spans, Whitehead can suggest a very intense kind of interconnectedness. The individual nature of the actual occasions does not mean their independence from all other occasions, but only contemporary ones. Whitehead (1978: 28) indeed goes so far as to say, 'Whenever we think of some entity, we are asking "What is it fit for here?" In a sense, every entity pervades the whole world.' To unpack this a little, we must consider what Whitehead understands by *internal relations*.

Phillips considers that a Hegelian doctrine of internal relations underlies all expositions of Holisms 1 and 2, and is the most important constituent of a philosophy of holistic organism. He uses as an example F. H. Bradley's *Appearance and Reality*. Bradley's doctrine of internal relations resembles Whitehead's in some respects although not in all.[6] Whitehead's most detailed exposition

---

[6] Whitehead has a very ambiguous attitude towards Bradley. Despite periodic penetrating criticisms of him, he comments, 'my final outcome is, after all, not so

of internal relationality is found in *Science and the Modern World*: 'The theory of relationships between events at which we have now arrived is based first upon the doctrine that the relatednesses of an event are all internal relations, so far as concerns that event, though not necessarily so far as concerns the other *relata*' (Whitehead 1938*a*: 147). The emptying of actual occasions into one another means that each actual occasion is, to some extent, determined by the actual occasions with which it is surrounded. Without them, the concrescing actual occasion would take a very different form. Thus Whitehead can say that if an occasion is extracted from its environment, its very existence would be destroyed. It is this formulative nature of relationships that makes them internal. Internal relationships have the power to affect and to change—in this case, to form—those who are involved in them. Every concrescing occasion is involved in a large number of internal relations with perished occasions which it is positively prehending.

However, Whitehead's explanation of internal relationships makes a further, key point: 'not necessarily so far as concerns the other relata'. The 'other relata' are the objective actual occasions being prehended by the actualizing occasion. They are complete; their subjectivity has perished, they cannot be changed by their relations. All relations are external to the objective actual occasion, and internal to the concrescing actual occasion. That is to say, the internal relations are one way—into the future. They are not *mutually* determined by one another.

This illustrates a significant difference between Whitehead's and Naess's views of internal relations. Naess defined an internal relation as 'An intrinsic relation between A and B so that without the relation, A and B are not the same things'.[7] These are reciprocal internal relations; Whitehead's are not reciprocal. If A is the complete, objective actual entity, it remains unaffected by its prehension by B, the concrescing actual entity. Naess thus envisages mutual and simultaneous interactions from different locations;

greatly different' (Whitehead 1978: xiii). Ford argues that in the early 1920s Whitehead himself held Bradleyan views on internal relations and that he developed his distinctive interpretation only later. Certainly, by the time Whitehead wrote *Process and Reality*, his views on the asymmetricality of internal relations were developed; and, as I made clear in the Introduction, it is with Whitehead's mature ideas that I am predominantly concerned.

[7] Thus Bradley's symmetrical internal relations have more in common with Naess than with Whitehead.

Whitehead envisages one-way, temporally staggered interactions from identical or surrounding locations. Internal relations in process thinking are successive, not simultaneous; asymmetrical, rather than symmetrical. It is the symmetrical, mutual nature of internal relations in much holistic philosophy—including deep ecology—which Hartshorne blames for its general lack of acceptance. The process understanding of internal relations, he argues, 'avoids the mysticism of wholes acting on their very own parts, a notion which would imply unrestricted and symmetrical internal relations between every part and every other, dissolving all definite structures into ineffable unity, a consequence which has caused clear thinkers to turn away from "holistic" or "organicist" doctrine' (Hartshorne 1962: 199). This process understanding of internal relations, according to Hartshorne, allows for the possibility of separation which is explicitly denied in most holistic metaphysics, including deep ecology, and explicitly contradicts Holism 1(c) (that the whole determines the nature of its parts). Indeed, this discreteness at the heart of process thinking limits its holism, certainly in Phillips's terms; one may perhaps describe process thinking as a 'restricted Holism 1'.

What effect does this have on the degree of interconnectedness in Whitehead's philosophy *vis-à-vis* that of deep ecology? It suggests interrelatedness of a different kind, although not necessarily of a lesser intensity. It allows Whitehead (1938b: 225) to state:

Thus, as disclosed in the fundamental essence of our experience, the togetherness of things involves some kind of doctrine of mutual immanence. In some sense or other, this community of the actualities of the world means that each happening is a factor in the nature of every other happening. The whole antecedent world conspires to produce a new occasion.

'Mutual immanence' is an expression which one might find in Holism 1 and certainly in the work of deep ecologists; but here again there is a terminological difference. Whitehead refers to the past and future being immanent in the present; deep ecology primarily to things which presently exist being immanent in one another (although this would, of course, also involve the past and future being immanent in the present).

This has interesting implications for the language of 'web' or 'field', and the tendency to dissolve the individual into the web in process thinking. Again, terminological caution is required here. In process thinking, 'individual' usually refers to the *actual occasion*, not to the human or non-human individual. To call a human being 'individual' is to speak with a high degree of abstraction. A human individual is more fundamentally seen as a society. Naess (1973: 80) makes a similar point, but about our language for human individuals rather than actual occasions: 'The total field model dissolves not only the man-in-environment concept, but every compact thing-in-milieu concept—except when talking at a superficial or preliminary level of communication.' For Naess, talking about objects is abstract, not because they are really societies of actual occasions, but because objects cannot be separated out from their environment. Naess (1989: 50) wants to escape from the idea of 'fixed, solid points' altogether, whilst 'retaining the relatively straightforward, persistent relations of interdependence'. Whitehead also rejects the concept of fixed solid points; but retains ultimate units, the actual occasions, which while neither exactly fixed nor solid, form the discrete elements at the base of his system. They cannot be reduced entirely to their relationships, because while these relations have, as I have said, a formulative part in their concretion, ultimately the freedom of the occasion determines its shape. What the occasion decides is *not* entirely governed by its relationships. Whitehead and Naess do, none the less, have something significant in common here: the treatment of the individual in its more usual sense: the enduring object, the plant, animal, or human. The disjunctive, distinct nature of the individual is weakened. For Whitehead, the individual becomes a society in the midst of other societies, albeit a closely knit one; for Naess, the individual dissolves into a web of interactions.

It remains to consider, briefly, the process response to Holism 2, which, while not explicit in deep ecological writing, would probably not be refuted by it. Could process thinkers accept that if one has the whole, it could not be explained by knowledge of its individual constituents and their interactions?

The two fundamental 'wholes' in process thinking are the actual occasion and God (in Hartshorne's terms, the cosmic organism). Taking only the actual occasion in this context (since this would seem an odd question to ask of God!) one can reframe this statement of Holism 2, 'Can the new actual occasion be explained by knowledge of its constituents and their interactions?' It is at this point that process thinking introduces a fresh dynamic. As described in Chapter 1, objective actual occasions, eternal objects (for Whitehead if not Hartshorne), and the initial aim provided by the primordial and the consequent nature of God are all vital elements in the concrescing of any actual occasion. But the way in which the occasion as a whole is finally actualized is dependent on its exercise of freedom; that is, on its own subjectivity. This certainly could not be predicted (Holism 1); but does it suffice as an explanation? (Holism 2). This again brings us to the question of the aim of the occasion, which was examined in Chapter 1. Can the choice of an occasion be explained, or is it purely arbitrary or irrational? Whitehead, while emphasizing that an occasion is more than the sum of its parts (Holism 1 (b)), certainly suggests that one could explain why an occasion made the choice it did (Whitehead 1978: 87). If this is the case, process thinking would not support Holism 2.

By comparing the holism of process thought to that of deep ecology, I hope to have indicated already some of the complexities of their relationship. These are further complicated when the concept of the extended self is taken into consideration.

The Extension and Realization of the Self in Deep Ecology

As early as 1974 in 'The Glass is on the Table', Naess expounds the concept of the extended self, and it is likely that this philosophy lay behind his formative paper on deep ecology in 1973. As with holism, at the root of Naess's concept of the extended self is the intuition that 'all things are ultimately one'. This intuition is interpreted by Naess in Spinozan terms: there is ultimately only one substance, God or Nature, of which everything which exists is a manifestation. This unity of substance immediately works to undercut the idea of radically different beings, or selves. Ultimately, all beings are one; their natures cannot be as disjunctive as we (in the West) are inclined to imagine. The 'Western' self is too narrowly constituted; there are, Naess argues, several selves:

The ego, the self with a small 's' and then this great Self, the Self with a capital 'S', the atman . . . the power of which gradually increases. You might still say the limits are those of your body, but there you would have to include units of your central nervous systems such as, for instance, those corresponding to the Milky Way and the Andromeda nebula in so far as you have sensuous or other bodily interactions with them . . .

(Naess 1974: 34)

Naess contrasts the idea of the self as identified with the human body and its traditional 'selfish' desires, to a broader self which stretches far beyond the individual, ultimately encompassing the vision that all is one and hence that one's self is everything and everything is in one's self: 'Humans can develop in such a way that in a sense, their selfs include the other selfs in a certain way' (ibid.).

Here, Naess envisages a kind of physically extended self: that inasmuch as one's body interacts with things as far away as the Milky Way, they are part of one's greater self. One cannot confine oneself to one's bodily limits in a strict sense because of physical interaction with what is outside the body. This develops the inter-connectedness which features so strongly in Naess's philosophy: since the individual is physically dissolved—'biologically we are just centres of interaction in one great field', as Naess tells Ayers—it is physically impossible to draw boundaries of self.

However, to suggest that this was all that Naess meant by his concept of the extended self would be misleading. Naess also describes his concept of self as: 'something like: if I hurt you, I hurt myself. Myself is not my ego, but something capable of vast development . . . ' This is a kind of psychological identification with other selves so that their pain becomes ours, and hence, in Naess's terminology, their selves part of our self. If we concentrate on developing our greater self, we can come to identify, and feel with, not only all other human selves, but with the Oneness at the basis of all that is.

Naess's concept of the extended self, and his twin concept of self-realization, are most fully developed in *Ecology, Community and Lifestyle* (1989). Here, again based on his intuition that all life is ultimately one, he urges identification with all that is: 'by identifying with greater wholes, we partake in the creation and mainte-nance of the whole. We thereby share in its greatness' (ibid. 173). The greater our identification with all that is around us, the greater our self-realization. In the light of this understanding of self, Naess (ibid. 197) places self-realization as the most basic norm of his

---

[8] Fox (1990: 220) qualifies this use of the word 'norm': it is not any kind of moral 'ought' but 'the overarching or most generally formulated positive goal or value

system.[8] Self-realization is greatest when those with whom one's self is identified are most realized too. As Naess comments, 'The higher the Self-realization attained by anyone, the more its further increase depends upon the Self-realization of others.' This leads him to advocate 'Self-realization for all living beings' (ibid. 197). Thus, from the concept of the extended self, Naess has derived an imperative to allow and even encourage the flourishing of all life:

> The greater our comprehension of togetherness with other beings, the greater the identification and the greater care we will take. The road is also opened thereby for delight in the wellbeing of others and sorrow when harm befalls them. We seek what is best for ourselves, but through the extension of the self, our 'own' best is also that of others. The own/not own distinction survives only in grammar, not in feeling. (ibid. 175)

Naess's concept of the extended self encompasses both physical and psychological identification with what lies outside the immediate human body. The self is in a constant state of change and process,[9] and may reach ever-greater depths of self-realization, achieved by ever-increased identification with others and with their realization. Ultimately, all selves are one, and our perception of division between them is due to our limited perspective.

This theme is taken up by more recent work in the deep ecology movement. Drengson (1988: 86–7), for example, comments: '[Deep ecology] directs us to develop our own sense of self until it becomes Self, that is until we realize through deepening ecological sensibilities that each of us forms a union with the natural world and that protection of the natural world is the protection of ourselves . . .' Protection of the non-human world thus can be justified as a protection of one's Self. Destroying the natural environment means destroying part of oneself or preventing oneself from reaching the fullest possible self-realization.

Fox is the most prominent exponent of extended-self theory in deep ecology, regarding it as deep ecology's 'defining characteristic'. In his early articles, Fox's emphasis falls on holism and explanations of the characteristics of holism which we have already investigated. It is Fox's insistence on the dissolution of

within his own attempt'. Thus, it is not binding on all, but only as part of Naess's system.

[9] As is made clear in Naess's unpublished paper 'Gestalt Thinking and Buddhism' (n.d.).

the boundaries between any individual and her environment that forms the basis of his concept of the extended self, or at least the physical aspect of it. The world is fundamentally one. As with Naess, on whom Fox is partially dependent, the extended self is not purely conceived in a physical sense. Fox opposes destruction of the natural world not because of its usefulness to us, or because of its value in or to itself, but because 'it is part of My/Our wider self; its diminishment is My/Our diminishment' (Fox 1986: 71–2). This suggests a psychological interpretation of the extended self, one which is developed in his later *Towards a Transpersonal Ecology* (1990). Drawing on the work of transpersonal psychologists, Fox argues like them, that 'trans' bears the meaning 'beyond' and so 'transpersonal ecology' means 'psychological identity with the ecological world beyond the confines of the person' or more particularly, beyond the selfish individual ego.[10] Fox urges deep ecologists to 'realize one's ecological, wider or big self' (ibid. 268).

To support this contention, Fox turns to physical field theory, using it as an image for the human psyche. As with the natural world, the psychological self has been wrongly conceived as narrow, atomistic, or particle-like. Our image of the self must change to become field-like or web-like. The key to this transformation for Fox, as Naess, is identification. Fox looks at modes of identification more carefully than Naess, suggesting that there are three different varieties: personal, ontological, and cosmological. Primary for Fox is ontological identification (identification with what exists, that which stands out of nothingness) and cosmological identification (identification with the All, the great underlying oneness of the cosmos). These must come prior to personal identification and provide a context for it. Personal identification suggests the priority both of those to whom we are closest and of the most personal beings—i.e. humans and mammals—and has no place for identification with nature in a wider sense without significant anthropomorphism. Ontological and cosmological identification, on the other hand, allow identification in a broader sense: 'impartial identification with all entities' (ibid.). Fox adds, as a coda, that he is not intending to oppose personal identification, but to shift emphasis from the personal to the cosmological

---

[10] While drawing vocabulary from transpersonal psychology, Fox does not advocate its methodology wholeheartedly, considering it to be anthropocentric in expression, if not in essence.

and ontological. That is to say 'ontologically and cosmologically based identification are seen as providing a context for personally based identification' (ibid.).

Fox, like Naess, links this closely with self-realization. Cosmological and ontological identification with all means, according to Fox, the desire to 'promote the freedom of all entities to unfold in their own ways; in other words, actions that tend to promote symbiosis'. Self-realization renders morality superfluous, since once one has identified oneself with all that is, the desire for self-realization dovetails with the desire of others to unfold in their own ways (ibid. 218). Thus there is no conflict and no need for moral guidelines.

For deep ecologists then, the extended self and self-realization are key metaphysical concepts. With their approach in mind, we can consider whether the extension and realization of the self have a role to play in process metaphysics. To explore this, it is first necessary to examine process conceptions of the self.

Process Thinking about the Extension and Realization of the Self

Central to process thought are the actual occasions, of which everything that exists including human beings are essentially composed. Whitehead (1978: 89) considers that 'the life of man is a historic route of actual entities which . . . inherit from each another'. The enduring personality is 'the historic route of actual occasions which are severally dominant in the body at successive instants' (ibid. 119).

It is the jurisdiction or control of the dominant actual occasion that creates the boundary of the individual human self. It generates unity within the individual: a 'special strand of unity within the general unity of nature' (Whitehead 1948: 183). That which is beyond the jurisdiction of the dominant occasion is beyond the body. However, the boundary is not tightly delineated. Whitehead leaves room for considerable movement and change. At a simple level, this is true of all that exists, even those enduring objects which lack a dominant actual occasion. Whitehead (1920: 120) insists, for instance, that while we think something like Cleopatra's Needle is a solid and enduring object, it is, in fact, an event or a society of events, subject to change: 'A physicist who looks on that part of the life of nature [Cleopatra's Needle] as a dance of electrons, will tell you that daily it has lost some molecules and found others . . . Where does Cleopatra's Needle begin, and where does it end?' If this is true of a 'democratic' society of actual occasions, lacking in a presiding occasion, it is also true of a 'monarchical' society such as a human being. Physically, the degree of interaction between individual humans and the world around them is immense. Constantly, new elements enter the body and old ones pass out. In Whiteheadian terms, one might say that constantly new concrescing occasions largely formed by prehending perished occasions from beyond the jurisdiction of the presiding occasion, are coming within the control of the presiding occasion. Similarly, other actual occasions, formed largely by prehending perished occasions from within the jurisdiction of the presiding occasion, are passing beyond its control.

This constantly changing pattern makes it impossible to physically confine the individual human self in process thinking. As early in his philosophical career as 1920, Whitehead (ibid. 107) comments:

The functions of the body shade off into those of other events, so that for some purposes, the percipient event is to be reckoned as merely part of the bodily life and for other purposes it may even be reckoned as more than the bodily life. In many respects, the demarcation is purely arbitrary, depending where on a sliding scale you choose to draw the line.

This understanding of the physical human self is closely related to Whitehead's approach to the psychological human self. Whitehead asserts that we have a peculiar 'intimacy of association' with our own bodies; they are for us more definite and distinct than the rest of the natural world. Having said this, the feelings that we have for parts of our body, of pain perhaps, or pleasure, are 'the feelings of derived feelings'. We are not immediately conscious of pain; rather, we feel the pain, for instance, of the actual occasions constantly coming to be in the stimulated or damaged nerve endings of our body. While 'feeling the body as functioning' is still our most primitive perception, it is not different *in kind* from feeling the rest of the world: the body is only a peculiarly intimate part of the world.

These factors certainly open the possibility of an extended self in process thinking. First, the boundaries of the physical self with the rest of the world are very loosely drawn. Secondly, there is no privileged immediate identification with, or feeling of, aspects of one's own body that is qualitatively different from one's ability to identify with or feel the world outside the body, or beyond the jurisdiction of the presiding actual occasion.[11] Feeling, or even identifying with, that which lies outside the body remains perfectly possible. Indeed, in some sense it is inevitable.

As we have already seen, according to Whitehead (1948: 91) any actual occasion 'has in its nature, a reference to every other member of the community, so that each unit is a microcosm, representing in itself the entire, all inclusive universe'. Thus, although the concrescing occasion negatively prehends some parts of the universe, and grades others according to relevance, the entire universe is necessary for each occasion to become what it is. This has considerable implications for the idea of the extended self. In one sense every actual occasion has an extended self, in that the entire past universe has gone into its composition. This is, of course, also true of the human being which, as a society of actual occasions, is intensely connected with the past world. The entire past world has made the self what it is. The distinction of the past of the self from the past general world, and the present of the self from the past general world, becomes blurred, and the separation of self from world more difficult.

This is not a surprising conclusion, in view of the observations made in Chapter 1 concerning the nature of the human self in process thinking. Even Hartshorne's idea of the dipolar self (with an unchanging essence and a constantly changing actuality) does not provide a strong sense of personal unity—hence the preference for the term 'personal sequence' rather than 'person'. Indeed, process thinking, as we have seen, tends to weaken understanding of the human self in two ways. First, the *unity* of the self tends to be fragmented into a society of occasions (albeit ones which are closely interlocking and governed by a dominant actual occasion). Consciousness is seen as narrowly selective. Secondly, the *permanence* of the self tends to be undercut, with the person becoming a constant flux of actual occasions. The concept of a substantial, permanent, united self is, according to process thinking, both an abstraction and a simplification of reality.

---

[11] Although as Sprigge points out (personal communication, 1993), this point could equally be made of Cartesianism!

This leads process thinkers to interesting perspectives on the concept of an extended self. Hartshorne argues that it is not only the past of one's self that merges into the more general past; it is also the future of one's self—or preferably one's personal sequence—that merges with the more general future. Thus it becomes impossible to separate one's own future self, and, as a corollary, one's own future interests, from the general future and general interests. Alongside this blending of the particular and general there is also the fact that since the 'self' is a constantly changing set of occasions, it becomes difficult for self-interest to exist at all. As Hartshorne (1970: 191) explains: 'Any future self, call it mine or not mine, which can benefit from my present act will be numerically a new and distinct unit of concrete reality. Hence, self interest has no privileged metaphysical base whatsoever.' Whatever happens in the future, whether or not it is perceived to be part of one's own personal sequence, is something quite new. Any act to benefit the future must be altruistic, since it cannot benefit one's present self, that is, the society of actual occasions currently constituting oneself. Thus Hartshorne can go on to say, 'We can love the other as ourselves, because even the self, as future, is also another.' In this sense, by limiting the self, Hartshorne has also extended it. The future is both not oneself and entirely oneself.

Thus process thinking suggests an understanding of the self based on inner plurality and a kind of ephemerality. This leaves the way open for some sort of concept of an extended self—at the most fundamental level, a physical one. This physically extended self has both similarities with and differences from that of Naess.

Naess explicitly comments that his understanding of the underlying oneness of existence derives from Spinoza. By looking at Whitehead's remarks on this aspect of Spinoza, we may discern how close Naess's and Whitehead's concept of the extended self might be. Whitehead (1978: 7) comments that 'the philosophy of organism is closely allied to Spinoza's scheme of thought'. However, he claims to *invert* Spinoza: 'Spinoza bases his philosophy upon the monistic substance, of which the actual occasions are inferior modes. The philosophy of organism inverts this point of view' (ibid. 81). Where Spinoza emphasizes the priority of the underlying Oneness, of which the occasions are but modes, Whitehead would emphasize the priority of the Many, of which the One is composed. 'The World', he says 'is primordially Many' (ibid.

349). This multiplicity at the heart of existence contrasts with Naess as well as Spinoza, founding the extended self on a different principle.

Despite this, the temporal interlocking of the Many in Whitehead means that, in practice, there is considerable similarity between process thinking and deep ecology. The absorption of the past into the present and of the present into the future leads to a temporal oneness in process thinking, similar in effect to the spatial oneness of deep ecology. The extended self across time becomes as the extended self across space. Both process thinking and deep ecology dissolve the human self—deep ecology into the One, process thinking into the Many. While these may seem to be diametrically opposed philosophies, they are identical in their result—the undercutting of a strong concept of an independent individual self. The physical self becomes more diffuse, and thereby extended.

What then of the response of process thought to psychological identification rather than the physical extension in deep ecology? As an obvious beginning one might say that because of the nature of the self in process thinking, the possible fields of identification shift. That is to say, if humans became aware of their own inner complexity, their contingency and interdependence with the world around them, the temporary nature of their current self, and the fact that their own future self is another self, then the possibility of extended identification is increased. In other words one could argue that recognition of the extended nature of the human self might lead to identification with an extended self. Whitehead (1938*b*: 29–30) himself hints at such an identification:

In fact the world beyond is so intimately entwined in our own natures that unconsciously we identify our more vivid perspectives of it with ourselves. For example, our bodies lie beyond our own individual existence. And yet they are a part of it. We think of ourselves as so intimately entwined in bodily life that man is a complex unity—body and mind. But the body is part of the external world—continuous with it. In fact it is just as much nature as anything else there—a river, a mountain or a cloud.

Here he reinforces his assertion that the human body is continuous with the natural world and that our natures are inextricably linked to our bodies, with which we identify. It is but a small step to move from this identification with the body (which is continuous with the rest of the natural world) to identification with the natural world (which is continuous with the body). The idea is certainly implicit in Whitehead's remarks. More explicit, perhaps, are the remarks of Cobb and Griffin (1977: 117):

The environment that is the true body would extend beyond it to all human beings and all creatures. The sense of mutual participation with all life and even with the inanimate world would radically alter the way in which we treat the environment. . . When we have existentially realized that we are continuous with the environment, that the environment is our body, then we will find new styles of life appropriate to that realization.

Here 'the sense of mutual participation' is very close to the idea of psychological identification. In Cobb and Griffin's mention of the inanimate world, there is a resemblance to Fox's cosmological and ontological identification: this participation goes beyond the personal, as perhaps does Whitehead's mention of rivers, mountains, and clouds. There is, then, considerable evidence to suggest that process thinking, physically at least, has a concept of the extended self similar to that in deep ecology. Does it also have a concept of self-realization?

Self-realization, in the context of the actual occasion, is vital in process thinking: it is the 'ultimate fact of facts' (Whitehead 1978: 222). It carries several nuanced ideas. First, realization means actualization, the process of coming to be. Whitehead frequently speaks of the realization of eternal objects, meaning their being brought into being from abstraction by actual occasions when they concresce. A second nuance is that of being fulfilled, of being realized, becoming what the occasion chooses to be, without hindrance. This self-realization, or satisfaction, is the attainment of value (Whitehead 1938a: 114). As was made clear in Chapter 1, the fullest self-realization that an actual occasion can achieve is maximum harmonious intensity of experience, taking into account the effects of its realization on other, future actual occasions. The aim should be, of course, at generating total maximum harmonious and intense experience for God rather than maximum individual self-realization, even if this means the sacrifice of experience for the occasion itself.

Moving beyond the scale of individual actual occasions to societies of occasions, in particular to the human being, similar principles apply. The individual human is encouraged to seek self-realization. However, Whitehead does not interpret this in Hobbesian fashion, as the individual human realizing herself at the expense of others. Rather, Whitehead identifies individual good/self-realization with social and cosmic good. Self-realization, even on the human level, is not a competitive activity; true self-realization is that which looks to maximum general good in the future, rather than to the projected future interests of the individual (which, as we have seen, are really those of another in any case). Self-realization for Whitehead is the aim at maximal future good of the cosmos.

This idea is not explicitly linked with that of the extended self in process thinking, although there is a natural connection. Whitehead (1938*b*: 161), for example, comments, 'It is the importance of others which melts into the importance of the self. Actuality is the self-enjoyment of importance. But this self-enjoyment has the character of the self-enjoyment of others melting into the enjoyment of the one self.' 'Self-enjoyment' as a concept is virtually identical with 'self-realization': the pleasurable experience of becoming actual.[12] But self-enjoyment, self-realization, cannot be achieved in isolation. It inevitably involves the self-enjoyment of others. Thus, the concept of the extended self in process thinking ties in very closely with self-realization *in its broadest sense*: where all that exists, or will exist, is a part of oneself.

Finally, then, we must consider how the concept of realizing the self in process thinking compares with that in deep ecology. Since process thinking begins at the level of the actual occasion rather than the human person, it inevitably has a somewhat different focus from deep ecology. Self-realization in process thinking is primarily concerned with the way in which an occasion concresces. However, there are extensive initial points of contact even here between process thinking and deep ecology.

Most actual occasions lack the sophistication to identify *psychologically* with other actual entities (except for dominant actual occasions in human beings); and an actual occasion is very clearly

---

[12] Becoming actual is always a pleasurable experience in Whitehead; all experience is valuable; evil is measured by degrees of value—value that is less than it might otherwise have been. The question as to whether this is a satisfactory explanation of evil is too large to be debated here!

discrete and therefore not *physically* identical with others. It is these two kinds of identification which, in deep ecology, mean that self-realization is extended self-realization. In process thinking, at the level of the actual occasion, the lure of God performs this function. It is this lure, providing the initial aim, which means that each concrescing occasion takes into account (or rather, is able to take into account, since it may choose not to do so) the interests of future occasions. Thus, for process thinking, as deep ecology, self-realization is that which is best overall, rather than best for the 'narrow' self. This is also true on the level of the human being, for Whitehead, as for deep ecologists. At the human level psychological identification is also possible.

One significant difference has, however, been glossed over here—a difference generated by the presence and role of God in the process system. For deep ecology, self-realization means the desire for realization for all. In process thinking, self-realization, both at the level of the occasion and at the level of the human self, means the desire for maximum realization of the consequent nature of God, a realization that can then be reflected back into the world through the prehension of other concrescing actual occasions. In other words, in a strange inversion, ultimate realization for process thinking aims at realizing the One, while ultimate realization for deep ecology is an aim at the realization of the Many (all that 'blossoms and flourishes'). This is of course, an over-simplification, since for deep ecology the Many are all expressions of the One; but the realization of the One is not perceived as an aim for deep ecologists. In a world without 'tragic conflict', to adopt Hartshorne's expression, this differentiation would be abstruse. However, in a world of conflict, the result is that process thinking and deep ecology respond differently, and face different problems. In a situation of conflict between two living beings, deep ecology primarily faces the problem of adjudication. If one identifies with both parties equally, as part of one's extended self, and wishes both of them to be maximally realized, how does one judge between them? The process system, in contrast, has a built-in principle of *adjudication*: that which provides maximum total richness of experience for the consequent nature of God. This raises problems of *justice*, rather than adjudication. Thus metaphysics issues in ethics, both for deep ecology and process thinking; and both approaches have important difficulties.

Problems with Holism and the Extension and Realization of the Self

This critique falls into two major categories: the *methodological* and the *substantial*. A methodological critique, while brief, is the necessary preliminary to a substantial critique; the methodological problem shadows many of the more specific problems of substance.

Methodology

Both deep ecology and process thinking are heavily indebted to certain interpretations of modern scientific investigation; in particular in the field of quantum physics. Both, however, fight shy of claiming to *derive* their ideas from modern science, preferring to speak, for instance, of 'inspiration'. However, there is little doubt that the language of 'scientists' such as Capra has shaped the expression and conceptuality of a significant amount of deep ecology, while Whitehead's own scientific background inevitably influenced his philosophical work. This raises important questions concerning the use of scientific theory in the construction of philosophical or metaphysical systems. Such uses of science have associated dangers.

First, many scientific theories are open to plural philosophical and sociological interpretation. A good example of this is evolutionary theory.[13] With the same data, the natural world can be seen to be a jungle red in tooth and claw, or a peaceful harmony of cooperating ecosystems. The fact that such plural interpretations are possible means that extreme caution is necessary when using scientific theory in the construction of a metaphysical system. The likelihood of neglecting either competing scientific theories derived from the same data, or competing philosophical interpretations of the same theory is very great.[14] This is specifically true of the use of quantum physics in deep ecology. Fox accepts an apparently oversimplified idealistic Copenhagen interpretation of quantum physics—an interpretation found universally in popular 'alternative' science writers such as Fritzjof Capra. In doing so, he neglects opposing scientific

---

[13] These uses of evolution are described by Midgley (1985) and Rachels (1991).
[14] This is not the place to examine work in the sociology and philosophy of science more fully. Issues about the social construction and uses of science are explored in the work of e.g. Kuhn (1962), Feyerabend (1993).

interpretations of quantum physics, such as the many worlds or alternative logic approaches.[15] He also neglects alternative philosophical interpretations of his preferred Copenhagen theory. Weizsacher, for instance, derives a much more strongly idealistic theme from the Copenhagen interpretation of quantum physics, and uses it to suggest the human mind-dependency of the natural world: an interpretation which Fox would reject.[16]

This is not intended to suggest that either Fox or the Copenhagen theory is necessarily mistaken; I am in no position to judge.[17] What is evident, however, is that quantum physics is open to a plurality of theoretical and philosophical interpretations; it can be read (as can many other scientific theories) politically, sociologically, philosophically, according to the climate of the time or the predisposition of the interpreter.

This 'reading' of scientific theory forms part of a more complex process of 'reading down' and 'reading up' in both deep ecological and process thinking. Whitehead, for example, takes as his starting-point human experience. The natural world, in the form of the actual occasions, is interpreted as being composed from something like human experience. This constitutes a kind of 'reading down' which is followed by a 'reading up' from the actual occasions into human society. Randall Morris (1986: 44) makes a similar point:

Not only do I believe that Whitehead considered human societies to exhibit the same principle as other societies, I also hold that he often writes as though an analogy exists between human individuals as a society and the interactions of actual occasions. In other words, human beings, while not of the same ontological status as actual occasions, appear to behave like actual entities in their mutual interactions.

Scientific theory (in Whitehead's case, quantum physics) is 'colonized' to support this reading of the natural world. (Indeed, as I suggested in Chapter 4, this is also true of Whitehead's treatment of evolutionary theory.) The result of such colonization is Whitehead's contention that 'the world of physics, described in terms of

---

[15] I am unqualified to comment on these scientific theories, and am indebted to Sylvan (1990: 86–90) for detailing the alternatives.

[16] C. F. von Weizsacher, *The History of Nature* (Chicago: Chicago University Press, 1949) as discussed by Marcuse (1972: 124).

[17] Sylvan (1985: 17), however, is prepared to judge, commenting that Capra 'extends the Copenhagen interpretation of quantum theory virtually to absurdity' giving it a 'wild, holistic, and anthropocentric interpretation'.

the transference of energy in the electro-magnetic field, has analogous properties to the sensory and emotional elements immediately experienced by us, as he describes the physical quanta of
energy as primitive throbs of emotional intensity' (Mays 1959:
19). It would not be unreasonable to suggest that Whitehead is
using quantum theory to support an interpretation of the world
which he already holds for other reasons, much as he used ecological theory to support his understanding of 'co-operation'
throughout nature. The problem with this, as with the deep ecological use of quantum theory, is that it is a partial interpretation,
neglecting competing alternatives. Scientific theories are selected
and interpreted according to their adherence to a pre-existing
philosophical or political agenda. This need not be a conscious
and cynical manipulation; rather a largely unconscious procedure
of innate sympathy with scientific theories that reflect (and reinforce) one's own view of the world.

For this reason, philosophical approaches which claim inspiration from particular scientific theories should be treated with the
utmost caution. Scientific theories have been used as support for a
wide range of political positions with results as extreme as geno-
cide. This particular case—the 'reading up' of certain interpretations of quantum physics into the world of normal human
perception—whilst leading to less extreme consequences, should
be treated with no less caution. Both process thinking and deep
ecology seem to be led into difficulties here. Even if their understanding of quantum physics is correct, the application of it beyond
the quantum level is extremely problematic.[18]

Substantial Critique: Holism

Of course, the philosophical concept of holism is not new with
deep ecology; nor are the problems raised by it. The first, and most
general, criticism of holistic thinking is its essential impossibility.
This is put most concisely by Russell: 'If all knowledge were knowledge of the universe as a whole, there would be no knowledge.'[19]

---

[18] Brennan (1988: 7) is, I think, making a similar point when he comments,
'Physics gives no special support either to idealism or to global holism—these
doctrines should be seen for what they are—metaphysical positions that are not
open to conclusive proof or refutation.'

[19] Russell, quoted in Phillips (1976: 29).

This applies directly to point 7 of my characterization of holism in deep ecology, if taken to the extreme: that the world is seamless and cannot be divided into independent parts, neither can parts of the world be analysed in isolation from the whole. Russell is essentially arguing that if one can only analyse the whole before one can have knowledge, one can never have knowledge. Phillips himself argues, in analogous vein, that one could never know any part of the world if one had to know the whole completely before one could know the part. Sylvan (1985: 12) raises a parallel point. Responding to Fox's claim that the perception of boundaries is a 'falling short' of deep ecological consciousness, he argues that, without boundaries, there could be no perception. Perception 'necessarily involves selection and discrimination and hence separation and boundaries'.

All these arguments contend that the very emphasis on undifferentiated wholeness in holistic thought renders it impossible. It is difficult for unmodified holism (which Sylvan calls 'extreme') to resist this argument: and some of the comments made by deep ecologists certainly sound as if they accept this degree of oneness. Naess's claim that there are no 'discrete and separable things' (point 3 of my characterization of holism) certainly lends itself to this interpretation. However, when faced with this question, deep ecologists deny that their holism is this thoroughgoing. Sylvan, for example, challenges Naess in his *Critique of Deep Ecology* by asking if Naess believes that there are 'No forests! No wilderness!' since nothing can be separated from the whole. Naess's response is to say '[Does Sylvan] think that *anyone* can be so silly?' (Naess 1985: 12). At the very least, this response suggests that Naess does not intend his earlier words to be taken at face value. In later work, Naess occasionally attempts to qualify his statements about holism: 'But the expression "drops in the stream of life" may be misleading if it implies that the individuality of the drops are lost in the stream. Here is a difficult ridge to walk: To the left we have the ocean of organic and mystic views, to the right the abyss of atomic individualism' (1989: 165). This statement is obviously intended as protection against the accusation that he is drowning in the 'ocean of organic and mystic views' and to suggest that he, himself, takes some kind of middle way between the two. In fact, this is the only evidence we have that he is not in the organic and mystic ocean, and since this remark runs contrary to the general tone of his work, it is difficult to take seriously.[20] Fox makes a more concerted attempt to come to terms with this accusation by suggesting that the images of knots in webs, fields of energy, and ripples on oceans, *while being perfectly acceptable*, are not his preferred choice. He (1990: 262) suggests the image of leaves on trees,[21] thus preserving both interconnectedness and individuality as well as impermanence. Since there are clear boundaries between leaves on trees, which appears to be the very reason why Fox uses the image, we can only assume that he has changed his mind and modified his holism accordingly.

Process thinking, at least in its expression in Whitehead, is much less easily accused of this lack of differentiation. This is because of the multiplicity which lies at its heart. Whitehead and Hartshorne attack dualism of mind and matter, not to suggest that there is an undifferentiated whole that contains both, but rather to propose a multiplicity of occasions which have both perspectives. This is not to say, however, that the problem of undifferentiated wholeness does not touch process thinking. Earlier Whitehead (1938b: 225) was quoted as saying, 'In some sense or other, this community of the actualities of the world means that each happening is a factor in the nature of every other happening. The entire antecedent world conspires to produce a new occasion.' For Whitehead, the whole world is implicated in the production of each actual occasion. Every occasion which ever existed is required for the production of a new occasion. But is there not here a failure to operate boundaries in time, much as deep ecology fails to operate boundaries in space? Is it not possible, and indeed on many occasions desirable, to say that one past event had no bearing on an event that followed it? Process thinking, of course, allows for the possibility of negative prehension: the concresing occasion selects what data it wishes to include, and which to reject, in its actualization. But is this enough? Is it really the case that everything which has ever happened is available to each occasion?

This argument seems to receive broad support from Ross (1983: 150), who comments (in a remark only obliquely related to his own argument):

---

[20] Capra (1982: 321) by whom Naess is influenced, actually advocates mystical concepts.

[21] He appears to be heavily dependent on Naess's remark about drops in oceans in *Ecology, Community and Lifestyle* although the dependence is unacknowledged.

It is fundamental that every occasion prehends other occasions. It is not so clear that every occasion must prehend the entire past world. Remote events in time or space do not appear to be relevant to each other even where the societies to which they belong are relevant. The principle of perspective [Ross's own interpretation of Whitehead] is compatible with events lost in time, having no relevance at all to the present. Whitehead's theory of experience does not permit this conclusion . . .

It is certainly possible to argue that, with respect to the past, process thinking also fails to make the necessary distinctions and to draw the necessary boundaries.

A second crucial criticism of holism is closely linked to the first: that, at root, things are only partially, rather than wholly, interdependent. This constitutes an attack on the concept of internal relations. There seems to be a certain amount of confusion around this question, so it is worth considering in some detail. The principle of internal relations, that is to say 'an intrinsic relation between A and B so that without the relation, A and B are not the same things', is a common characteristic of holistic writing. It is also the most commonly attacked. Phillips (1976: 155) for example, makes this his most basic criticism of holistic thought: 'A thing can still be the same thing when one of its characteristics is altered, for most characteristics are accompanying characteristics; and furthermore, most things are defined by reference to a cluster of characteristics, in which one or two characteristics can leave or join without the thing being different.' This point is made in varying ways by Sylvan and Brennan. Both want to emphasize that there are relationships which are not constitutive or necessary. Sylvan comments, for example, that the fact that A passed by B in a street does not make their relationship constitutive. Brennan (1988: 124), in a more biological analysis, distinguishes between supervenient and essential qualities and relationships. A supervenient quality, he maintains, is not essential to make A, A; it is still A whether or not it interacts with B or C. In other words, there are interactive but not internal relationships, which are not essentially determinative.

There are several responses which holists might make to this. They might argue that the internality of relations is only intended to operate at the fundamental level of interaction in the universe: for instance, Fox might argue that universal internal relations occur at the quantum level, while individual humans behave rather differently. This would be a very unusual argument for a deep ecologist to make, however, since it entails the drawing of boundaries and distinguishing between levels. A second, more likely argument, might be to suggest that even passing someone on the street really does change both parties, however infinitesimally; that all interactions actually do affect one's essential being—that everything is constantly being changed and shaped by what is around it. In other words, a holist might continue to affirm the primacy of internal relations. This is certainly what Fox (1986: 17) suggests in his response to Sylvan's critique.

At this point, both holists—in this case represented by deep ecologists—and those criticizing the holistic approach seem to be setting themselves at unnecessary odds. Holists insist that all relationships must be internal; their attackers that none are. But it seems obvious that some relations are internal and some are not. There are some relationships without which I would undoubtedly be a different person; these are internal relationships, constitutive of what I am in a fundamental sense. There are also relations which do not have such an effect. Even these two distinctions are not clear-cut; rather, there is a sliding scale of the degree to which I am affected by different relations.

This does not, however, let the holists off the hook, since the argument of holists such as Naess is that *all* relations are internal. To admit any non-internal relations in fact nullifies the whole position of unreformed holism, since it means the creation of distinctions and boundaries and the suggestion that there are things which are not interconnected in any profound sense. Thus, without a significant reform of the fundamental root of their holism, it is impossible for holists to admit the existence of relations which are not internal. Yet it seems impossible to deny that some relations are not internal. This is surely a blow at the heart of unmodified holistic thinking—and more particularly at the heart, in this context, of deep ecology.

How does this affect the modified holism of process thinking? Can Whitehead be attacked in a similar way? Whitehead is happy to admit the existence of certain external relations (that of the objective actual occasion that is being prehended by the concrescing occasion) as well as to insist that there is *no relation at all* between simultaneously concrescing actual occasions. Thus he is not open to the criticism that he advocates universal internal relations. However Whitehead's doctrine of internal relations remains problematic. He asserts, 'If you abolish the whole, then you abolish its parts; and if you abolish the part, then you abolish *that* whole' (Whitehead 1978: 288). The first clause states, quite comprehensibly, that if the whole is destroyed, inevitably the parts go with it. The second part of the clause, however, suggests that if one part of the whole goes, *something* may go on, *but it will no longer be the same* whole as before. In other words, the parts are constitutive of the nature of the whole.

The most obvious whole in process thinking, and the wholes meant in this context, are actual occasions. Thus Whitehead is arguing that everything that an actual occasion prehends is constitutive of its being. Without it, the occasion would no longer be the same: 'the relatednesses of an event are all internal relations, so far as concerns thatevent' (Whitehead 1938a: 82). All *active* relations are, thus, internal. The only non-internal relationship that Whitehead concedes, that of the objective actual occasion to the concrescing one, is a passive relationship. The objective actual occasion is after all perished, and being used as fodder for the new occasion. Where there is subjectivity, that is to say, in the concrescing actual occasion, all relationships are internal. Everything prehended is, therefore, essential to make the occasion what it is; had it prehended just very slightly different data, it would have been a different occasion. Thus, Whitehead is affirming that there are no interactive but non-essential, non-internal relationships. So Whitehead is, like deep ecology, open to the criticism that he cannot account for non-internal but interactive relationships.

Within the process tradition, some later thinkers have attempted to modify this Whiteheadian view. Ross (1983: 150) for instance, argues that his process philosophy of perspectives avoids the difficulties inherent in Whitehead's doctrine of internal relations. Birch and Cobb (1981: 87), however, reinforce Whitehead's view of internal relations:

An electromagnetic event, for example, cannot be viewed as taking place independently of the electromagnetic field as a whole. It both participates in constituting that field as the environment for all the events and also is constituted by its participation in that field. In abstraction from that field it is nothing at all. It does not have independent existence and then relate to the field. It is constituted by the complex interconnections which its place in the field gives to it. The same is true when the event in question is the functioning of a gene, a cell or a rabbit. This functioning does not exist in itself apart from its total environment and then relate to the environment. It is a mode of interacting, of being affected and affecting.

This passage is an important one since it illustrates both methodo-logical and substantial problems. Birch and Cobb have 'read down' into their understanding of electromagnetic fields an interpretation of internal relationships of which they already approve (whether or not it is accurate or merely one of many interpretations I do not know). Then they have 'read up' from the electromagnetic field into the world of normal perception: a rabbit. They then suggest that the rabbit and the electromagnetic event have the same rela-tions with their environment; that a rabbit does not exist in itself apart from its total environment. This seems rather odd. Certainly, a rabbit needs an environment, and indeed, must of necessity have one; but the relationship which a rabbit has with its environment is radically different from that which an electromagnetic event has with *its* environment. The rabbit is not an electromagnetic event, but a society which persists over time; movement to a different field would not in any meaningful sense make it a different rabbit. This argument of Birch and Cobb's comes from a combination of failure to draw boundaries between the level of the micro (the electro-magnetic field) and the level of the macro; together with a con-tentious doctrine of internal relations. The methodological problem shadows and supports the substantial problem; perhaps if Birch and Cobb had not been so aware of electromagnetic fields they might not have drawn such extreme parallels.

There is no doubt that, in this respect at least (although not necessarily where ecological *value* is concerned) Birch and Cobb, in *The Liberation of Life*, have driven process thinking closer to deep ecology—possibly due to the influence of Capra, with whom both are evidently familiar. This has the effect of making their work more open to the criticisms made of deep ecology. As we have seen, however, these difficulties are present in the work of White-head himself; Birch and Cobb merely accentuate this and drive it to its logical conclusion.

These two criticisms of holistic thought form the centre of a nexus of questions about deep ecology and process thinking. Ancil-lary concerns about the relations of wholes and parts and the objection to so-called 'mechanism' and 'reductionism' are also raised. These have, however, been adequately dealt with else-where.[22] I hope only to have raised some issues which question the understanding of holism in both deep ecology and process thinking.

Substantial Critique: The Extension and Realization of the Self

The concept of extension and realization of the self as it appears in deep ecology is found in similar form in the work of T. H. Green and Bradley. However, direct reference to these philosophers is very rarely made in deep ecological writing; Naess only explicitly mentions Eastern philosophical writing as an influence on this element of his thought. It seems likely that the emphasis on self-realization (without a direct link to the extended self) in Western liberal political and philosophical thought may have been of signi-ficance here. This liberal tradition, while examined as an influence on Whitehead and Hartshorne by Randall Morris, has not been considered as a source for deep ecology. Yet liberal philosophers (albeit with application only to the human) can sound very like deep ecologists. Hobhouse (1951: 561), for instance, comments: 'Instead of the rule of self-repression, we have the idea of expan-sion, of harmonious self development which . . . blossoms into the full flower of human excellence conceived as the realisation of many-sided capacities, physical, moral, intellectual and spiritual.' If one were to construe Hobhouse's self as an extended self here, this statement would echo deep ecological thinking closely. It also highlights the problems which this approach poses for deep eco-logy, in particular with its claim to be 'ecological'. The background for Hobhouse's remarks is a world of harmonious co-operation, where human individuals, in interaction, develop and realize them-selves and their potential. Deep ecologists move in a similar world, where extended human selves include the great Oneness of the world, enveloping them in one great Self, allowing all to develop and realize their fullest potential.

---

[22] Brennan (1988) has an illuminating chapter on the relationship of wholes and parts in which he concludes that wholes and parts are as real as one another, neither more nor less so. Sylvan (1985; 1990) approaches the issue of mechanism; while Phillips (1976) argues that holists (in particular those supporting Holisms 1 and 3) have an unnecessarily jaundiced view of the 'reductionism' of science, commenting that many scientists would object only to Holism 2.

Presented in this way, two problems become obvious. The first is that of humanization and other associated issues; the second is that of conflict. 'This ideological approbation can only be (human) self serving. One must ask if humanity is naturalized in such self-realization, or is nature merely humanized?' (Luke 1988: 81). Luke's question penetrates to the heart of the problem of the extended self; ultimately arguing that deep ecology, in Hegelian vein, projects humanity's alienated self-understanding onto the natural world, and seeks to find its own realization and permanence in it. By 'thinking like a mountain' one can find a way of coming to terms with one's own impermanence. 'One may survive physically', Luke argues, 'in fact, within other humans, whales, grizzlies, rainforests, mountains, rivers and bacteria; or (psychologically in faith) as an essential part of an organic whole (ibid.).[23]

Luke's argument reflects one particular strand of a general criticism of the extension and realization of the self in ecological terms: that it is thoroughly anthropocentric, and even egocentric. First, it begins from the concept of the individual human self, which is of primary importance, even though it has been extended to include everything that is. So Sylvan can say that it presupposes the belief that the only real motivation and interests that we have concern ourselves, and that this doctrine of the extended self is for 'people raised and hooked on a narrow self' (Sylvan 1990: 73). Ultimately, it is the human self that matters and that should be realized. As a direct result of this, the non-human natural world becomes valuable purely as an instrument of human self-realization. Of course, deep ecologists argue that realization of the expanded self lies in the fulfilment of others; but it is the motivation that is at issue here. Fox (1986: 71-2) says explicitly that the non-human world should be protected not because of its value in and to itself, but because 'it is part of My/Our wider self; its diminishment is My/Our diminishment'. This kind of remark prompts Andrew Dobson's comment that it involves a return to the original sin of anthropocentrism: 'It seems clear that the principle of self-realization described above, although it generates concern for the non-human world, generates it for human providential reasons . . . diluting the non-anthropocentrism that is held to be central to an ecological

[23] Sometimes deep ecological writing sounds as if it is deliberately laying itself open to this interpretation. Note e.g. Seed's comment, 'Love the plump worms you will become' (Naess 1988*b*).

perspective' (Dobson 1990: 60). This would only be perceived as an *ecological* criticism of deep ecology by those who attribute value to the non-human natural world other than the human-instrumental. This would, however, include ethical statements by deep ecologists themselves, notably in the Eight-Point Platform, where the non-instrumental value of non-human life is emphasized. There seems to be some unresolved inner contradiction here.

These reservations are, in fact, not only ecological, but also apply to the treatment of fellow humans. We would surely find it rather strange if someone were to claim that they had not harmed me because I was part of their own self, and they did not want to harm themselves. We would expect not to be harmed because we were respected as individuals, as others, with value in ourselves. The deep ecological concept of the extended self fails to acknowledge otherness. Value is only assigned as an extension of oneself, not to others in their own right. Oneself is the ultimate source of value.[24] Plumwood (1993: 174) calls this the 'Death of the Self' in deep ecology; the 'essential tension between different and alike is lost; only one element, the Self, is left'.

There are other, concomitant problems with this approach. The argument that you are part of myself, and therefore I will not hurt you, is not necessarily convincing. It would also be possible to argue that if I hurt the 'you' part of me, but gained in the 'me' part of me, the act is justified. Indeed, one could justify anything that benefited me on the grounds that I was also paying the cost, in another part of me: i.e. you. This may seem abstruse, but could have powerful political implications, some of which already hover on the so-called 'fascist' edge of the deep ecology movement, and are expressed in the more extreme material in *Earth First!*[25] This leads to the second part of my critique of the extended self—the problem of conflict. 'Human nature is such that with sufficient, all-sided maturity we cannot avoid identifying ourselves with all living beings, beautiful or ugly, big or small, sentient or not . . .' (Naess 1988*b*: 19). Here Naess puts forward the case for impartial identification. But this offers no solution to the problem of conflict

---

[24] Brennan (1988: 143) makes the criticism that deep ecology extends identification only to the living, and thereby is making an arbitrary divide. This critique is unjustified, since, as we have seen, Fox's ontological and cosmological identification do not specify the living (although admittedly Fox is writing after Brennan).

[25] See e.g. some of the material in J. Davis (1991).

between different elements of that with which one is identified. There is a genuine failure to come to terms with the reality that, in a limited world, conflicts are inevitable. This seems to be based on the fundamental conviction that the world could operate entirely harmoniously, and that the realization of the extended self could include the full realization of all that exists. But of course, this is not so; the realization of one living being is often inevitably at the expense of another. This failure to acknowledge conflict means that, as Luke (1988: 92) points out, 'no criteria [are advanced] for deciding between alternatives when such acts are necessary' How can there be, when all are subsumed into one's extended Self?

This leaves deep ecology (which seems not to have resolved this issue) with three possible alternatives. It could adopt the original ethical position by which it stood: that all that exists has an equal right to blossom and flourish. This generates extreme problems, as we saw in Chapter 3. Secondly, it could adopt some kind of hierarchical structure based on diversity, complexity, essential need, etc. (some moves have already been made in this direction). Thirdly, which has been the cause of the most controversy, at least in the United States, one could follow the fascist path I identified above. This alternative serves to illustrate that while the concept of the extended self may be in origin human-centred, in result it can be misanthropic in the extreme. If one's extended self is identified with all that exists, its interests become those of everything that exists. The interests of the Earth thus come first (hence *Earth First!*). The advocacy of a rapid decrease in human population by, for example, release of the smallpox virus, the spread of AIDS, and the abandoning of the starving (all of which have been advocated, although not in the mainstream of *Earth First!*) follow hard on the heels of such views. This brings to a head the question of whether personal identification can coexist with onto-logical/cosmological identification, as Fox seems to hope. Is it possible to have both a particular personal identification with individuals and an identification with all that exists, wanting the fulfilment of both? Are not the two in irreconcilable conflict? A subsidiary problem which follows from this identification with everything is that of identifying with what we might call evil. One must identify not only with the forest, but with the developer; not only with the starving, but with the oppressor; not only with the Jews, but also with Hitler. At the root of the problem is a failure of discrimination in deep ecology. The affirmation that everything should realize its potential denies the political reality of the world in which we live.[26]

It should be clear from this that the extension and realization of the self in deep ecology generate insuperable problems—and these are by no means all of them. How far, if at all, do these problems also apply to process thinking? When characterizing process thinking about the extension and realization of the self earlier, it was suggested that its emphasis was much more on physical than psychological extension, largely because of its focus on actual occasions, most of which are too primitive to evince any kind of psychology. Where process thinkers have advanced human psychological identification views they are vulnerable to entirely the same critique as deep ecology. However, this is not something at which Whitehead does more than hint; and it is not taken up, as one would expect, were it to be a key ecological theme, by Birch and Cobb in *The Liberation of Life*.

Nevertheless, as will have become evident in earlier chapters, process thinking (certainly that of Whitehead) is at least partly vulnerable to exactly the same criticisms as those which arise from the psychologically extended self, although for different reasons. Whitehead's uneasiness about conflict, such as that involved in predation, became clear in Chapter 4. His movement in the same co-operative world as Hobhouse and Naess means that he envisages the actual occasions working in harmony with one another to achieve an overall good. Williams and Hartshorne, as we have seen, admit much more forcefully the inevitability of conflict and of competition between actual occasions, thus indicating that this is not a *necessary* problem of process thinking in the same way that it is a necessary problem for the psychologically extended self. As further insulation from this criticism, process thinking has a built-in adjudicative principle: that of maximizing richness of experience. Where conflict is acknowledged, such as by Hartshorne, the correct resolution is that which achieves maximum richness of experience for God. Deep ecology has no such principle.

Process thinking is, however, vulnerable to the criticism that it has no real place for 'otherness' in the sense of 'not being me or like

---

[26] This point in fact forms one of the criticisms of deep ecology by social ecology, spearheaded by Murray Bookchin. See, for instance, Bookchin (1982).

me'. This is not because it subsumes the world into an extended self, but rather because it assumes that the world is composed from self-actualizing experiencing occasions. The world is humanized, transformed into a place composed from rudimentary human beings. Human experience in fact becomes both the model and the standard for the entire universe. This kind of humanization is, however, unlikely to result in the environmental fascism and misanthropy possible from the deep ecological position. The value concept of richness of experience is inexorably tilted towards humanity, and the ultimate aim is at the best consequences for God, not the Earth. Thus process theologians are unlikely to advocate, for example, the release of the smallpox virus or the spread of AIDS, since human beings contribute the richest experience to God.

What is particularly striking here is that, without a strong concept of the psychologically extended self, process thinking draws some similar conclusions to those of deep ecologists. This similarity raises one further—and fundamental—question about the extended psychological self in deep ecology: *How necessary is it?* Or, to be more precise, how necessary is it to propose an extended self in order to identify with other organisms? How far, in fact, is identity possible, beyond a kind of sympathy? This is a question Ayer raises in conversation with Naess:

Well, I share your moral sentiments, but I think that what you've been saying is very largely just false . . . of course, I sympathise with you, and if you are hurt I shall be sorry, but I shan't be hurt in the same way. It's indeed true—empirically true—that to a rather limited extent human beings sympathise with one another, with people they know and like and feel close to; but to say that they are one in any literal sense is just false. (Ayer, in Elders 1974: 32)

Naess fails to counter this satisfactorily; and, as this study has suggested, it is perfectly possible for a similar practical position to be derived without resort to the psychological concept of the extended self. Ayer also argues that resort to the *physically* extended self is unnecessary. He insists that personal identity can only be found within the identity of the body; one's self does not and cannot extend beyond this. Here we return to the problem of boundaries and distinctions which characterized my critique of holism. The question of the physically extended self seems to be partly a question of a failure to perceive boundaries, and partly the problem of confusing different kinds of language.

Let us take, for example, Whitehead's (1920: 120) use of Cleopatra's Needle, which daily gains and loses molecules, so that one can ask, 'Where does it begin, and where does it end?' This may be true in a scientific sense, on a micro-level, but on a macro-level, it is quite clear where Cleopatra's Needle begins and ends. For all normal purposes, Cleopatra's Needle has distinct boundaries. The same is true of my own body. Similar questions arise when one considers the extended self over time, as elaborated by Hartshorne, when he comments that all acts with a view to the future are altruistic, since the future is composed from new selves. But what meaning could 'altruistic' have here? If all deeds are altruistic to the same degree, then the word loses its meaning, since it would be impossible to be anything other than altruistic. If there are degrees of altruism, then presumably it would be more altruistic to act for the future selves which have least in common with one's own present self; which makes the statement that all acts are altruistic rather empty. In any case, how can one, in common-sense terms, understand this argument of Hartshorne? Why would one, for instance, ever apply for a job, since it isn't going to be oneself that gets it anyway, but a future self which may or may not have any special relationship to one's present personal sequence? In fact, Hartshorne's argument leads to absurdity, as does any strong argument for a physical self extended over time and space. Haunted by 'reading up' from scientific theory, and stricken with an inability to draw boundaries, doctrines of an extended physical and psychological self cause process thinking, but more particularly deep ecology, insuperable problems.

In conclusion, then: this chapter began with the question whether the use of Whitehead's name as support for deep-ecological ideas was a tag without philosophical baggage. In an attempt to answer this question, two metaphysical concepts central to deep ecology, that of holism and the extension and realization of the self, were compared with similar aspects of Whitehead's metaphysics. In both areas, process thinking had extensive points of contact with deep ecology, but also some significant differences, largely stemming from an emphasis on the individual nature of the actual occasion, on time over space, and the lack of a developed psychological concept of the extended self. These differences acted, as a general rule, to protect process thinking from some of the flaws in deep ecology, although where process thinking shared similar conceptuality, it was also vulnerable to the same critique.

So is the use of Whitehead's name by deep ecologists a tag without baggage? This entirely depends on how specific the tag is about the baggage to which it is referring. To claim, as a general statement, that Whitehead is either a source for deep ecology, or is, in essence, conceptually similar, would be to claim too much; to say that Whitehead and deep ecology bore little or no resemblance would be equally misleading. If deep ecologists wish to use process thinking to support their own work, they must be very specific about which aspect of it they are using. Those who claim baggage in ignorance of its content may find themselves in unprecedented difficulty when they arrive at Customs! With or without the support of process thinking, deep ecology generates numerous, seemingly intractable difficulties. Its metaphysics raises questions about the significance of wholes and parts, the value of individuals and the resolution of conflict, with all their ethical implications; questions which deep ecology fails to address satisfactorily. Process thinking, as we have seen, avoids the worst of these difficulties. However, as I shall go on to suggest in the conclusions, this does not mean that process thinking is itself satisfactory.

Conclusions

In the preceding chapters of this book, I have explored the fundamentally consequentialist, totalizing, and experience-centred nature of process ethical thinking. In particular I have considered the kind of environmental ethics that might flow from process thinking, in comparison with other existing forms of environmental ethics. This exploration has raised a number of difficulties for process approaches to environmental ethics, some of which are peculiar to process thinking; others of which are shared by approaches to environmental ethics with which process thinking has some similarities. In these conclusions, I will be discussing these difficulties at more length; proposing, where possible, ways forward for process thinking, and making some general comments concerning the ability of process thinking to address environmental questions.

The difficulties I have identified cluster around four key areas:

1. The interlinking questions about *integrity* and *replaceability* within process approaches to environmental ethics (particularly noted in Chapters 2 and 3);
2. The issue of *resolving conflict* between two different sources of value in process thinking; that arising from the intensity and harmony of experience produced by actual occasions themselves, and that arising from contrasts between different *kinds* of experience (noted in Chapters 2, 3, and 4);
3. The issue of the *comparative value* of human and non-human life, both in terms of the added intensity of experience attributed to human life in comparison with non-human life, and in terms of the added richness created for the divine life by contrasts between the experiences of different individual human beings and different human cultures (noted in Chapters 3 and 4). I will call this 'the double claim to superiority';
4. The *humanizing nature* of the process interpretation of the universe in terms of experiencing actual occasions (noted in Chapter 5).

These four difficulties are not all of a similar kind. Some are fundamental to the nature of process thinking; others are in principle resolvable although such a resolution may be in practice difficult or partial.

Beginning, then, with the first difficulty: I argued in Chapter 1 that the true individuals in process thinking are actual occasions, including (in Whitehead's terms) the consequent nature of God (or, in Hartshorne's terms, the cosmic organism). All other 'individuals' are more fundamentally *societies* of actual occasions, even though they may have a dominant actual occasion which acts as a unifying force. This societal understanding of organisms tends to undercut the concept of persistent, bounded, and enduring 'things' and 'organisms'; these diffuse into a constant flow of changing experience. Combined with totalizing consequentialism, this characteristic of process thinking may lead to the sacrifice of organisms (if such a sacrifice promotes increased total richness of experience) and the possibility of replaceability even for 'high-grade' organisms (provided that total richness of experience remains constant or increases by the substitution).

As was argued in Chapters 1 and 2, sacrifice and substitution may be ethically justified amongst human beings as well as in environmental ethics. Despite the affirmation of the uniqueness of individual human experience in process thinking, even human beings are, in certain circumstances, replaceable. It is the pattern created for the divine life by the contrast of one unique flow of experiences with another which generates value. Providing the patterned contrast is maintained (albeit by a different individual) it is difficult to argue that value is necessarily lost by replacement.

This difficulty is fundamental to process thinking in the Whiteheadian tradition at least. It is an element which it would be difficult to adapt or resolve. Value is contributory; God sums the value generated by actual occasions and within Himself; the system must therefore be consequentialist and totalizing.

Perhaps the best response to this 'difficulty' is to ask how far it is a difficulty at all. Clearly, from a non-consequentialist point of view (such as that of Regan or Taylor) the conclusions of process ethics in this respect are unacceptable. However, for someone who regards consequentialism of one form or another as an appropriate ethical framework, the conclusions of process thinking in this respect may not create new difficulties. As we have seen, consequentialists—both individualists and collectivists—have made a substantial contribution to writing in environmental ethics. It would seem odd to reject process thinking about environmental ethics for characteristics shared with perhaps the majority of writing in environmental ethics. After all, the problems of justice and replaceability are not significantly more acute for process thinking than for other consequentialist approaches. For this reason, I will not pursue this 'difficulty' further here.

The second difficulty (raised in Chapters 2, 3, and 4) is not so much (as the first) a judgement from outside the process system about system inadequacies, but rather an unresolved difficulty internal to the system—that of two apparently incommensurable value-generating principles: the richness of experience felt by actual occasions, and the harmonious intensity generated by contrasts between different kinds of experiences within the divine life. This is a particularly acute difficulty, as we have seen, within environmental ethics where many ethical problems involve the resolution of conflict between high-grade experiencers (such as human beings) and different kinds of experience (such as might be produced in areas of high biodiversity). Little seems to have been written about this difficulty in the tradition of process thinking, including in material specifically addressing environmental questions. Birch and Cobb, for instance, who half acknowledge the two value-generating sources, do not address the relative significance of each source or suggest what might constitute ethical behaviour in situations of conflict.

Rather surprisingly, perhaps, the existence of two potentially conflicting sources of value generation suggests that a kind of moral pluralism is present in the process system. However, it is important to consider this pluralism carefully, since as Wenz (1993) has recently pointed out, moral pluralism can take many different forms. Wenz's own classification of moral pluralisms is of use here. He distinguishes three forms of moral pluralism: extreme, moderate, and minimal. Extreme moral pluralism, in Wenz's classification, is characterized by 'alternations between different ethical theories' (ibid. 65)—theories such as utilitarianism or Kantianism. Clearly, process thinking does not fall into this category—the consequentialist, totalizing approach to ethics is consistent throughout. Secondly, Wenz characterizes moderate moral pluralism as a single, overarching theory, 'pluralistic in the sense that it contains a variety of independent principles, principles that cannot be reduced to or derived from a single master principle' (ibid. 69). Does process thinking fall into this category? Are the principles crudely expressed as 'Maximize richness of experience!' and 'Maximize contrast!' independent principles that cannot be reduced to or derived from a single master principle? The answer to this question is surely negative. The two principles *can* be derived from a single master principle—maximizing harmonious intensity for the divine life. Moral pluralism in process thinking is at a less profound level than this.

There remains a third category in Wenz's classification of moral pluralism—what he calls 'minimal pluralism', defined as a moral theory which 'merely lacks a universal algorithmic decision procedure'. Indeed, Wenz goes on to argue that all known moral systems are at least this pluralistic (i.e. there are no monistic systems which provide a perfect algorithmic decision-making procedure in all circumstances).

If Wenz is correct in this last point, it is clear that minimalist moral pluralism encompasses a spectrum of possibilities. After all, it is certainly possible to imagine a moral system less pluralistic than process thinking as I have portrayed it (for instance, a revised version of process thinking where only one of the two value-generating elements discussed above contributed to the harmonious intensity of God's experience). None the less, process thinking does appear to be only minimally pluralistic in Wenz's terms; the problem is one of working out what produces the best result in practice, rather than that there is any deep-rooted incommensurability of principles in theory. Since God is the sum of all value, there ought always to be a single best act in any situation of conflict (although it is possible that two different actions, based on the two different principles of value-generation could produce the same amount of harmonious intensity for God, and hence could be morally indistinguishable from one another).

The problem, then, appears to be one of knowledge in practice rather than one of conflict in theory. How can we know which principle has priority, which principle generates greater harmonious intensity for the divine life? One possible, but rather dangerous, way of addressing this question would be to maintain that the divine 'lure' would indicate to humans which action or set of actions would best maximize harmonious intensity in a situation where this was unclear. However, such a position would be little different from that of moral intuitionism with all its accompanying difficulties. It seems better to assume that we can have no special knowledge and proceed accordingly. Of course, comfort can be taken that on many occasions these two value-generating principles do not conflict, and may even be mutually reinforcing. Where they do conflict, there would seem to be several ways of attempting to resolve the dilemma. The first would be to decide on some kind of general hierarchy of principle: either that maximizing richness of high-grade experience always trumps the maximization of contrasts between different kinds of experience or the other way around. This, however, seems rather simplistic. Better, perhaps, would be the imposition of a 'VanDe Veerian' superstructure onto the two principles. This would mean that in any conflict of principle, priority would be given to the principle apparently more seriously affected by the conflict. Let me explain what I mean by this.

In Chapter 3, I discussed a case proposed by Regan concerning a choice between the life of a human being and a single rare wildflower. Let us vary the case (since the introduction of a human creates new difficulties) and replace the human with a fairly common mammal such as a deer. Clearly the wildflower, as it is rare, allows for the continued existence of unusual contrasts in the world, whilst the deer (which will not be replaced if it is removed) produces high-grade experience. In this case—unless the flower was the last reproductively able member of its species—it would seem likely that the richness of experience lost if the deer was killed would outweigh the contrast produced by the wildflower, since other members of that species exist elsewhere and in itself it produces minimal richness of experience (although I will be considering some more issues about the value of plant species in process thinking shortly). In contrast, however, where a similar choice must be made between a single deer and a whole wildflower meadow with a range of rare species growing together in a unique combination, one might conclude that the principle of maximizing contrast outweighed that of maximizing richness of experience for high-grade experiencers.

This attempt at adjudication does not help a great deal in tricky choices such as that between a wildflower meadow and a herd of cows, the situation discussed at the end of Chapter 3. In such a case one might have to consider factors such as the number of wild mammals dependent on the meadow, the kind of lives which the cows would experience whilst living in it, and so on. Such schemes as I am proposing here are at the best vague and open to dispute (characteristic of utilitarian-type systems in general, of course, not just of process thinking) but they do at least provide some sort of guidelines for making decisions when principles conflict. As both Sprigge[1] and Wenz (1993) point out, this degree of difficulty in practical decision-making is common in ethical systems. Because of the near-universal nature of this problem, it would seem hard to reject process approaches to environmental ethics because of it. But clearly, someone wishing to pursue environmental ethics in a process tradition needs to work on this problem in more detail than I am able to undertake here.

We move on, then, to consider the third difficulty facing process approaches to environmental ethics: the double claim to superiority. It is important to note that, like the first difficulty but unlike the second, this is only problematic from particular perspectives. Some process thinkers may wish to bite the bullet here and to say that this is just what the world is like. Humans just do produce richer experience than other animals, and provide God with individualized instead of species-representative contrasts. However, since the double claim to human superiority is so much at odds with many positions in environmental ethics, it is an area which process thinkers may wish to revisit, in order to retain a reputation as an environmentally sensitive philosophy. It seems to me that some relatively minor reformations of process approaches such as those of Whitehead, Hartshorne, and Cobb, could at least ease the difficulties caused by the double claim of superiority.

Because of the double nature of the claim (both in terms of contrasts and richness of experience), in almost all situations of ethical conflict the claims of humans can trump those of non-humans. This was apparent in Chapter 4 when I discussed a case where new human populations were expanding into a wildflower meadow and the richness of experience and individualized contrasts produced by the humans seemed to outweigh the 'low level' of experience and the species contrasts produced within the wildflower meadow.

[1] In a personal communication to the author, 1993.

Do such conclusions, however, spring from the fundamental nature of process systems in the Whiteheadian tradition, or do they merely represent what has been proposed to date, by thinkers such as Hartshorne and Cobb? Both Cobb and Hartshorne, for instance, assume that with the exception of human beings and possibly some few other 'top' mammal species, the experiences generated by living organisms are primarily representative of their species, rather than of themselves as individuals. However, if one were to revise these approaches by emphasizing the individuality of the experiences produced by individuals of non-human species, a far more complex pattern of contrasts would be set up. A chicken, for instance, would not produce generically 'chickeny' experiences but the experiences of that-chicken-in-particular. Affirming such experiential individuality in a much wider range of living organisms (fish, birds, mammals, for instance) would mean that they counted for much more when in conflict with human beings—they are not immediately trumped by the double claim of superiority. Such a revision, whilst making a considerable difference to the environ-mental ethic that might flow from process thinking, does not seem to me to introduce fundamental change, but merely boundary adjustments—adjustments which seem fully in the spirit of the 'gradualism' of process thinking, where no abrupt divide is en-visaged between human experiences and those of non-humans.

However, it must be acknowledged that this revision does not resolve the problem of the wildflower meadow, which both collect-ivist consequentialists and most individualist deontologists in environmental ethics would wish to protect against human devel-opment. This is due to the difficulty of extending emphasized individuality of experience into the plant world—because plants in process thinking have no dominant actual occasion (or, in Hart-shorne's terms, they are quasi-organisms). Thus, they are not individuals in the same sense as the other organisms which we have discussed—the whole is not more unified than the most unified of parts. How might this be addressed? Could it be argued that the cells of a plant actualize the individuality of the plant, and thus provide contrasts with other plants? This is rather difficult to maintain, since if the plant has no 'individuality' as such it is not clear what the cells would be manifesting. It would also, I think, be difficult to maintain that the cells themselves, as individuals, pro-duced valuable contrasts with one another (and even if one did maintain this, since human bodies are composed from large numbers of cells as well, this would not necessarily provide an ecological gain!)

An alternative response, perhaps, might be to make a rather larger revision of the process tradition (in line with objections by biologists, cited in Chapter 3) and to argue that plants do have dominant actual occasions, or (in Hartshorne's terms) that they are true organisms. This does not seem to undermine any fundamental element of process thinking, merely to realign it to reflect ecological concerns. If plants were acknowledged—in some sense at least—to have a dominant actual occasion, an individuality, then contrasts between individual plants could reflect not just their species, but also their individuality.

This emphasized individuality of experience which I am proposing—for all kinds of non-human organisms—could, of course (in line with process thinking on other matters) be a thing of degree. The experiences produced by all living organisms would, in part, be representative of their species, but also, in part, representative of their individuality. (It would be important to maintain some degree of species-experience, otherwise there would be no incentive for preservation of rare species, or for preferring a wildflower meadow to a grass ley.) The proportion of individual and species-representative experiences would vary: a plant, for instance, might have a higher proportion of species-representative experience and a lower proportion of individual experience; mammals might have much more individuality of experience, and much less species-representative experience.

The result of this revision is a much flattened, more inclusive, hierarchy of value generated by contrasts. This hierarchy could be flattened still further if the values of the contrasts generated between different species was reassessed—perhaps even to the point where the contrasts between species outweighed those between individual human beings and the richness of experience produced by individual human beings. Hartshorne's comments on this matter, discussed in Chapter 4, have at least admitted the possibility of this; more thoroughgoing revisions could be made here. A similar flattening of the value hierarchy found in the 'richness of experience' element of the double claim to superiority can also be proposed (as I suggested at the end of Chapter 2). With a reassessment of the relative significance of human and non-human production of harmonious and intense experience, the value-gap between humans and non-humans can be narrowed considerably (making Whitehead's use of expressions like 'with humans the Rubicon is crossed' inappropriate). Dombrowski has already taken steps in this direction, with his more radical animal protection position (despite its difficulties, discussed in Chapter 3). A more thoroughgoing shift towards re-evaluating the intensity of non-human experience in comparison with human experience, could provide a significant 'flattening' of this part of the human–non-human hierarchy.

These revisions certainly weaken the double claim to superiority in process thinking. It seems unlikely, for instance, that after such a revision, human development of the wildflower meadow discussed earlier would be ethically acceptable. If the contrasts between all individual organisms (including plants) could be felt by God, the significance of inter-species contrasts was elevated, and a higher weighting was given to non-human richness of experience, this might overwhelm the double human claim of superiority—in this case at least.

Despite all these revisions, however, some environmental ethicists (deontologists such as Paul Taylor and critics of animal-liberation positions such as Rodman) would argue that this hierarchy, albeit flattened, still presents a value-tilt towards human beings; humans are still at the top of the hierarchy and ultimately produce more value than members of other species. In the end, such questions about the persistent double claim to superiority in process thinking are inseparable from the fourth difficulty raised by process approaches to environmental ethics, discussed in Chapter 5: the problem of 'humanization' or 'anthropomorphization' of the universe, from God to the atomic particles. If the universe is modelled on human experience, it is not surprising that when non-humans are judged against it they are found to be lower on the hierarchy.

This humanizing aspect of process thinking has been the subject of critical comment from a variety of sources, not all of them environmental. Gunton, for example, objects not so much to the humanization of the universe, but to the humanization of God in process thinking: God, like the rest of the universe, is modelled on human experience which constitutes 'an example on which to found the generalised description of metaphysics' (Gunton 1972:

90). Indeed, a further point could be made here. It is not so much human experience that has been generalized into the universe—if, indeed, such a phenomenon can be said to exist at all—but rather, Western liberal experience. The self-actualizing, self-creative aspect of the actual occasion resembles very closely the liberal understanding of humanity portrayed in the writing of T. H. Green and L. T. Hobhouse, as Morris has argued. That this limited representation of human experience should be the interpretative filter through which the entire universe is understood elevates a regional, temporal, species, race-, and gender-specific concept into a universal and eternal principle. The effects of such an approach on environmental ethics are, as we have seen, to create a hierarchy with those species that are most like (Western liberal white male) humans at the top and those which are least like (Western liberal white male) humans at the bottom. One might describe this as what Primo Levi (1989: 61) calls 'selfishness extended to the one who is closest to you' or 'us-ism'. As Plumwood (1993: 130) comments about process thinking: 'The criterion of experience builds in an anthropocentric hierarchy, since it conceives of the world of nature as similar to, but of a lesser degree, than the human world, rather than as simply different.' Unlike the three former difficulties discussed, this difficulty is fundamental to the nature of process thinking but not shared by some other ethical systems. It is not possible to reform the pan-experiential understanding of process thinking—this is one of its most important and distinctive elements. Neither can one argue here that process thinking is, in this respect, in the same position as other ethical approaches and so should not be rejected where they are not. Yet surely this 'humanization' of the universe does present a difficulty for a system attempting to come to terms with ecological questions. Indeed, this objection to process thinking could be taken one step further, if we extend an attack on deep ecology by Jim Cheney (1989: 293–325) to process thinking.

Cheney (ibid. 302) argues that deep ecology, like Stoicism, is a metaphysical system designed to give its adherents security during a time of upheaval: for the Stoics, the collapse of the Empire; for deep ecologists, the 'shattering of the security of modernism'. In these insecure external conditions, deep ecology is projected as an historical, timeless, uncontextual system, which provides a 'unifying framework in which others can be encountered without risk'.

For Cheney, the metaphysics of deep ecology is an insulation against encountering otherness. Everything can be fitted into a secure overarching framework (an especially secure framework when it is composed from one's own, extended self); 'otherness' can be controlled and loses its alien nature. Deep ecology is thus, for Cheney, a colonizing or totalizing system, attempting to subsume the entire universe into its own interpretative categories.

Although Cheney has not written a critique of process metaphysics, it is clear that a similar critique could be made of it. Like deep ecology, process thinking is a universal system, subsuming the universe into its own interpretative categories. For the deep ecological 'Me' which encompasses the universe, process thinking substitutes a plurality of tiny 'me's' which humanize and familiarize the world, diluting any sense of difference. This kind of conceptual colonization of the world, Cheney argues, is symptomatic of the need to control and dominate. Although process thinking claims freedom and self-creation is a primary concern, the very fact that it interprets the world in such a way is, from this perspective, symptomatic of its need to control. The only freedom allowed to the non-human world is the freedom to behave like a human being 'writ small'. The world is not allowed to be truly Other, to stand outside the governing structure of self-actualizing experience.

Cheney's argument obviously extends to all all-embracing metaphysical systems, and thus has implications for a variety of approaches to environmental ethics other than deep ecology and process thinking. In place of such systems, Cheney (1991: 325) advocates local and contextual approaches to ethics: 'We cannot tell *the* story of the world and then lay down rules for how we are to respect that world. Our (ethical *and* ecological) stories are positioned stories, and we can only just keep on telling and retelling them, and contesting the various tellings.' Certainly (especially feminist) environmental ethicists seem to have increasingly moved towards developing such contextual approaches to ethics, which recognize their own provisional and positioned nature, in a way that contrasts sharply with process thinking (and with many of the other approaches to environmental ethics explored in this book). Cheney's ideas, and those of others like him, are controversial, and not just in environmental ethics. To pursue this question further would open up an extensive moral debate which I do not wish to pursue here. (But see Wenz 1988 and 1993; Stone 1987;

Plumwood 1993; Callicott 1992.) Fortunately, for the purposes of this study, it is not necessary to come to firm conclusions about this debate. Cheney's argument that universalist metaphysical systems in general are dominating and controlling, suppressing difference and familiarizing the Other, is but a final twist to the difficulty raised by process thinking in this respect. Even if Cheney is mistaken about the nature of universalist metaphysical systems *in general*, this does not undermine the argument that process systems *in particular* manifest just such controlling, familiarizing characteristics.

These particular characteristics of process thinking—its anthropomorphic interpretation of the universe which acts as legitimation for its accompanying double claim of human superiority—distinguish it from other forms of utilitarianism (such as that of Singer in Chapter 2) and indeed from all the other kinds of environmental ethics considered in this book. And clearly, these characteristics are peculiarly problematic in the construction of an environmental ethic. Although I have, in this conclusion, suggested several ways in which process ethics might be revised in the light of concerns raised by other approaches to environmental ethics the difficulties of the double claim to superiority and the humanization of the universe seem to be irresolvable. From the perspective of many environmental ethicists (myself included) these difficulties mean that process thinking is unable to generate an environmental ethic adequate to meet some of the most profound questions raised in the current environmental debate.

To return, then, to the point at which I began: Paulos Mar Gregorias's advice to listen to process theology with respect. Having (I hope) listened respectfully in this book, I conclude that the 'intellectual alternative' provided by process theology to alleviate the 'eco crisis' is, ultimately, an unsatisfactory one.

References

ARMSTRONG-BUCK, SUSAN (1986), 'Whitehead's Metaphysical System as a Foundation for Environmental Ethics', *Environmental Ethics*, 8/3: 241–61.

—— (1991), 'What Process Philosophy can Contribute to the Land Ethic and Deep Ecology', *Trumpeter*, 8/1: 29–34.

ATTWELD, ROBIN (1983), *The Ethics of Environmental Concern* (Oxford: Basil Blackwell).

—— (1987), *A Theory of Value and Obligation* (London: Croom Helm).

—— (1990), 'Deep Ecology and Intrinsic Value: A Reply to Andrew Dobson', *Cogito*, Spring issue: 60–5.

—— (1991), *The Ethics of Environmental Concern*, 2nd edn. (Athens, Ga.: University of Georgia Press).

BENTHAM, JEREMY (1943), 'An Introduction to the Principles of Morals and Legislation', in William Hampson (ed.), *A Fragment on Government and an Introduction to the Principles of Morals and Legislation* (Oxford: Basil Blackwell).

BIRCH, CHARLES (1990), 'Christian Obligation', in Charles Birch, William Eakin, and Jay McDaniel (eds.), *Liberating Life* (Maryknoll, NY: Orbis Books), 57–73.

BIRCH, CHARLES, and COBB, JOHN (1981), *The Libration of Life* (Cambridge: Cambridge University Press).

BLACKSTONE, WILLIAM (ed.) (1974), *Philosophy and Environmental Crisis* (Athens, Ga.: University of Georgia Press).

BOHM, DAVID (1980), *Wholeness and the Implicate Order* (London: Routledge & Kegan Paul).

BOOKCHIN, MURRAY (1982), *The Ecology of Freedom* (Palo Alto, Calif.: Cheshire Books).

BOTKIN, DANIEL (1991), *Discordant Harmonies* (Oxford: Oxford University Press).

BRADLEY, F. H. (1946), *Appearance and Reality* (1893; Oxford: Oxford University Press).

BRENNAN, ANDREW (1984), 'The Moral Standing of Natural Objects', *Environmental Ethics*, 6/1: 35–56.

—— (1986), 'Ecological Theory and Value in Nature', *Philosophical Inquiry*, 8/1–2: 66–951988),

—— (1988), *Thinking about Nature: An Investigation of Nature, Value and Ecology* (London: Routledge).

BUBE, PAUL CUSTODIO (1988), *Ethics in John Cobb's Process Theology*, American Academy Series, 62 (Atlanta: Scholars Press).

CALLICOTT, J. BAIRD (1980), 'Animal Liberation: A Triangular Affair', reprinted in Scherer and Attig (1983), 54–72.

—— (1984), 'Non-Anthropocentric Value Theory and Environmental Ethics', *American Philosophical Quarterly*, 21/4: 299–308.

—— (1985), 'Intrinsic Value, Quantum Theory and Environmental Ethics', *Environmental Ethics*, 7/3: 257–75.

—— (1986), 'The Search for an Environmental Ethic', in Regan (ed.) (1986).

—— (ed.) (1987), *Companion to a Sand County Almanac* (Madison: University of Wisconsin Press).

—— (1988), 'Animal Liberation and Environmental Ethics: Back Together Again', *Between the Species*, 4/3: 163–9.

—— (1989), *In Defense of the Land Ethic* (Albany, NY: State University of New York Press).

—— (1990), 'The Case Against Moral Pluralism', *Environmental Ethics* 12/2: 99–125.

—— (1991), *Fisheries: A Bulletin of the American Fisheries Society*, 16/2: 23–7.

—— (1992), 'Can a Theory of Moral Sentiments Support a Genuinely Normative Environmental Ethic?', *Inquiry*, 35: 183–98.

—— (1994), 'Moral Monism in Environmental Ethics Defended', *Journal of Philosophical Research*, 19.

CAPRA, FRITJOF (1982), *The Tao of Physics* (London: Wildwood House).

CARPENTER, JAMES (1988), *Nature and Grace* (New York: Crossroad).

CARRUTHERS, PETER (1992), *The Animals Issue: Moral Theory in Practice* (Cambridge: Cambridge University Press).

CHASE, A. (1986), *Playing God in Yellowstone: The Destruction of America's First National Park* (New York: Harcourt Brace Jovanovich).

CHENEY, JIM (1989), 'The Neo-Stoicism of Radical Environmentalism', *Environmental Ethics*, 11/4: 293–325.

—— (1991), 'Callicott's "Metaphysics of Morals"', *Environmental Ethics*, 13/4: 313–25.

CHRISTIAN, WILLIAM (1967), *An Interpretation of Whitehead's Metaphysics* (1959; New Haven: Yale University Press).

CLARK, HENRY (1981), 'Process Thought and Justice', in Cobb and Schroeder (eds.) (1981), 132–54.

COBB, JOHN (1966), *A Christian Natural Theology* (London: Lutterworth).

—— (1972), *Is It Too Late? A Theology of Ecology*, Faith and Life Series (Beverly Hills, Calif.: Benzinger, Bruce, & Glencoe).

—— (1973), 'Ethics, Ecology, Theology', in Daly (ed.) (1973), 307–20.

COBB, JOHN (1979), 'Christian Existence in a World of Limits', *Environmental Ethics*, 1/2: 149–58.

——and DALY, HERMAN (1990), *For the Common Good* (London: Green Print).

——and GRIVIN, DAVID (1977), *Process Theology: An Introductory Exposition* (Belfast: Christian Journals).

——and SCHROEDER, WIDICK, W. (eds.) (1981), *Process Philosophy and Social Thought* (Chicago: Centre for the Scientific Study of Religion).

COMMONER, BARRY (1972), *The Closing Circle* (London: Jonathan Cape).

DALY, HERMAN (ed.) (1973), *Towards a Steady State Economy* (San Francisco: W. H. Freeman).

DAVIS, JOHN (ed.) (1991), *Earth First! Reader* (Salt Lake City: Peregrine Smith).

DAVIS, KAREN (1989), Letter to the Editor, *Between the Species*, 5: 242.

DEVALL, BILL, and SESSIONS, GEORGE (1985), *Basic Principles of Deep Ecology* (Salt Lake City: Peregrine Smith).

DOBSON, ANDREW (1990), *Green Political Thought* (London: Unwin Hyman).

DOMBROWSKI, DANIEL (1988), *Hartshorne and the Metaphysics of Animal Rights* (Albany, NY: State University of New York Press).

DOOLEY, PATRICK (1986), 'The Ambiguity of Environmental Ethics: Duty or Heroism?', *Philosophy Today*, 30/1–4: 48–57.

DOYLE, JAMES F. (1977), 'Schweitzer's Extension of Ethics to All Life', *Journal of Value Inquiry XI*, 1: 44–50.

DRENGSON, ALAN (1988), Review of Devall and Sessions' *Deep Ecology*, in *Environmental Ethics*, 10/1: 83–9.

EAGLETON, TERRY (1990), *The Ideology of the Aesthetic* (Oxford: Basil Blackwell).

ELDERS, FONS (ed.) (1974), *Reflexive Waters* (London: Condor Books, Souvenir Press).

ELLIOT, ROBERT, and AARON, GARE (eds.) (1983), *Environmental Philosophy* (St. Lucia: University of Queensland Press).

EMMET, DOROTHY (1933), *Whitehead's Philosophy of Organism* (London: Macmillan).

ENGEL, J. RONALD, and ENGEL, JOAN GIBB (1990), *Ethics of Environment and Development* (London: Belhaven Press).

FEINBERG, JOEL (1974), 'The Rights of Animals and Unborn Generations', in William Blackstone (ed.) (1974), 43–68.

FEYERABEND, PAUL (1993), *Against Method* (1975; London: Verso).

FLADER, SUSAN (1974), *Thinking like a Mountain: Aldo Leopold and the Evolution of an Ecological Attitude toward Deer, Wolves and Forests* (Columbia, Mo.: University of Missouri Press).

FORD, LEWIS (1984), *The Emergence of Whitehead's Metaphysics* 1925–1929 (Albany, NY: State University of New York Press).

FOX, WARWICK (1984*a*), 'Deep Ecology: A New Philosophy of our Time?', *Ecologist*, 14/5–6: 194–200.

—— (1984*b*), 'The Intuition of Deep Ecology', *Ecologist*, 14/5–6: 144–9.

—— (1984*c*), Review of Birch and Cobb, *The Liberation of Life*, in *Ecologist* 14/4: 178–82.

—— (1986), 'Approaching Deep Ecology: A Response to Richard Sylvan's Critique of Deep Ecology', *Environmental Studies Occasional Paper*, 20 (Hobart: University of Tasmania).

—— (1990) *Towards a Transpersonal Ecology* (Boston: Shambhala Press).

FRANKENA, WILLIAM (1979), 'Ethics and the Environment', in Goodpaster and Sayre (eds.) (1979), 3–20.

FREY R. G. (1983), *Rights, Killing and Suffering* (Oxford: Basil Blackwell).

—— (ed.) (1985), *Utility and Rights* (Oxford: Basil Blackwell).

FRITZELL, PETER (1987), 'The Conflicts of Ecological Conscience', in Callicott (ed.) (1987*b*), 128–48.

GAMWELL, FRANKLIN (1981), 'Happiness and the Public World: Beyond Political Liberalism', Cobb and Schroeder (eds.) (1981), 38–54.

GARE, ARRON (1995), *Postmodernism and the Environmental Crisis* (London: Routledge).

GLEASON, H. A. (1952), 'Delving into the History of American Ecology', *Bulletin of the Ecological Society of America*, 56: 7–10.

GOODPASTER, KENNETH (1979), 'From Egoism to Environmentalism', in Goodpaster and Sayre (eds.) (1979), 21–35.

—— (1983), 'On Being Morally Considerable', in Scherer and Attig (eds.) (1983), 31–9.

—— and SAYRE, K. (1979), *Ethics and Problems of the 21st Century* (Notre Dame, Ind.: University of Notre Dame Press).

GRIVIN, NICHOLAS, and BENNETT, DAVID (1984), 'The Ethics of Triage', *Discussion Paper in Environmental Ethics* (Canberra: Australian National University).

GUNTON, COLIN (1972), 'A Comparison of the Doctrine of God in Process Theology and in Karl Barth', D.Phil. thesis, Oxford University.

HARGROVE, EUGENE (1989), *The Foundations of Environmental Ethics* (Englewood Cliffs, NJ: Prentice Hall).

—— (ed.) (1992), *The Animal Rights/Environmental Ethics Debate* (New York: State University of New York Press).

HARTSHORNE, CHARLES (1936), 'The Compound Individual', *Philosophical Essays for A. N. Whitehead* (New York: Longmans, Green), 193–220.

—— (1962), *The Logic of Perfection and Other Essays in Neoclassical Metaphysics* (La Salle, Ill.: Open Court).

HARTSHORNE, CHARLES (1970), *Creative Synthesis and Philosophic Method* (London: SCM).

—— (1972), *Whitehead's Philosophy* (Lincoln, Nebr.: University of Nebraska Press).

—— (1974*a*), 'The Environmental Results of Technology', in William Blackstone (ed.) (1974), 69–78.

—— (1974*b*), 'Beyond Enlightened Self Interest: A Metaphysics of Ethics', *Ethics*, 84/3: 201–16.

—— (1975), *Beyond Humanism: Essays in the Philosophy of Nature* (1937; Gloucester, Mass.: Peter Smith).

—— (1979), 'The Rights of the Subhuman World', *Environmental Ethics*, 1/1: 49–60.

—— (1981), 'The Ethics of Contributionism', in Ernest Partridge (ed.) (1981), 103–7.

—— (1984), *Creativity in American Philosophy* (Albany, NY: State University of New York Press).

—— (1987), *Wisdom as Moderation* (Albany, NY: State University of New York Press).

—— and REESE, WILLIAM (1953), *Philosophers Speak of God* (Chicago: University of Chicago Press).

HOBHOUSE, L. T. (1951), *Morals in Evolution: A Study in Comparative Ethics* (London: Chapman & Hall).

HUNT, MURRAY, W. (1980), 'Are Mere Things Morally Considerable?', *Environmental Ethics*, 2/1: 59–65.

JAMES, WILLIAM (1911), *Some Problems in Philosophy* (London: Longmans, Green).

JAMIESON, DALE (1990) 'Rights, Justice and Duties to Provide Assistance: A Critique of Regan's Theory of Rights', *Ethics*, 100: 349–62.

JOHNSON, A. H. (1983), *Whitehead and his Philosophy* (Lanham, Md.: University Press of America).

JOHNSON, LAWRENCE (1991), *A Morally Deep World* (Cambridge: Cambridge University Press).

KANTOR, JAY (1980), 'The "Interests" of Natural Objects', *Environmental Ethics*, 2/2: 163–73.

KATZ, ERIC (1985), 'Organism, Community and the Substitution Problem', *Environmental Ethics*, 7/3: 241–53.

KEVER, SUSAN, KING, SALLIE, and KRAFT, STEVEN (1991), 'Process Metaphysics and Minimalism: Implications for Public Policy', *Environmental Ethics*, 13/1: 23–47.

KUHN, THOMAS (1962), *The Structure of Scientific Revolutions* (Chicago: University of Chicago Press).

LANGFELDT, GABRIEL (1979), *Albert Schweitzer: A Study of his Philosophy of Life* (London: Allen & Unwin).

LECLERC, IVOR (ed.) (1961), *The Relevance of Whitehead* (London: Allen & Unwin).

LEOPOLD, ALDO (1968), *A Sand County Almanac* (1949; Oxford: Oxford University Press).

——(1979), 'Some Fundamentals of Conservation in the Southwest', *Environmental Ethics*, 1/2: 131–58.

LEVI, PRIMO (1989), *The Drowned and the Saved* (1988; London: Abacus, Sphere Books).

LOCKWOOD, MICHAEL (1979), 'Killing and the Preference for Life', *Inquiry*, 22: 157–70.

LOMBARDI, LOUIS (1983), 'Inherent Worth, Respect and Rights', *Environmental Ethics*, 5/3: 257–70.

LUCAS, GEORGE R. (1985), 'Evolutionist Theories and Whitehead's Philosophy', *Process Studies*, 14/4: 287–300.

LUKE, STEPHEN (1988), 'The Dreams of Deep Ecology', *Telos*, Summer issue, 65–92.

McDANIEL, JAY (1989), *Of God and Pelicans* (Louisville, Ky.: Westminster/John Knox Press).

MACKIE, J. L. (1978), 'The Law of the Jungle', *Philosophy*, 53/206: 455–65.

——(1979), *Ethics: Inventing Right and Wrong* (1977; Harmondsworth: Penguin).

McTAGGART, John (1921), *The Nature of Existence* (Cambridge: Cambridge University Press).

MARCUSE, HERBERT (1972), *One-Dimensional Man* (1964; London: Sphere Books).

MAR GREGORIAS, PAULOS (1980), *The Human Presence: An Orthodox View of Nature* (Madras: Christian Literature Society).

MARLENE RUSSOW, LILY (1981), 'Why do Species Matter?', *Environmental Ethics*, 3/2: 101–12.

MAYS, WILLIAM (1959), *The Philosophy of Whitehead* (London: Allen & Unwin).

MERCHANT, CAROLYN (1990), 'Environmental Ethics and Political Conflict: A View from California', *Environmental Ethics*, 12/1: 45–69.

——(1992), *Radical Ecology* (London: Routledge).

MIDGLEY, MARY (1983) *Animals and Why they Matter* (Harmondsworth: Pelican).

——(1985), *Evolution as a Religion* (London: Meuthen).

MILL, JOHN STUART (1950), *The Philosophy of Scientific Method*, ed. E. Nagel (New York: Hafner).

——(1979), *Utilitarianism* (1861; Glasgow: Fontana).

MILLER, HARLAN B. (1988), 'Comment on Callicott', *Between the Species*, 4/3: 171–3.

MILLER, PETER (1983), 'Do Animals Have Interests Worthy of Our Moral Interest?', *Environmental Ethics*, 5/4: 319–34.

MOLINE, JON (1986), 'Aldo Leopold and the Moral Community', *Environmental Ethics*, 8/2: 99–120.

MORRIS, RANDALL (1986), 'Process and Politics: Towards a Political Theology Based on the Thought of A. N. Whitehead and Charles Hartshorne', D.Phil. thesis, Oxford University.

MOSKOP, JOHN (1980), 'Mill and Hartshorne', *Process Studies*, 10/1: 18–33.

NAESS, ARNE (1973), 'The Shallow and the Deep Long-range Ecology Movement: A Summary,' *Inquiry*, 16: 75–98.

—— (1974), 'The Glass is on the Table', in Elders (ed.) (1974), 30–7.

—— (1977), 'Spinoza and Ecology', in Hessing (ed.), *Speculum Spinozanum 1677–1977* (London: Routledge), 418–26.

—— (1984a), 'A Defence of the Deep Ecology Movement', *Environmental Ethics*, 6/3: 265-70.

—— (1984b), 'Intuition, Intrinsic Value and Deep Ecology', *The Ecologist*, 14/5.6: 201-4.

—— (1985), 'Response to Richard Sylvan's Critique' (unpublished).

—— (1988a), 'Basics of Deep Ecology', *Resurgence*, 126: 4–7 (transcription of 1987 Schumacher Lectures).

—— (1988b), 'Self-Realization: An Ecological Approach to Being in the World', in J. Macey, J. Seed, A. Naess, and J. Fleming (eds.), *Thinking Like A Mountain: Towards a Council of All Beings* (London: Heretic), 19–29.

—— (1989), *Ecology, Community and Lifestyle*, trans. David Rothenberg (Cambridge: Cambridge University Press).

—— (1990), 'Sustainable Development and Deep Ecology', in J. R. Engel and J. G. Engel (1990), 87–97.

—— (n.d.), 'Gestalt Thinking and Buddhism' (unpublished, n.d.).

NAIRN, THOMAS (1988), 'Hartshorne and Utilitarianism: A Response to Moskop', *Process Studies*, 17/3: 170–9.

NASH, RODERICK FRAZIER (1989), *The Rights of Nature: A History of Environmental Ethics* (Madison: University of Wisconsin Press).

O'NEILL, JOHN (1993) *Ecology, Policy and Politics* (London: Routledge).

PALMER, CLARE (1995), *Animal Liberation, Environmental Ethics and Domestication*, OCEES Research Paper, 1.

PARWT, DEREK (1984), *Reasons and Persons* (Oxford: Clarendon Press).

PARTRIDGE, ERNEST (ed.) (1981), *Responsibilities to Future Generations* (Buffalo, NY: Prometheus Books).

—— (1986), 'Values in Nature—Is Anyone There?', *Philosophical Inquiry*, 8/1–2: 96–110

PHILLIPS, D. C. (1976), *Holistic Thought In Social Science* (Stanford, Calif.: Stanford University Press).

PLUMWOOD, VAL (1993), *Feminism and the Mastery of Nature* (London: Routledge). (See also under Routley, Val.)

POLS, EDWARD (1967), *Whitehead's Metaphysics* (Carbondale, Ill.: Southern Illinois University Press).

RACHELS, JAMES (1991), *Created from Animals: The Moral Implications of Darwinism* (Oxford: Oxford University Press).

RAWLES, KATE (1990), 'Animal Welfare and Environmental Ethics', MA thesis, State University of Colorado.

REGAN, TOM (1982), 'The Nature and Possibility of an Environmental Ethic', *All That Dwell Therein: Animal Rights and Environmental Ethics* (Berkeley: University of California Press), 187–205.

—— (1984a), *The Case for Animal Rights* (London: Routledge).

—— (ed.) (1984b), *Earthbound: New Introductory Essays in Environmental Ethics* (New York: Random House).

—— (ed.) (1986), *Matters of Life and Death* (New York: Random House).

RODMAN, JOHN (1977), 'The Liberation of Nature', *Inquiry*, 20: 83–145.

—— (1983), 'Four Forms of Ecological Consciousness Reconsidered', in Scherer and Attig (eds.) (1983), 82–92.

ROLSTON, HOLMES (1988a), *Environmental Ethics* (Philadelphia: Temple University Press).

—— (1988b), 'Human Values and Natural Systems', *Society and Natural Resources*, 1: 271–83.

—— (1989), *Philosophy Gone Wild* (1979; Buffalo, NY: Prometheus).

—— (1990), 'Biology and Philosophy in Yellowstone', *Biology and Philosophy*, 5: 241–58.

—— (1992), 'Religion in an Age of Science: Metaphysics in an Era of History', Review Article, *Zygon*, 27/1: 65–87.

ROSS, STEPHEN (1983), *Perspective in Whitehead's Metaphysics* (Albany, NY: State University of New York Press).

ROUTLEY, RICHARD, and ROUTLEY, VAL (1980), 'Human Chauvinism and Environmental Ethics', in Don Mannison, Michael McRobbie, and Richard Routley (eds.), *Environmental Philosophy*, Monograph 2 (Australian National University). See also under Sylvan, Richard, and Plumwood, Val.

SAPONTZIS, STEVE (1982), 'The Moral Significance of Interests', *Environmental Ethics*, 4/4: 345–58.

—— (1984), 'Predation', *Ethics and Animals*, 5: 27-38

SCHERER, DONALD, and ATTIG, THOMAS (eds.) (1983), *Ethics and the Environment* (Englewood Cliffs, NJ: Prentice Hall).

SCHILLP, PAUL (1951), *The Philosophy of A. N. Whitehead* (1941; New York: Tudor Press).

SCHWEITZER, ALBERT (1970), 'Ethics of Compassion', *Reverence for Life: Sermons*, trans. Reginald Fuller (1966; London: SPCK).

—— (1986), *My Life and Thought: An Autobiography* (1933; London: Allen & Unwin).

SCHWEITZER ALBERT (1987), *The Philosophy of Civilization* (Including *Civilization and Ethics*) (1923; Buffalo: Prometheus Books).

SESSIONS, GEORGE (1977), 'Spinoza and Jeffers on Man in Nature', *Inquiry*, 20: 481–528.

SHEPARD, PAUL (1969), 'Ecology and Man—A Viewpoint', in P. Shepard and D. McKinley (eds.), *The Subversive Science* (Boston: Houghton Mifflin), 1–10.

SHRADER-FRECHETTE, KRISTIN (1981), *Environmental Ethics* (Pacific Grove, Calif.: Boxwood Press).

—— (1990*a*), 'Biological Holism and The Evolution of Ethics', *Between the Species*, 6/4: 185–92.

—— (1990*b*), 'Biology and Ethics: Callicott Reconsidered', *Between the Species*, 6/4: 195–6.

SINGER, PETER (1972), 'Famine, Affluence and Morality', *Philosophy and Public Affairs*, 1/3: 229–43.

—— (1976), *Animal Liberation*: Towards an End to Man's Inhumanity to Animals (1975; St Albans: Paladin Books, Granada).

—— (1979*a*), 'Killing Humans and Killing Animals', *Inquiry*, 22: 145–56.

—— (1979*b*), *Practical Ethics* (Cambridge: Cambridge University Press).

—— (1979*c*), 'Not for Humans Only: The Place of Nonhumans in Environmental Issues', in Goodpaster and Sayre (eds.) (1979).

—— (1981), *The Expanding Circle: Ethics and Sociobiology* (Oxford: Oxford University Press).

SMART, J. C. C. (1987), 'Utilitarianism and Generalized Benevolence', *Essays Metaphysical and Moral* (Oxford: Basil Blackwell), 283–92.

—— and WILLIAMS, BERNARD (1973), *Utilitarianism: For and Against* (Cambridge: Cambridge University Press).

SPRIGGE, T. L. S. (1987), 'Are There Intrinsic Values in Nature?', *Journal of Applied Philosophy*, 4/1: 21–8.

—— (1990), *The Rational Foundations of Ethics* (1988; London: Routledge).

—— (1991), 'Some Recent Positions in Environmental Ethics Examined', *Inquiry*, 34/1: 107–28.

STACKHOUSE, MAX: (1981), 'The Perils of Process: A Response to Sturm', in Cobb and Schroeder (eds.) (1981), 103–14.

STONE, CHRISTOPHER (1987), *Earth and Other Ethics* (New York: Harper & Row).

SUCHOKI, MARJORIE (1988), *The End of Evil* (Albany, NY: State University of New York Press).

SYLVAN, RICHARD (1985), 'A Critique of Deep Ecology' *Radical Philosophy*, 40: 2–12 and 41: 10–22

—— (1990), 'A Critique of (Wild) Western Deep Ecology: A Response to Warwick Fox's Response', *In Defence of Deep Environmental Ethics*,

Discussion Paper in Environmental Philosophy, 18 (Canberra: Australian National University), 37–91.

—— (n.d.), 'Moral Matters Matter—Environmentally?' (unpublished).

TAYLOR, PAUL (1981), 'The Ethics of Respect for Nature', *Environmental Ethics*, 3/3: 191–218.

—— (1986), *Respect for Nature: A Theory of Environmental Ethics* (Princeton, NJ: Princeton University Press).

THOMPSON, PAUL (1995), *Spirit of the Soil: Agriculture and Environmental Ethics* (London, Routledge).

VANDE VEER, DONALD (1979), 'Interspecific Justice', *Inquiry*, 22: 55–79.

VARNER, GARY E. (1991), 'No Holism Without Pluralism', *Environmental Ethics*, 13/2: 175–9.

VITALI, THEODORE (1990), 'Sport Hunting: Moral or Immoral', *Environmental Ethics*, 12/1: 69–82.

WARREN, MARY ANNE (1983), 'The Rights of the Nonhuman World', in Elliott and Gare (eds.) 109–34.

WENZ, PETER (1988), *Environmental Justice* (Albany, NY: State University of New York Press).

—— (1993), 'Minimal, Moderate, and Extreme Moral Pluralism', *Environmental Ethics*, 15/1: 61–74.

WESTON, ANTONY (1991), 'On Callicott's Case Against Pluralism', *Environmental Ethics*, 13/3: 283–6.

WHITEHEAD, A. N. (1920), *The Concept of Nature* (Cambridge: Cambridge University Press).

—— (1926), *Religion in the Making* (Cambridge: Cambridge University Press).

—— (1928), *Symbolism: Its Meaning and Effect* (Cambridge: Cambridge University Press).

—— (1938a), *Modes of Thought* (New York: Macmillan).

—— (1938b), *Science and the Modern World* (1925; Harmondsworth: Pelican).

—— (1948), *Adventures of Ideas* (1933; Harmondsworth: Pelican).

—— (1978), *Process and Reality: An Essay in Cosmology* (1929; corr. edn., ed. David Griffin and Donald Sherburne (New York: Free Press).

WILLIAMS, DANIEL DAY (1961), *in* Leclerc (ed.), (1961) 356–72.

ZIMMERMAN, MICHAEL (1983), 'Towards a Heideggerian Ethos for Environmental Ethics', *Environmental Ethics*, 5/2: 99–132.

Index